W9-CHB-001

The Return of the Public in Global Governance

Many international relations scholars argue that private authority and private actors are playing increasingly prominent roles in global governance. This book focuses on the other side of the equation: the transformation of the public dimension of governance in the era of globalization. It analyzes that transformation, advancing two major claims: first, that the public is beginning to play a more significant role in global governance, and, second, that it takes a rather different form than has traditionally been understood in international relations theory. The authors suggest that unless we transcend conventional wisdom about the public as a distinct sphere, separate from the private domain, we cannot understand the dynamics and consequences of its apparent return. Using examples drawn from international political economy, international security, and environmental governance, they argue that "the public" should be conceptualized as a collection of culturally specific social practices.

JACQUELINE BEST is an Associate Professor in the School of Political Studies at the University of Ottawa. She is author of *Governing Failure: Provisional Expertise and the Transformation of Global Finance for Development* (2014) and *The Limits of Transparency: Ambiguity and the History of International Finance* (2005) and co-editor, with Matthew Paterson, of *Cultural Political Economy* (2010).

ALEXANDRA GHECIU is an Associate Professor at the Graduate School of Public and International Affairs and Associate Director of the Centre for International Policy Studies. Her publications include *NATO in the "New Europe": The Politics of International Socialization after the Cold War* (2005) and *Securing Civilization?* (2008).

The Return of the Public in Global Governance

Edited by

Jacqueline Best and Alexandra Gheciu

CAMBRIDGE
UNIVERSITY PRESS

CAMBRIDGE
UNIVERSITY PRESS

University Printing House, Cambridge CB2 8BS, United Kingdom

Published in the United States of America by Cambridge University Press,
New York

Cambridge University Press is part of the University of Cambridge.

It furthers the University's mission by disseminating knowledge in the pursuit of
education, learning and research at the highest international levels of excellence.

www.cambridge.org
Information on this title: www.cambridge.org/9781107052956

© Cambridge University Press 2014

First published 2014

Printed in the United Kingdom by Clays, St Ives plc

A catalogue record for this publication is available from the British Library

Library of Congress Cataloguing in Publication data
The return of the public in global governance / edited by Jacqueline Best and
Alexandra Gheciu.
    pages cm
ISBN 978-1-107-05295-6 (Hardback)
1. Globalization–Social aspects. 2. Public interest. 3. International
organization. 4. International economic relations. 5. Security,
International. 6. International relations. I. Best, Jacqueline, 1970-
II. Gheciu, Alexandra.
JZ1318.R485 2014
327.101–dc23 2013046727

ISBN 978-1-107-05295-6 Hardback

Contents

Contents

Figure and tables

Contributors

RITA ABRAHAMSEN is Professor in the Graduate School of Public and International Affairs at the University of Ottawa.

DEBORAH AVANT is the Sié Chéou-Kang Chair for International Security and Diplomacy and Director of the Sié Chéou-Kang Center for International Security and Diplomacy in the Josef Korbel School of International Studies at the University of Denver.

STEVEN BERNSTEIN is Professor in the Department of Political Science at the University of Toronto.

JACQUELINE BEST is Associate Professor in the School of Political Studies at the University of Ottawa.

ALEXANDRA GHECIU is Associate Professor in the Graduate School of Public and International Affairs at the University of Ottawa.

VIRGINIA HAUFLER is Associate Professor in the Department of Government and Politics at the University of Maryland.

ERIC HELLEINER is the Faculty of Arts Chair in International Political Economy in the Department of Political Science at the University of Waterloo.

ANNA LEANDER is Professor (MSO) in the Department of Management, Politics, and Philosophy at the Copenhagen Business School.

MATTHEW PATERSON is Professor in the School of Political Studies at the University of Ottawa.

TONY PORTER is Professor in the Department of Political Science at McMaster University.

MICHAEL C. WILLIAMS is Professor in the Graduate School of Public and International Affairs at the University of Ottawa.

Acknowledgements

This project grew out of a series of conversations about recent changes in governance practices in our two fields of study, international political economy (IPE) and international security. As we discussed both recent events and current scholarship, we were struck by the remarkable parallels in the changes that had recently been taking place in these seemingly very different areas of global life: in both IPE and international security, public actors and public concerns seemed to be on the rise. And yet the form of these new public dynamics was clearly different from what we had witnessed in the past. Evidently, these were changes worth paying attention to and exploring further.

In order to dig further into these questions, we brought together a group of international scholars in the spring of 2009 for a workshop at the University of Ottawa, who examined the changing relationship between public and private in issue areas including finance, security, global development, and the environment. Many further conversations later, this book is the ultimate product of those initial discussions.

Like any collaborative project, this book is the product of a great many minds, their dialogue and debate, and their considerable effort.

First among those we would like to acknowledge for those efforts are, of course, our contributors, who have persisted with this project through its long gestation period, commented on and contributed to the book's theoretical framework, and reworked and refined their chapters. They have produced some superb scholarship in the process.

We would also like to thank those who participated in the original workshop, whose early contributions and conversations also made this volume possible, including Ole Jacob Sending, Len Seabrooke, Rod Hall, Randall Germain, Eleni Tsingou, and Arne Rückert.

A number of people have also been generous enough to read the entire manuscript, or at least large portions of it, including our editor at Cambridge, John Haslam, as well as Duncan Snidal, Chris Reus-Smit, and several anonymous reviewers. This project is much stronger as a result of the valuable feedback that we received from them. We would also like to thank Alex Wendt for his support for the project at certain key stages in its development.

This volume would not have been possible without the invaluable research and editorial assistance from several graduate students – Christopher Leite, Natalie Britton, and Robert McNeil. Phillipe Roseberry and Judy Meyer also provided excellent organizational support for the original workshop.

This project was funded through a grant from the Social Sciences and Humanities Research Council of Canada, and through the generous support of the Centre for International Policy Studies, the Faculty of Social Sciences, and Office of the Vice-President, Research at the University of Ottawa.

I

Introduction

1   Introduction

Jacqueline Best and Alexandra Gheciu

Although there has been much discussion among international relations scholars about the extent to which the relationship between public and private in global governance is changing, much of that attention has been focused on the rising role of private governance, authority, and actors. This volume focuses instead on the other side of the equation: our interest is primarily in the transformation of the public dimension of global governance. As we analyze that transformation, we advance two major claims: first, that the public is beginning to play a more significant role in global governance, but, second, that it takes a rather different form than has traditionally been understood in international relations (IR) theory. Rather than a bounded realm or space, we argue that the public must be conceptualized as a collection of social practices.

The return of the public

No matter where we look, the public seems to be playing an increasingly important role in our lives. This is particularly striking given that, after a couple of decades of neoliberal governance that extolled the virtues of the private sphere (particularly the market), many experts thought that the public – and particularly the state – had irrevocably lost its once privileged position in the world. Take, for instance, the recent examples of state intervention to address the financial crisis largely perceived as the outcome of the reckless behavior of private actors (primarily financial institutions). Or consider the new rules that came into effect after 9/11 and that impose unprecedented demands on institutions such as private banks to cooperate with public authorities, including by disclosing confidential information about their clients. Think, also, about the ways in which the transnational flows of goods, people, and services have been subjected to unprecedented levels of monitoring by public authorities – suffice it to mention the new security arrangements at airports – in a situation in which states and intergovernmental international organizations fear that such flows could facilitate the operations of terrorist and criminal organizations. Finally, let us recall the multitude of government-, UN-, and EU-sponsored efforts to create a more effective system of environmental governance that would, among other things, significantly change the ways in which private corporations conduct their business.

Based on all these (and many other) examples, we could be very tempted to conclude that, after a couple of decades of neoliberal governance, the public is back with a vengeance. But is it? Yes, and no. As this volume argues, the public is indeed back, but not as we knew it. We suggest that unless we transcend the conventional wisdoms about the category of public, we cannot understand the dynamics and consequences of its apparent return.

The concept of the public is a fundamental category in political theory, and has long shaped modern liberal thought and practice. Although various liberal scholars have different views of the relative merits and power of public vs. private objects and subjects, the assumption of a clear distinction between public and private realms has been at the heart of liberalism's "art of separation" – to borrow Michael Walzer's (1984) term. As we explain in the next chapter, the public/private divide has also been central to thinking about international relations. While in recent years a host of scholars have drawn attention to the shifting and blurring of the boundary between public and private, for the most part their analyses have not challenged the assumption that public and private are ontologically separate domains of social life, governed by different logics and associated with specific sites. On this view, it ought to be possible at any given time and in any given place to determine, based on their location, whether a particular organization, group, or individual acts in a public or a private capacity.

The problem with this perspective, this volume suggests, is that it does not enable us to see that whether an actor is regarded as public or private depends much more on what they are seen to be *doing*, than on where they are *located*. As the empirical contributions to this volume demonstrate, in many instances the public is back, but it is not where or what it is supposed to be, according to conventional wisdom. We suggest that it is only by transcending the view of the public as a separate, distinct entity or social space and by embracing the view of public as practice that we can understand the nature and consequences of the contemporary "return of the public." This is what we set out to do in this volume.

The public as practice

Drawing inspiration from the "practice turn"[1] in international relations and social theory, we argue that the best way to understand the novel

---

[1] See in particular Adler 2005; Adler and Pouliot 2011a and 2011b – also Bourdieu 1990; McMillan 2008 and 2009; Schatzki 1996; Schatzki, Knorr Cetina, and von Savigny 2001.

forms of "public" that are currently emerging internationally is to see them as public practices. Understanding the public as practices, we suggest, enables us to develop a more nuanced appreciation for the complex ways in which different forms of public are gaining in significance – allowing us to open up the black box of the public and to examine the multiplicity of actors, objects, and subjects that are implicated.

As we discuss at greater length in the next chapter, we define practices as meaningful patterns of activity that enable individuals and communities to reproduce their world. Such practices are often tacit or habitual – the everyday practices through which we engage in our social and political lives – although they can also take more self-conscious and strategic forms. This means that practices are both ideational and material: they take concrete forms, as specific actions and techniques, but only have meaning within a particular social and ideational context. Some of the practices discussed in this volume include concrete techniques for soliciting public feedback and participation, for structuring spaces of deliberation, and for providing public goods like security.

One of the most common ways of understanding practices today is through the idea of "communities of practice." This particular under-standing of practices emphasizes what we are calling in this volume the *reinforcing* character of certain practices: the ways in which they can be used to stabilize the rules, norms, and boundaries of a particular way of life – by, for example, reinforcing an international organization's claims to authority by developing new practices of public consultation. Yet practices can also be used to *transform* a given set of background assumptions, or redefine the boundaries of taken-for-granted categor-ies. Not surprisingly, given that this volume seeks to examine a moment of disruption and transition in global governance, many of the kinds of public practices being discussed by our contributors take this second form, as actors in the environmental, economic, and secur-ity domains seek to redefine the meaning and scope of the public in global governance.

As we discuss in the next chapter, we define public practices as patterns of activity that involve an understanding in a given society at a particular moment in time that something is of common concern. By conceptualizing the public as a set of practices, rather than as a bounded domain or sphere, we are emphasizing the contested and historically contingent character of what we call public. This reconceptualization enables us to disaggregate the public, examining the ways in which different kinds of actors and activities get counted as public in different contexts. It also allows us to consider the politics involved in defining a particular good, procedure, or actors *as* public, revealing the power relations involved in defining what counts as public or not.

What is at stake in this return and reconstitution of the public? We suggest that the present reconstitution of the public dimension of governance can be seen as a moment of disruption – partially in response to the perceived limitations of neoliberal ideas and practices of the public that were prominent in previous years. Contributors to this volume provide somewhat different answers in response to the question "What has changed?" but they agree that recent transformations – for instance, the global financial crisis, changes in the field of security after 9/11, and climate change – have all challenged previously taken for granted definitions of the public, as well as boundaries between the public and private. Each of these crises has forced a redefinition of what counts as a public object or subject, just as it has forced a rethinking of the previously dominant public logic. To understand the nature and implications of this moment of disruption, we argue, we need to examine practices through which particular understandings of the public objects, subjects, and logics of action are defined, enacted, and contested.

Contributions

By examining the ways in which the public is constituted through historically specific practices, the chapters included in this collection seek to make several significant contributions to the IR literature. The project makes an important contribution to the significant literature on public and private in global governance, both building on and challenging the existing literatures on private authority, public goods, and the global public sphere.

We also formulate a theoretical framework for the study of the public in global governance that can be applied to a range of IR subfields to help us understand the complex interactions among them. This book demonstrates the ways in which the same patterns in the transformation of the public are occurring in IPE, international security, and the global environment.

This volume also contributes to the recent IR and sociological bodies of literature on "the turn to practice" by extending the analysis of practices to a previously undertheorized area. Thus, we explore the ways in which practices help to construct and change some of the most fundamental categories (public objects and subjects) that shape our understanding of – and actions within – the world of international politics. Through its emphasis on the concrete practices, mechanisms, and techniques through which the public is constituted, this volume makes an important contribution to debates in IR about the relationship between the material and the ideal. Practices, by their very nature, bridge this divide: they are informed by particular understandings but take material form – as a set of techniques for making financial derivatives open to public scrutiny, or a set of consultation mechanisms for dealing with poor communities.

In addition, our focus on practices enables us to contribute to a better understanding of the exercise of power in international relations. After all, as Barnes has noted, "To engage in a practice is to exercise a power. [. . .] what is called the active exercise of a power may equally be called the enactment of a practice" (quoted in Adler and Pouliot 2011a: 30). In this volume, we examine the exercise of power through the practices of inclusion, exclusion and authorization involved in constituting certain subjects or objects as "public."

Finally, contributors to this volume seek to enhance our understanding of the public by examining the normative dilemmas and challenges associated with contemporary forms of the public. Thus, one of the recurring themes in this volume is that some of the recent transformations in the fields of international political economy, security, and environmental governance have worrying implications, as some of the recent practices of publicness provide a much thinner basis for legitimacy than the democratic processes that – in modern (liberal) political thought – are conventionally associated with the public domain.

Overview of the book

Each of the chapters that make up this book contributes to the theoretical and empirical robustness of our central claims. Thus, despite their different empirical foci, our contributors share a commitment to exploring the constitutive effects of practices on the objects and subjects identified as "public" in a specific context. As noted above, many of our contributors have already carried out research that challenges conventional assumptions regarding the boundaries between the public and the private realms, arguing that categories of public and private cannot be treated as fixed.[2] Our volume takes that line of argument a step further through a systematic examination of the dynamics and implications of the historically specific practices through which the "public" is constructed. It is on the basis of such a systematic set of analyses that we seek to explain the present efforts to reconstitute the public dimension of governance in response to recent crises in the fields of IPE, security, and environment governance.

[2] See, for example: Abrahamsen and Williams 2007, 2009, and 2011; Avant 2005; Cutler, Haufler, and Porter 1999; Gheciu 2008; Haufler 2007; Porter 2005.

The next chapter (Chapter 2), by Best and Gheciu, provides a theoretical framework for the other chapters in this book, and for the broader claims that the contributors make about the need to reconceptualize the global public. If the public is in fact re-emerging in global governance, then how can we conceptualize it? In order to answer this question, Best and Gheciu begin by considering whether the existing literatures on the public and private in global governance can provide enough insight into the changes that we are currently witnessing, allowing us to recognize the re-emergence of the public and to understand its novel characteristics. Having identified both the strengths and weaknesses of the existing scholarship in resolving these puzzles, they go on to develop a framework for making sense of the evolving role and character of the public in global governance. They suggest that the best way of understanding the re-emergence of the public is to approach it as an evolving set of practices rather than as a bounded sphere, state-based authority, or natural set of goods. Drawing on the evidence provided by contributions to this volume, Best and Gheciu then develop a theoretical framework for understanding the public as practice in global governance.

If we are to develop a conception of the public that is historically and culturally attuned, then it is important to consider contemporary shifts in the light of their history. The chapters by Avant and Haufler (Chapter 3) and by Helleiner (Chapter 4) do exactly that: they consider recent changes in the constitution of the public through a historical lens. In their chapter entitled "The dynamics of private security strategies and their public consequences," Avant and Haufler examine the relationship between Western profit-seeking, helping, and ruling organizations in the management of violence during nineteenth-century imperial expansion, late nineteenth-century modernity, the Cold War, and contemporary global governance. Through their analysis, they demonstrate that changes in the practices of ostensibly private firms and NGOs have played an important role in shaping the conception of the public that prevails in a particular historical context. Their historical analysis demonstrates that the clear distinctions between public and private that we take for granted today were the product of social practices in a specific historical context. Thus, at the start of the history they examine, there was no distinctive boundary between public and private. As Avant and Haufler explain, only over time did the state and private actors come to be seen as entities operating in separate spheres. Furthermore, "By the start of the twenty-first century, the public and private were once again merging – but in a new way, in which the state is no longer equated with the public. This may presage a transformation of the public through the manner in which security is provided – through transparent and accountable processes. What those who provide security do, rather than who they are, is increasingly important for organizations claiming to be acting on behalf of the public."

Helleiner, in his chapter, considers the rise of new public-constituting practices in the context of the recent financial crisis. In his examination of the move to regulate derivatives, he considers how policy-makers across the world have stated clearly that they now consider derivatives markets to be a proper subject for global public policy. These declarations of the "publicness" of derivatives markets have been accompanied by internationally coordinated initiatives to boost market participants' use of various private central counterparties, exchanges, electronic trading platforms, and trade depositories. Yet, Helleiner notes that while derivatives have been redefined as a public concern, the proposed new forms of regulation remain quite distinct from the post-war Bretton Woods era, as, "the publicness of OTC markets is being constructed in more ways than simply through a 'return of the state.'" These new governance practices also point to a narrowing of the "public" being served by the international financial order: "When broader political issues relating to fairness and participation in governance are addressed, policy-makers' vision of the 'public' seems to narrow suddenly to include only the participants in the markets themselves." As Helleiner concludes, this suggests that the content of both the distinct narratives and the specific mechanisms that generate "publicness" in turn influence the very identity of the public being constituted by these practices.

The next five chapters apply these insights into the changing character of public practices to several contemporary issue areas. In her chapter "The 'demand side' of good governance: the return of the public in World Bank policy," Best (Chapter 5) looks at recent changes in the World Bank's development policies. Bernstein's piece, "The publicness of non-state global environmental and social governance" (Chapter 6), and Paterson's chapter, "Climate re-public: practicing public space in conditions of extreme complexity" (Chapter 7), both consider different aspects of the evolution of environmental governance, while Gheciu focuses on the changing practices of security provision in her chapter, "Transforming the logic of security governance in Europe" (Chapter 8). Finally, Leander's chapter, "Understanding US national intelligence: analyzing practices to capture the chimera" (Chapter 9) examines the opaque world of "top secret" security services.

Best's contribution examines recent efforts by the World Bank to foster the "demand side" of good governance and poverty reduction. Having spent the better part of a decade trying to improve the supply of these developmental goods, whether by the international financial institutions themselves or by borrowing states, Bank staff are now focusing on the other side of the equation. In the simplest terms, this means encouraging poor people, civil society groups, parliaments, and market actors to stand up and demand better governance, better services, and better efforts to reduce poverty. In other words, this new governance strategy seeks to create new kinds of public: to foster the formation of public groups, to encourage them to engage in particular kinds of public speech, and to hope through those means to create a more responsive and accountable public sector. The chapter suggests that if we are to understand what is involved in this return of the public, as well as what is at stake, we need to move beyond the more traditional conceptions of the public. We are witnessing neither simply a shift in private authority, nor a new kind of public good, nor a return of the public sphere. Instead, Best suggests, we can best capture recent changes by understanding them as a new kind of public logic, in which the various practices that we associate with the public and the private have been disaggregated and recombined in new and potent ways. Yet, Best argues, these efforts have not been entirely successful to date: her chapter thus points out the potential limits of recent efforts to constitute a new kind of public.

In the realm of global environmental and social governance, Bernstein also finds some important changes underway. Non-governmental actors play an increasingly salient role in creating environmental and social standards in areas such as fisheries, labor practices, forestry, climate change, apparel, and a wide range of commodities that are traded internationally. In so doing, they have developed a new repertoire of governance systems – such as product labeling and producer certification – that they have sought to define as public. Using the ISEAL Alliance to support his claims about the growing importance of non-state governance systems, Bernstein argues that "the language of public and private as distinctive forms of global governance offers limited analytic traction." As he explains, ISEAL members (which include actors such as the Marine Stewardship Council, the Rainforest Alliance, Fairtrade International, and Forest Stewardship Council) are increasingly relying on claims to their public authority. Like Best and Gheciu, Bernstein suggests that these empirical transformations raise some difficult normative questions and have some potentially problematic implications. One of the key problems, Bernstein argues, is that in practice it can be difficult to achieve publicity for these initiatives beyond elites or those with specialized knowledge. Thus, the risk is that the reconstitution of public authority "legitimizes the slicing up of a divisible transnational 'public' – made up in practice of elites engaged in particular issues or market sectors – in the absence of a globally constituted public."

Matthew Paterson further enhances our understanding of the reconstitution of the public in the realm of environmental policy by exploring how the public is being practiced in global climate politics. Paterson begins by elaborating how climate change can be understood as a classic case of a public goods problem, but also as a problem of extreme complexity, or as a "superwicked" problem. He suggests that the combination of these features has helped to engender a practice of the public that seeks to recreate classical forms of public space – an agora for deliberation – that are oriented towards the type of open-ended learning and deliberation that the characteristics of complexity entail. The relationship between "public" and "private" is thus to be sought less in the characteristics of specific actors or institutions than in the qualities of the interactions between them. Paterson's chapter explores this claim through an analysis of the legitimating practices of "private" climate governance, the notion of "learning by doing" that pervades a range of climate governance discourses, and the organization of public space in recent international climate change negotiations.

Gheciu's chapter examines the dynamics and implications of domestic security practices carried out in post-communist Eastern Europe, with a special emphasis on Bulgaria and Romania. She argues that contemporary providers of a key public good (security) in those countries are not confined to a particular space or institutional domain. Rather, they are both global and national, state and non-state, new yet often with strong connections to old (communist) organizations. Those actors can be understood as "communities of practice" that have emerged in a specific historical context – particularly post-Cold War processes of liberalization – and, by mobilizing material and symbolic sources of power, have contributed to the reconstitution of the "public" in particular ways. Practices of security provision carried out in contemporary Bulgaria and Romania have a profound impact on those societies by redefining norms of acceptable behavior by public actors and by a responsible demos, reshaping understandings of who has the right to provide public goods, legitimizing new techniques of protection, and introducing an ethic of care of the public that is not provided by the state.

Leander's chapter attempts to come to terms with the chimerical nature of US National Intelligence since 9/11. In her view, this can only be achieved by moving beyond the public/private divide and understanding this security field as a hybrid set of practices. Leander's chapter starts from the observation that there has been an extraordinary growth in intelligence activity since 9/11. "This 'public' is returning" and "expanding at impressive speed," she notes. Yet, the exact nature of this public transformation "is surprisingly difficult to pin down."

The problem, according to Leander, is that efforts to "capture" US National Intelligence tend to (re-)produce its elusiveness. She draws on a 2-year-long investigative project about "Top Secret America" carried out by a team of twenty journalists from the *Washington Post*. Not only do the journalists – who have gone through all available public documentation – consider that the nature and scope of US National Intelligence escape their control and understanding, so do insiders at all levels including the director of the CIA and the Secretary of Defense. As Leander explains, the reason this expansion of the public is so difficult to capture is its hybridity – and particularly the chimerical side of this hybridity. The chimerical nature of US National Intelligence is produced by public and private practices that obscure its expansionary nature, as well as the reflexive processes through which it is reproduced. To come to terms with this phenomenon therefore requires an approach that conceptualizes the public as practice. The advantage of such an approach is that it can make the creation of the public/private divide endogenous to the analysis rather than treat it as an exogenously given point of departure.

The volume concludes with two chapters – the first by Tony Porter and the second by Rita Abrahamsen and Michael Williams – whose primary aim is to situate our understanding of the reconstitution of the public in a broader theoretical perspective. Porter's chapter looks forward, to where the changing character of the public might take us in the future, while Abrahamsen and Williams' chapter looks backwards, in order to understand the historical roots of the more traditional conceptions of the public that we are now leaving behind.

Porter's chapter, entitled "Constitutive public practices in a world of changing boundaries" (Chapter 10), takes a step back from detailed issue-specific cases, and considers the broader context within which the contemporary transformation of public (and private) practices is occurring. Using as a lens the cases of border security and internet governance, Porter considers the various ways in which the practices of global governance are growing in complexity. As he points out, "Once upon a time – indeed not that long ago – it was quite easy to say what was public and what was private." This is no longer the case, as we can no longer easily assume that public practices are those associated with the state and its citizenry. He suggests that the growing complexity of the global public is echoed and enabled by several other new forms of complexity – in the increasing entanglement between ideas and materiality, and in the fading distinction between the national and the international. As Porter notes, although the internet resembles the public sphere of old, it also more complex: both material and ideal, public and private, national and transnational. The internet "is not a free-floating cyberspace that operates independently of humans or objects, but instead consists of humans and objects that are coordinated and governed through a complex set of practices and institutions." Moreover, he suggests, many of the key actors involved in the internet's governance are engaged in intense debates about its public or private character. Although the internet and its governance therefore involve public practices, they remain both complex and contested.

Abrahamsen and Williams (Chapter 11) conclude this volume with a reflection on the implications that this return and reconceptualization of the public has for IR scholarship. The central question that they seek to answer in their chapter, "Publics, practices, and power," is: what or where is the public? They suggest that in order to understand how the character of the public is changing today, we have to look back in history, arguing "the dominance of state-centrism [in IR theory] is a largely unrecognized inheritance of attempts to determine what or where the public is, and what therefore qualifies as legitimate, or properly public, power." Although the site of the public has become far more complex today, they suggest that the central problems that early political thinkers like Hobbes and Hume sought to address in their emphasis on the state remain with us today: at the heart of these challenges is the difficulty of ensuring that the public in fact represents the will of the people. They conclude by examining some of the most recent calls to return the public to the people, and suggest that "while the place of the public is perhaps more puzzling than ever, it is by no measure disappearing."

REFERENCES

Abrahamsen, Rita, and Michael C. Williams. 2007. "Securing the city: private security companies and non-state authority in global governance." *International Relations* 21(2): 237–53.
2009. "Security beyond the state: global security assemblages in international politics." *International Political Sociology* 3(1): 1–17.
2011. *Security beyond the State: Private Security in International Politics.* Cambridge: Cambridge University Press.
Adler, Emmanuel. 2005. *Communitarian International Relations: The Epistemic Foundations of International Relations.* New York: Routledge.
Adler, Emmanuel, and Vincent Pouliot. 2011a. "International practices." *International Theory* 3(1): 1–36.
2011b. *International Practices.* Cambridge: Cambridge University Press.
Avant, Deborah. 2005. "Private security companies." *New Political Economy* 10(1): 121–31.
Bourdieu, Pierre. 1990. *The Logic of Practice.* Translated by R. Nice. Stanford, CA: Stanford University Press.

Cutler, Claire A., Virginia Haufler, and Tony Porter, eds. 1999. *Private Authority and International Affairs*. New York: State University of New York Press.
Gheciu, Alexandra. 2008. *Securing Civilization? The EU, NATO and the OSCE in the Post-9/11 World*. Oxford: Oxford University Press.
Haufler, Virginia. 2007. "The private sector and governance in post-conflict countries." In *Governance in Post-Conflict Societies: Rebuilding Fragile States*, edited by Derick W. Brinkerhoff, pp. 143–60. New York: Routledge.
McMillan, Kevin. 2008. "The emergence of international governance: practices of European politics, 1700–1848." Ph.D. dissertation, Columbia University.
    2009. "'The conduct of conduct': great-power management in the Concert of Europe." Presentation, University of Ottawa.
Porter, Tony. 2005. "The private production of public goods: private and public norms in global governance." In *Complex Sovereignty: Reconstituting Political Authority in the Twenty-First Century*, edited by Edgar Grande and Louis W. Pauly, pp. 68–92. Toronto: University of Toronto Press.
Schatzki, Theodore. 1996. *Social Practices: A Wittgensteinian Approach to Human Activity and the Social*. Cambridge: Cambridge University Press.
Schatzki, Theodore, Karin Knorr Cetina, and Eike von Savigny, eds. 2001. *The Practice Turn in Contemporary Theory*. New York: Routledge.
Walzer, Michael. 1984. "Liberalism and the art of separation." *Political Theory* **12**(3): 315–30.

2 Theorizing the public as practices: transformations of the public in historical context

Jacqueline Best and Alexandra Gheciu

If the public is in fact returning as a major force in global governance, then how do we go about making sense of it? This is the central question examined in this chapter. In order to answer it, we begin by considering whether the existing literatures on the public and private in global governance can provide enough insight into the changes that we are currently witnessing, allowing us to recognize the re-emergence of the public and to understand its novel characteristics.

Having identified both the strengths and weaknesses of the existing scholarship in resolving these puzzles, we go on to develop our own framework for making sense of the evolving role and character of the public in global governance. We suggest that the best way of understanding the re-emergence of the public is to understand it as an evolving set of practices rather than as a bounded sphere, state-based authority, or natural set of goods. What counts as public depends more on what is *done* than on whether an individual or institution is associated formally with what we traditionally define as the public or private realm. Over time, particularly in moments of transition such as the present moment, what counts as public gets contested and renegotiated through transformational practices. In other words, we suggest that distinctions between public and private – just like distinctions between the national and the global, or economics and security – are themselves forms of power-laden practices, which reflect and in turn shape the characteristics of the broader social context in which they are enacted.

We conclude by providing a broad overview of some of the transformations currently taking place in the constitution of the global public, drawing together some of the empirical and theoretical insights provided in the essays that follow.

Engaging the existing literature

Although the public has not received a great deal of attention in international relations (IR) scholarship in recent years, there nonetheless exists a rich scholarship on the concepts of public and private in global governance. Before we develop our own analytic framework for making sense of the changes taking place in political economy, global security, and the environment, we need to determine what insights can be derived from this existing scholarship. We focus on three key literatures here because of their prominent role in global governance scholarship: analyses of the rise of private authority, the global public sphere, and the role of global public goods. We ask two central questions of each analytic approach: do they recognize the re-emergence of the public as a global force, and can they help us to understand the particular characteristics of the public in its present form? We suggest that while each of these literatures provides us with some insight into each of these questions individually, none can provide an adequate insight into both. Although our analysis will therefore build on these literatures, it will also depart from them in significant measure.

Private authority

Paradoxically perhaps, we would like to start our examination of the ways that the public has been conceptualized with a brief discussion of recent research on privatization. We do so because this body of literature relies on very specific – though sometimes implicit – assumptions about the conventional role of the public dimension of governance. These are coupled with assumptions regarding the growing inability (or unwillingness) of the public to perform some of those conventional functions. The narrative that emerges is highly seductive, yet, in our view, unable to capture the complexity of the reconstitution of the public in the age of globality.

A host of IR scholars – as well as sociologists and political theorists – has persuasively argued that, particularly against the background of the triumph of neoliberal policies over the past two decades, the world has witnessed an unprecedented proliferation (and empowerment) of private actors and private authority in global governance. Thus, the increasingly globalized flows of capital, ideas, goods, and people coupled with neoliberal policies that extolled the virtues of the market and called for a "roll-back of the state" created unprecedented opportunities for private actors, and served to legitimize their involvement in areas from which they had previously been excluded. The prevailing view within this body of literature is that the contemporary rise to prominence of private actors and private authority is a relatively new phenomenon, marking a shift away from the conventional (state-based) patterns of national and international governance.[1] In essence, in many cases and issue areas ranging from environmental governance to political economy and security, private actors are now routinely performing some of the functions traditionally seen as falling exclusively within the purview of the modern state.[2] For some of the scholars who focus on this topic, the growing power of private actors can amount to a serious challenge to the modern, Weberian state, while for others processes of privatization can reinforce – and often have reinforced – Weberian notions of statehood and sovereignty.[3]

The literature on privatization has provided many valuable insights into the changing landscape of global governance, not least by pushing analysis away from the traditional IR focus on state-based processes and institutions of governance. Yet, these scholars' emphasis on the rise of private authority and the influence of private actors has meant that they are not always attuned to the shifting role of the public in global governance. The fact that what appear to be private actors (NGOs, civil society, firms) are increasingly engaged in public practices (such as processes of public deliberation and the pursuit of public purposes) is too easily viewed as simply another example of the rise of private authority – missing the crucial ways in which these practices are redefining those actors as public because of what they do, not where they are situated (as chapters by Avant and Haufler [Chapter 3] and Best [Chapter 5] in this volume point out).

If the private authority literature is therefore an inadequate guide to the shifting role of the public, it does nonetheless provide us with some insight into the complex character of that emergent public, and its continued interdependence with forms of private authority.[4] Best's

---

[1] Pattberg 2005; Ruggie 2004; Thirkwell-White 2006; Van Harten 2005 – to cite but a few relevant works. Some scholars, however, argue against the novelty of private actors and private authority in global governance (e.g. Mugge 2006). There are also those who remind us that the Weberian conception of the state is a normative model, and should not be treated as the empirically accurate description of some past golden age of statehood (Abrahamsen and Williams 2006; Bernstein, Chapter 6, this volume).

[2] See, for instance, Abrahamsen and Williams 2011, 2009, and 2006; Avant 2005; Hall and Bierstecker 2002; Kamat 2004; Leander 2005; Percy 2007. Also relevant are Cutler 2003; Cutler, Haufler, and Porter 1999; and Haufler 2007.

[3] Krahmann 2003; Hall and Biersteker 2002; Poincignon 2005. See also Avant's argument that the marketization of security delivers a blow to state power by challenging the ability of modern states to control the use of force (Avant 2006). In the field of international political economy, particularly interesting are Germain 2007 and Cooley 2003. For analyses of the ways in which privatization has reinforced Weberian conceptions of statehood and sovereignty see also Leander 2006 and 2009.

[4] For a very interesting analysis of public/private interdependence, see the account of the politics of global regulation provided by Walter Mattli and Ngaire Woods (2009). Their analysis of global regulatory change contrasts outcomes that entrench narrow interest to

chapter in this volume, for example, demonstrates the ways in which a logic of privatization continues to underpin some of the emergent public practices in international development. Yet, whereas the contributions to this volume point to the impossibility of understanding public and private as distinct or coherent categories, the private authority literature tends to assume that public and private actors remain entities that continue to display the characteristics and practices associated with two distinct spheres of action. As Anna Leander notes in her chapter (Chapter 9, this volume), whether such literatures focus on "revolving doors" between public and private, the "capture" of the state by private interests (or vice versa), or the shifting of boundaries between public and private, the assumption remains that, even as actors move between them or seek to control one another, public and private remain separate and bounded entities.[5]

This conceptualization cannot capture some of the most interesting aspects of the contemporary transformations in global governance.[6] By treating the individuals and organizations that are playing these new roles as if they were still just private actors, such analyses miss the ways in which their construction as "public" endows them with special attributes. For example, as we see in several contributions to this collection, under certain conditions non-state actors can come to be seen as agents who perform important public functions. Through their constitution as public subjects, such actors are empowered to participate in practices of governance in ways that are not available to those regarded as purely private actors. At the same time, their constitution as public subjects also means that those actors are expected to comply with a certain set of norms and rules (such as norms related to their duty to advance the public good, as well as norms of transparency and accountability); to the extent that they are perceived as failing to comply with such norms, their involvement in practices of governance can be contested (Bernstein, Chapter 6, this volume).

Moreover, the attributes associated with "publicness" change depending on the historical and cultural context. As Avant and Haufler (Chapter 3, this volume) show, not only have firms and NGOs played

those that fulfill broader public purposes; their argument is that we should not assume that regulatory change is necessarily the result of actions by public officials against reluctant private sector groups. Contrary to conventional wisdom – which might suggest that public and private actors would by definition play different roles – Mattli and Woods show that entrepreneurs for change can be public officials, NGOs, but also (under certain circumstances) private sector actors.

[5] Evans 1996; Hellman, Jones, and Kaufmann 2003; Seabrooke and Tsingtou 2009.
[6] Our point is similar to the argument provided by Abrahamsen and Williams 2009.

important roles in the provision of security as a public good, but by using varying security practices in different historical eras, they have helped to constitute different kinds of public authority. At the same time, in situations in which the behavior of those actors was perceived as inconsistent with the norms associated with the pursuit of the public good, their involvement in practices of governance came to be contested. These findings suggest that what is needed is an analysis of the kinds of practice that emerge in a specific historical context and enact the "public" by mobilizing particular (material and non-material) forms of power. It is only through a sensitivity to the historical context in which specific practices are enacted that we can capture the broader dynamics associated with the constitution of a particular type of public at a given moment in time.[7]

The public sphere

Another body of literature that focuses on the concept of the public is the scholarship on the public sphere. In the field of IR, the preoccupation with the public sphere is a relatively recent phenomenon; among philosophers and political theorists, however, the concept of the public sphere has a long and distinguished intellectual history.[8]

Among contemporary scholars, Jürgen Habermas stands out as one of the most influential theorists of the public sphere.[9] According to Habermas, the public sphere is "a realm of our social life in which something approaching public opinion can be formed" (Habermas 1974: 51). In his view, the public sphere "can best be described as a network for communicating information and points of view" (Habermas and Rehg 1996: 360). For Habermas, it is important to differentiate between the center of a democratic political system and the periphery. In contrast to the democratic state institutions (parliaments, governments, and courts), which are located at the center of the political system, processes of public communication are situated at the periphery,

---

[7] For instance, as Porter (Chapter 10, this volume) demonstrates, the contemporary reconstitution of the public occurs in the context of – and is profoundly shaped by – the growing complexity of contemporary international practices.

[8] Some of the earliest discussions of the division between public and private spheres date to ancient Greece, where *public* meant the realm of politics, and *private* the domains of family and economic life. From the eighteenth century forward, liberal political theory has focused heavily on the public sphere, conceptualizing it as central to the establishment (and protection) of democracy.

[9] Although there have been many criticisms of Habermas – including criticisms of the Westphalian assumptions of his treatment of the public – his conception of the public sphere remains among the most influential in IR. See, for instance, Fraser 2007.

but play a crucial role in supervising the processes that take place at the center. It is at the level of civil society that citizens' views on governance are formed and their demands are articulated.

While it might be tempting to conceptualize it as a physical, territorially bounded domain, the public sphere – as Charles Taylor has persuasively argued – needs to be understood as de-territorialized common space for reasoned argument about matters of common interest.[10] From its emergence in the eighteenth century, Taylor has noted, the public sphere transcended "topical spaces" (that is, the kinds of common space arising from assembly in some particular locale). The public sphere "knits together a plurality of such spaces into one larger space on non-assembly" (Taylor 1992: 229). And, in contrast to the influential argument that in the Westphalian international system there never was a public domain apart from the sphere of states,[11] Taylor demonstrates that the original public sphere exceeded any one state and was linked to the idea of "civilized Europe" (Taylor 1992: 234).

The vision of a public sphere that transcends any particular state has been further developed by several prominent IR scholars. Particularly influential has been Thomas Risse's argument that, in numerous instances, international actors engage in processes of argumentation, deliberation, and persuasion – as a distinct mode of social interaction, to be differentiated from strategic bargaining and rule-guided behavior.[12] According to him, apart from utility-maximizing action and rule-guided behavior, actors often engage in truth-seeking, with the aim of reaching a mutual understanding via reasoned consensus.

In recent years there has also been growing (though by no means universal) support for the idea that, contrary to the conventional view of a state-based international order, an emerging transnational public sphere is already reshaping international politics and has the potential to help bring about a fundamental transformation of world order.[13] According to these scholars, the work of global civil society actors is crucial for the emergence of a public sphere in global politics. In particular, we are often reminded that NGOs and transnational social movements have played a crucial role in triggering transnational public debates on global governance, and have helped to infuse more transparency and accountability into institutions and practices of governance.[14]

---

[10] Taylor 1992.   [11] See Ruggie 2004, 504–05   [12] Risse 2000.
[13] On the potential democratizing power of such forces, see Archibugi, Held, and Koehler 1998; Falk 1995; Held 1995.
[14] Fraser 2007; Scholte 2004.

This literature on the public sphere and global civil society provides important insights into the increasingly complex involvement of non-state actors (particularly NGOs) in processes of global governance. Because of its attention to the emergence of a particular kind of global public – a public sphere – this literature provides us with some useful tools for recognizing the return of the public in global governance. As a number of the chapters in this book attest, in fields ranging from environmental governance (both Bernstein [Chapter 6] and Paterson [Chapter 7]), to international security (Avant and Haufler [Chapter 3]), and international development (Best [Chapter 5]), many of the emergent public practices that we are witnessing bear considerable resemblance to those tradition-ally associated with the liberal public sphere – practices of deliberation, participation, publicity, and transparency.

Yet, we suggest that this literature cannot capture the full complexity of the reconstitution of the public dimension of governance in the con-temporary era. First, there is a tendency in much of this literature to treat the public sphere as if it were a relatively coherent type of social space, which involves a specific logic: this is the space of deliberative processes arising out of people's recognition of their dwelling together in a common world. Although global civil society is often viewed as a new form of global public sphere, it is assumed that this new public domain is characterized by the same practices of debate, truth-seeking, and public-opinion formation that characterized the public sphere in liberal democratic societies. As in the case of the traditional (national) public sphere, these practices both rely upon and help to further reinforce fundamental liberal rights – although, in the case of the global public sphere, the boundaries of the community of individuals endowed with those rights no longer coincides with the borders of the territorial state. Taylor has argued persuasively, however, that the modern public sphere emerged in particular historical circumstances, and was constituted by specific sets of shared understandings about its nature and purpose.

Moreover, several of the contributions to this volume suggest that although we are witnessing the re-emergence of some practices that appear like those characteristic of the liberal public sphere, in fact they are often much thinner than the kind of robust, democratic, and deliberative processes that we traditionally associate with the public sphere. For example, both efforts to regulate derivatives and to improve development outcomes by fostering local demand for good governance involve a certain degree of public participation. Yet, as Helleiner points out in the case of derivatives (Chapter 4, this volume), the public who get to participate turn out to be a very small group of insiders, while as Best suggests in the case of good governance initiatives, the form that participation takes often looks more like marketing surveys than open-ended debate and deliberation.

Second, the literature on global civil society and the global public sphere tends to assume a much tidier division between public and private than the chapters in this volume suggest is the case in practice. At least in some historical contexts, some NGOs can enact practices that seem much closer to those conventionally attributed to public authorities and/or private, profit-seeking actors.[15] In other words, the boundaries between public authorities, the public sphere, and the private realm are more complicated than the public-sphere literature would seem to suggest. Moreover, far from being pre-given and fixed, these boundaries – and the communities of practice that they contain – are constantly constructed, reconstructed, and sometimes challenged through the transformative practices of particular networks of actors, networks that often defy the conventional divides between public and private. Although the literature on the public sphere therefore provides us with important insights into some of the aspects of the return of the public that we are witnessing today, it nonetheless tends to miss the complexity, fluidity, and sheer messiness of the processes currently underway.

Public goods

The final common conception of the public in IR scholarship is that of public goods. Like many other influential concepts in the discipline, the category of public goods is one that has been borrowed from economic theory – more specifically, from neoclassical economics and public choice theory.[16] In Paul Samuelson's classic formulation, a public good is one that is both non-excludable and non-rival.[17] In other words, it is something like clean air: it is impossible to restrict its availability to certain people, and its consumption by some does not reduce its availability to others.

Public goods pose a particular public policy challenge at both domestic and international levels: since people cannot be excluded from consuming a public good, whether or not they have paid for it, there is always a risk (a significant one if one accepts the economic assumption that individuals are rational maximizers) that they will refuse to pay for its provision. Hence both the "free rider" problem – the likelihood that people will consume the good without paying for it – and the problem

---

[15] Cooley and Ron 2002.
[16] Classic public-choice texts include: Buchanan and Tullock 1962; Downs 1957; Olson 1971.
[17] Samuelson 1954.

of underprovision – when enough people stop paying for the production of the good that it actually ceases to be produced altogether. This is what institutionalist economists would describe as a classic example of market failure, in which market forces alone are unable to ensure the adequate production and distribution of a crucial good.[18] At the domestic level, the problems of public goods and free-riding provide a kind of minimalist justification for state regulation – state coercion can provide the incentive to comply (by reducing air pollution for example), thus ensuring that an important public good is protected. This conception of public goods thus has some implications for the concept of public authority: it is assumed that the state legitimately exists only because it can ensure the provision of certain kinds of non-excludable, non-rival goods. This particular conception of the public therefore sees it as a largely negative, residual category that fills a gap left by market failures.

These assumptions about the character of the public have been largely retained in the main strands of IR literature that have drawn heavily on the idea of public goods. Theoretically driven neoliberal institutionalist scholars have sought to use the concept to examine the challenges and possibilities of providing public goods on a global scale. Relying heavily on Mancur Olson's logic of collective action, together with Douglass North's institutionalist economics,[19] they have examined the extent to which regimes and international organizations can provide public goods in the absence of state-like coercive force. Robert Keohane's *After Hegemony* is of course the classic formulation of a public-goods-based explanation for the existence of regimes as institutions that reduce problems of market failure and collective action dilemmas.[20] Later debates between neoliberal and neorealist scholars on the relevance of international institutions, as well as ongoing research into the provision of global public goods, also hinges on the question of whether public goods such as a liberal trading regime can be provided in the absence of a hegemon.[21] A more normative, policy-oriented group of analysts have also recently used the concept to argue for greater provision of global public goods. The UNDP's Inge Kaul has been particularly vocal in arguing for an expansion in what is defined as a global public good, and in using the concept to argue for a more robust set of international institutions capable of providing such goods on a global scale.[22] While

---

[18] Coase 1960; North 1990; Williamson 1975.
[19] North 1990; Olson 1971.   [20] Keohane 1984.
[21] See: Gowa 1989; Oye 1986; Snidal 1985; Stone, Slanchev, and London 2008.
[22] Kaul, Grunberg, and Stern 1999. For an analysis of the emergence of this branch of global public-goods thinking, see Carbone 2007.

this second group has been arguing for a more positive kind of public good, they have relied explicitly on the more negative, neoclassical economic conception of the public to make their case.[23]

One of the most interesting recent contributions to the public-goods literature comes from John Ruggie. He suggests that we are witnessing the beginning of a fundamental reconstitution of the global public domain, "away from one that equated the public in international politics with states and the interstate realm to one in which the very system of states is becoming embedded in a broader, albeit still thin and partial, institutionalized arena concerned with the production of global public goods" (Ruggie 2004: 500). This book builds on Ruggie's argument regarding the transformation of the spatial map of global governance, involving the problematization of a host of new political economy, security, environmental issues in public terms. Yet, we also seek to transcend some of the limitations of Ruggie's account, including his functionalist account of the public domain as the realm concerned with the production of public goods, and seek to develop a more nuanced account, which pays attention to the multiple meanings of the "public" in contemporary processes of governance.

Given its emphasis on the role of public goods, these various strands of literature do provide us with some tools for recognizing the re-emergence of the public in global governance. As chapters by Paterson (Chapter 7) and Helleiner (Chapter 4) point out respectively, recent changes in climate and financial governance have been driven in part by efforts both to redefine what counts as a public good and to reconstitute the institutional mechanisms for managing it. Yet both of these authors move significantly away from more traditional public-good assumptions in their conception of the public. The public goods literature treats the public as a remarkably thin – even negative – category. The public is defined as something that exists naturally because it cannot be subdivided, priced, bought, and sold like normal private goods. Public goods themselves are not seen to be variable or dependent efforts to construct them as such: the definition of something as a public good depends merely on its being non-excludable and non-rival. In contrast to this conception of public goods as natural, both Paterson and Helleiner emphasize the constructed and contested nature of these emergent public goods.

Each of these literatures gets something right and something wrong. The private-authority literature reminds us that the character of these

---

[23] This point is made very effectively by Coussy 2005. For a more pragmatic critique of the concept as used by the UN, see Long and Woolley 2009.

new publics remain intimately connected to the private domain, yet it does not take seriously enough the specifically public character of these new actors and processes. The scholarship on the public sphere points out that many of these practices bear striking resemblances to more traditional liberal conceptions of public processes, but misses the other forms that this newly emerging public also takes. At the same time, the literature on public goods points to the ways in which these more deliberative public processes are often linked to far thinner and more instrumental economic conceptions of the public, but in the process misses the much thicker forms of public practice that are also being developed and enacted.

Ironically, in spite of their considerable differences, the literatures on private authority, the global public sphere, and global public goods all exhibit certain similar weaknesses. Each tends to treat the public as a coherent space or site, thereby reproducing the liberal tendency to think about public/private as ontologically separate domains of social life, marked by their distinct (pre-given) logics and associated with specific institutional locations. Therefore they fail to understand that its characteristics are socially constructed, and thus potentially subject to contestation, particularly during times of socio-cultural disruption. It is only by embracing a conception of the public as practices that we can shed light on the socially constructed, historically specific nature of the public and its relationship with the private. On this basis, it becomes possible to see contemporary interrogations and movements of protest not as a dangerous skepticism and potentially catastrophic move away from the "natural" relationship between public and private realms (as some neoliberals, in particular, would suggest), but as a historically specific interrogation and contestation of a particular definition of the public.

Conceptualizing the public as practice

It is against the background of the limitations of existing theories about the public that we argue for a "turn to practice" in the study of the evolving role of the public domain of global governance.[24] In turning to practice, we depart from conceptions of the public as a clearly defined and bounded space, type of good or form of authority. Instead, we examine the practices – and the power associated with those practices – through which common understandings regarding the nature and boundaries of the public are defined, and subjects, objects, and "rules

---

[24] On the importance of practices in IR see in particular Adler and Pouliot 2011.

of the game" for public action are constituted in specific political contexts. From this perspective, definitions of the public that are taken for granted in mainstream IR need to be understood as the outcome of historically specific practices. For instance, as Abrahamsen and Williams (Chapter 11, this volume) argue, the dominance of state-centrism in IR is often "an unspoken (and sometimes unrecognized) consequence of complex historical attempts to determine what or where the public is, and its relationship to the private."

Conceptualizing practices

Scholars have tended to describe the growing interest in practices as a "turn to practice" rather than as "practice theory" because of the broad range of different theorists who have found the concept of practices useful.[25] As the concept of practices has begun to enter the theoretical vocabulary of IR scholars, they have drawn on a diverse range of different social theorists – with security scholars tending to draw on Pierre Bourdieu, while IPE scholars have relied more on Michel Callon and Bruno Latour.[26] In calling for a turn to practice in our conceptualization of the public, we are not therefore proposing a new singular grand theory,[27] but rather trying to demonstrate the usefulness of the idea of practice for IR theory today.

Practice is a very broad category, containing a range of different kinds of actions, claims, and understandings. For the sake of clarity in conceptualizing the role and character of practice in global governance, we are therefore making several basic distinctions among different kinds of practices, which should be understood as heuristic devices rather than absolute categories. We suggest that it is useful to think of practices as bringing together the *ideal* and the *material* in new ways, and as more or less *reinforcing* or *transformative* in their social dynamics.

Practices can be defined as knowledge-constituted, meaningful patterns of socially recognized activity that structure experience and that

---

[25] Some of the major social theorists and philosophers associated with the practice turn include: Bourdieu 1977 and 1990; Callon 1986; Dreyfus 1991; Hacking 2002; Latour 1986 and 1987; Schatzki 1996; and Taylor 1992. These scholars have all in turn, although in different ways, been inspired by the foundational work of Heidegger (1962) and Wittgenstein (1958).

[26] Security scholars: see Abrahamsen and Williams 2011; Gheciu 2008; Pouliot 2008; Williams 2007. IPE scholars: see Best 2009; Langley 2008. For an interesting analysis of the ways in which these traditions can be combined see Leander 2011.

[27] This is similar to the position adopted by Adler and Pouliot 2011.

enable agents to reproduce or transform their world.[28] As this definition demonstrates, practices always bring together the *ideal* and the *material*; therefore, as Porter argues (Chapter 10, this volume), analyses that focus on practices – such as those developed in this collection – transcend the dichotomy between the material and the ideational realms that has shaped much of the conventional IR approaches. It might be tempting to interpret particular types of practices (such as the use of particular technologies) as not having much to do with the ideational realm. Yet, as the contributions to this volume show, particular techniques, institutional arrangements, or uses of technology are possible only because those who participate in them share a set of inter-subjective ideas about the meaning and appropriate use of that technology. For example, as Gheciu (Chapter 8, this volume) demonstrates, in the 1990s Bulgaria witnessed the proliferation of practices of security provision that revolved around a particular use of stickers. Those stickers signified that vehicles and shops that displayed them were protected by the powerful "insurance" companies that often had close connections to organized crime. In that context, a whole set of inter-subjective ideas – shared not only by participants in those practices but by society at large – about the power and *modus operandi* of those insurance companies and about the inability or unwillingness of the state to control them enabled the use of the stickers as a relatively effective (albeit deeply problematic) instrument of protection.

The relationship between the material and the ideal goes both ways, however, as Porter (Chapter 10, this volume) demonstrates. Porter points out that the ideas and assumptions that make border security possible gain much of their power from the fact that they are embedded into and enabled by specific material objects and procedures – including electronic passports, airline security procedures, and the growing use of biometrics. These material artefacts are not merely expressions of pre-given ideas about border security but instead play a role in enabling and shaping norms and assumptions. At the same time, the very forms of materiality that we take for granted are becoming more virtual and abstract. As Porter suggests, "the border itself, which previously was seen as fixed by the physical properties of the terrain across which it ran, is increasingly constructed in complex ways by new legal and technical

---

[28] See Swidler 2001: 79. This is very similar to the definition proposed by Adler and Pouliot: "practices are socially meaningful patterns of action, which, in being performed more or less competently, simultaneously embody, act out, and possibly reify background knowledge and discourse in and on the material world" (Adler and Pouliot 2011: 4)

ideas" – as it extends beyond the physical boundaries of the state and also includes sites within it.

In other practices, discourse itself plays the primary role in constituting particular objects and subjects. In examining this side of the world of social practices, we are building on a rich, largely Foucauldian, body of literature that examines the role of discursive practices in constructing, reproducing, and sometimes changing the world in particular ways.[29] The key role of discursive practices in constituting public subjects and objects is highlighted by several contributors to this volume. For instance, Helleiner (Chapter 4, this volume) examines the narratives through which, in the aftermath of the 2007–08 financial crisis, policy-makers and societal groups across the world have sought to define derivatives markets as a proper subject for global public policy. A strong emphasis on discursive practices can also be found in Best's chapter (Chapter 5). In her analysis of recent efforts by the World Bank to foster the "demand side" of good governance, Best highlights the way in which the Bank has encouraged poor people, civil society groups, parliaments, and market actors to engage in particular kinds of public speech, demanding better governance and more efforts to reduce poverty. Yet, it is important to note that these discursive practices are not disconnected from the material world. Thus, policy-makers seeking to define derivatives markets as a subject for global public policy, and the World Bank seeking to foster the demand side of poverty reduction depend on material artefacts such as modern technology and concrete institutional arrangements to disseminate their ideas and to seek to implement them. Those forms of materiality – their possibilities and limitations – in turn help to shape the ideas that inform them.[30]

Partly because of the way that they bring together the material and discursive dimensions of social life, practices play an important role in *reinforcing* and/or *transforming* social relations (often both at once). One of the most common ways of conceptualizing practices in IR today is through the idea of communities of practice, which emphasize the way

---

[29] Foucault 1980; Foucault *et al.* 1991.

[30] The concept of "affordances" is particularly useful for understanding how material objects can influence not just norms and ideas but also various forms of human agency. This concept points to the ways in which the material form of certain objects encourages particular kinds of practices and discourages others. As scholars in science and technology studies (STS) have argued, focusing on the power of screens and other technical devices, complex objects like computers can actually "configure the user" and thus help to constitute certain forms of subjectivity. One only needs to think of the ubiquity of the smartphone and its integration into everyday life to recognize the ways in which this object has altered our relationship with the world and one another (Norman 1988; Woolgar 1991).

in which practices are embedded in particular routines and organizations, and reproduce existing communities by translating often tacit understandings into concrete actions.[31] Inscribed in practices are forms of background knowledge and dispositions – or, to employ a Bourdieusian term, a particular *habitus* – that predispose actors to interpret reality, and respond to that reality, in specific ways.[32] From this perspective, to understand why, in a specific historical setting, particular objects and subjects are recognized as public while others are not, it is important to take into account the prevailing inter-subjective understandings and dispositions that incline actors to accept particular classifications, and to explore the specific forms of power that are both reflected in and reproduced through a specific *habitus*. Such everyday practices and assumptions can operate at a very basic level, making possible certain things that we take for granted, such as our basic understanding of security or the market; Michel Callon suggests, for example, that in order for a liberal market to be created, people have to learn to calculate in particular ways – to perceive their labor, their dwellings, their livelihood through the lens of profit and loss.[33] This is a conception of practices that emphasizes their role in *reinforcing* and reproducing an existing community and its key values, categories, and assumptions.

Many of the practices that help to reproduce our conceptions of the public operate in this way. Various concepts of public authority, public goods, public actors, and the public sphere are part of our everyday taken-for-granted vocabulary and embedded in our background understandings of political and social life. Although some of these conceptions of the public might rise to the level of conscious thought and some might even be contested, many operate below that level – linked to ways of being in the world. Anyone who has spent more than a couple of days in a different country quickly comes to feel how different kinds of things, practices, spaces, conversations, etc. are understood as subject to public

---

[31] Following Adler, we define communities of practice as consisting of "people who are informally as well as contextually bound by a shared interest in learning and applying a common practice" (Adler 2005: 15). As Adler explains, "communities of practice are a configuration of a *domain of knowledge*, which constitutes like-mindedness, a *community of people*, which 'creates the social fabric of learning,' and a *shared practice*, which embodies 'the knowledge the community develops, shares and maintains'" (Adler 2005: 15) [emphasis in original].

[32] Bourdieu, 1977. In this section, we draw on the works of several IR scholars who have applied the work of Bourdieu to international politics: in particular, Abrahamsen and Williams 2011; Adler 2008; Gheciu 2008; Leander 2008 and 2011; Pouliot 2010; Williams 2007.

[33] Callon 1998. For a more thorough description of this process, see Best and Paterson 2010: Introduction.

debate, authority, or responsibility. Many of these ways of demarcating the public are mundane (in Australia, public barbecues are ubiquitous; in France, state officials clean up after citizens' dogs). Yet many of these everyday practices add up to important definitions of what counts as public and what does not, and who gets to participate in defining it.

Yet not all practices work to reinforce and reproduce the understandings and boundaries of existing communities. Others are more transformative, working to contest and ultimately change taken-for-granted values and categories. Thus, as several contributions to this volume (including those by Bernstein [Chapter 6] and Paterson [Chapter 7]) demonstrate, particularly at moments of disruption such as the present, there are many different actors who challenge conventional wisdom about the nature, limits, and proper role of the public, and act strategically in an effort to establish a new *habitus* and new institutional arrangements in their fields of activity. Even in those cases, however, the balance between transformative and reinforcing practices can be complicated. For example, practices can transform a domain previously dominated by private practices by creating new institutional arrangements with a public character, but at the same time reinforce the practices of publicness themselves. By the same token, in some cases failed attempts at transformation could reinforce the unique legitimacy of the state as the sole realm of the public.

Even when particular sets of actors seek to create a new *habitus* and define new "rules of the game" – in our case, new rules concerning the nature and functions of the public – they often mobilize broader background understandings and norms that can help them secure legitimacy in that process of transformation. For instance, as Gheciu (Chapter 8) points out, those who seek to redefine the rules of the game concerning the nature and powers of actors that provide public security often mobilize socially accepted forms of material or symbolic capital such as sophisticated technology and expertise in the provision of security. To cast themselves – and secure recognition – as effective security providers, those actors often invoke broader inter-subjective understandings that prevail in a given society. As we find out in some of the empirical chapters in this volume (e.g. Bernstein, Chapter 6), much of the contestation around efforts to create new rules of the game revolves around debates about whether the new norms and institutional arrangements being proposed are consistent with prevailing (generally liberal) teleological and procedural norms of public responsibility.

The contributions to this volume provide a rich array of examples as to how the public can be conceptualized as practice – some reinforcing existing "rules of the game" and existing communities of practice in a particular field, while others explicitly seek to challenge and transform existing rules and communities of practice. Reinforcing practices are carried out by an existing community of individuals that are recognized – and seek continued recognition – as actors who can identify and act in the name of the public interest or public good. Take, for instance, the case of the World Bank, as examined in Best's chapter. As Best shows (Chapter 5), recent years have marked a shift in its practices of governance: in contrast to its previous emphasis on the supply side of good governance, the Bank now focuses on the demand side of the equation. In some ways, this move can be seen as an effort to transform the definition and scope of the public – by defining good governance as a global public good, and by seeking to engage a new range of actors as public. At the same time, however, this is a case of community reinforcing practices, in which the Bank staff and management seek to reinforce their role as the community of practitioners that can be trusted to prescribe and help implement the correct "rules of the game" in efforts to achieve economic development. In other words, the recent change in emphasis can be seen as an expression of the Bank's effort to secure continued international recognition as an institution that has the ability to identify and effectively address a key matter of common concern (development).

As several contributions to this volume demonstrate, in other instances practices can be much more transformative, specifically seeking to alter not only existing rules of the game but also established communities of practice. For instance, Avant and Haufler (Chapter 3) shed important light on historical efforts to redraw the boundaries of existing communities of practice in the field of security, to include in those communities a whole new set of actors recognized as legitimate participants in the definition and enactment of the public interest. To take just one example: by the mid nineteenth century in Britain, the growing power of parliament – and the openness of that institution – allowed a venue for debate on what the British public interest should be. The voices of some religious groups and others argued that the government had a responsibility to define the British public interest according to the views of the British public. Importantly, this redefinition of the community of actors involved in debates about matters of common interest placed constraints on the types of practices that could be carried out in the name of protecting the British public interest. If British forces were to be used to generate security in imperial territories, these territories should be under the control of the British government (acting in the British public's interest). This led to a consolidation of British government power over its colonies and restricted the activities in which overseas – now seen as private – companies could engage.

Very interesting examples of transformative practices can also be found in Bernstein's accounts of transnational governance (Chapter 6, this volume). Bernstein examines efforts to establish public transnational governance in social and environmental issue areas, in a situation in which conventional (intergovernmental) processes have failed to deliver authoritative and effective rules, or where multilateral rules exist but are too limited in their effects. He shows that transnational governance organizations engage in a broad set of strategic practices in an effort to secure authority to pursue public goals – in other words, to change the nature of the community of practitioners involved in the provision of social/environmental public goods.

Focusing on climate change governance, Paterson (Chapter 7, this volume) explores the ways in which the failure of traditional means of resolving public goods problems has spawned a whole range of forms of governance that are not centered on states. These experiments involve the inclusion in deliberation about climate change of new (non-state) actors; indeed, in recent years we have witnessed the emergence of transnational, hybrid, partnership-based forms of governance. The transformative practices examined by Paterson go beyond the redefinition of the nature of actors who can participate in the public space of climate change. Importantly, the qualities of this new type of public space are different from the authoritative decision-making conventionally associated with the public domain. Paterson argues that, given its character as a complex ("superwicked") problem, public practices surrounding climate change are predominantly characterized by a focus on inter-subjective learning. In spite of these important innovations, however, Paterson also notes that these new public practices also reinforce certain existing hierarchies of power. The emerging practices of climate change governance are both transformative and reinforcing in their character.

The public as practice

How then do we apply this conception of practice to the public in global governance? We define as public those goods, actors, or processes that are recognized by the community in which they are carried out as being of common concern. This definition of the public captures a core assumption underpinning the different ways in which the term "public" is generally used: a public good is a good that is of common (rather than exclusive) concern or use; a public actor acts on behalf of the common (rather than a particular) interest; and a public process is one that allows the general public or demos (not a select group) to understand and participate in debates about those issues that concern them.

Based on this conception of the public, we define public practices as actions that involve an understanding in a given society at a particular moment in time that something is of common concern. Such practices are often embedded and taken for granted – part of our background understandings about how to go about our daily lives as political, economic, and social actors. More explicit, transformative practices tend to arise when the boundaries around the public become subject to debate: current debates about the appropriate response to the financial crisis, for example, have led to more explicit claims about the appropriate scope of public authority in this area and efforts to create new kinds of financial practices that are subject to greater public scrutiny and control.[34] By understanding these claims as a kind of public-making practice, we are arguing that this is not simply a matter of shifting responsibilities from one pre-existing (private) domain to another (public) one. Nor is it simply a question of expanding the scope of the public. It is instead a set of practices that seek to claim particular problems, actors, or processes *as* public – or of common concern – and in doing so, that effectively work to constitute those issues as public. In other words, public-making practices are performative: they seek to create the things that they describe.

There are many different kinds of public practice. A public practice may work to define *who* counts as the public (who will be consulted, who gets to speak, who has the authority and/or responsibility to govern in the name of the public),[35] *what* counts as public (what kinds of issues are of common concern and what kinds of speech count as public), and *how* the public is enacted (how public processes of debate or publicity should proceed, what are the rules of public accountability). Thus, to extend our initial definition of the public as practice, a public practice is an action that involves an understanding that someone counts as a member of the public, something is of common concern, or that some process is public.

Once we begin to see the public in terms of key practices, we need no longer assume that it should look like a stable, coherent space or sphere, in which actors, concerns, and processes are all located. We can instead begin to disaggregate the public. This means understanding it as a construction involving certain actors or processes at certain moments,

---

[34] Such forms of public authority include but are not limited to the state, as is revealed by Helleiner's analysis (Chapter 4) of the regulation of derivatives markets and Bernstein's discussion (Chapter 6) of the different kinds of publicness in social and environmental governance.

[35] As Abrahamsen and Williams point out (Chapter 11, this volume), there is a very long history of political debate, from Hobbes onwards, precisely around this question of who has the authority to represent the people as a public authority.

and not at others. It also means that what counts as a public actor, process, or problem is open for renegotiation, particularly at certain moments of transition. And it means that what is seen as public will depend as much on what is *done* as on where an issue, actor, or institution is located.

In moving towards a conceptualization of the public as practices, we suggest that the processes governing the definition and enactment of public subjects and objects share interesting similarities with those of securitization highlighted, in particular, by the Copenhagen school of IR. Securitization theorists argue the act of naming something a security problem is performative: by defining an issue as an existential threat, authoritative actors are able move it beyond ordinary politics. According to Buzan, Waever, and de Wilde, the key therefore is to understand "who securitizes, on what issues (threats), for whom (referent object), why, with what results, and not least, under what conditions" (Buzan, Waever, and de Wilde 1998: 32). In a similar vein, our volume asks: Why do we treat a particular subject or object as public? What are the consequences of designating that particular subject/object as public? In addressing these questions, our contributors, like the securitization scholars, pay close attention to discursive practices through which something or someone is defined as a public subject or object. At the same time, however, our contributors also emphasize the material dimension of practices, which are often marginalized in the securitization literature. As we shall see, a close attention to the particular techniques, technologies, and/or institutional arrangements associated with particular practices is often needed if we are to understand how, exactly, the public is constituted.

Some implications

Several things follow from this initial definition of public practices. First, the fact that someone claims or acts as though a particular problem, process, or actor is public does not necessarily mean that they will be successful. As Latour has argued in the context of the production of scientific claims, the success of any attempt to render something a scientific fact depends not simply on the skill in representing it as such, as but also on the number of other people who accept it as a fact.[36] The most successful public practices will be those that are taken entirely for granted (or "black boxed," to use Latour's terminology). Yet even these may be subject to contestation and revision at a

---

[36] Johnson 1988; Latour 1987.

different moment in time, as we will discuss in our brief history of public practices in the next section.

Second, public practices always involve power. For example, within the worldviews in which the public is positively valued, the claim that X is a public issue or Y speaks on behalf of the public has powerful normative overtones that seek to trump more selfish, individual concerns. Even when public practices are implicit understandings rather than explicit statements, they still carry a powerful moral punch. Yet, because public practices are partial, incomplete, and contested, efforts to define an actor, problem, or process as public tend to include some things or people while excluding others. Some actors may be defined as legitimately working in the public interest (in participating in neighborhood security patrols for example), while others (in many societies, vigilantes) are not. Some forms of expression and speech (newspapers) may count as part of the public sphere, while others (graffiti) may not. Some issues (certain kinds of financial derivatives products for example) may be initially seen as a private matter, and then redefined as being of public concern. Each of these public-defining acts can work to empower some actors and disempower others, redrawing the boundaries not just of public and private but also of legitimate and illegitimate action. For instance, Paterson (Chapter 7, this volume) demonstrates that the legitimacy of new, transnational forms of governance in the area of climate change is widely contested, precisely on the basis of normative claims that climate change should be addressed through public rather than privatized means. These claims about privatized governance in turn give rise to an interesting set of legitimation strategies adopted by the actors involved in such governance projects, specifically through making claims about the "public" character of their projects. To analyze the practices through which the public is defined, enacted, and contested, several contributors to this volume engage in an analysis of the various forms of power that facilitate processes of designating certain objects and subjects as public. While drawing on different theorists to help them conceptualize power, contributors such as Best, Bernstein, Gheciu, and Leander share an interest in focusing on more subtle, productive, and not just coercive forms of power.[37]

Third, if public-defining practices are performative, that means that the definitions of the public contained in political, economic, and IR theory also have constitutive effects. As noted above, in spite of the growing interest in private actors and private forms of authority, the field

---

[37] Barnett and Duvall 2005.

of IR continues to be informed by assumptions regarding the separation between the public and the private spheres. We argue, instead, that these separations are themselves forms of practice, which both reflect and contribute to the reproduction of particular forms of power. Those who define global public practices through the lens of the public sphere tend to focus on certain things as public (forms of discourse, statements, publicity, arguments) and to downplay others (forms of power and authority). Similarly, those who define the public in terms of public goods frame the problem in terms of efficiency and functionality, and tend to ignore questions of debate and power.

These broader overarching conceptions of the public (as goods, sphere, authority, etc.) are each a kind of *public logic* – bringing together a cluster of practices and organizing them in a way that privileges certain kinds of public practice over others. A conception of the public as practices therefore invites a study not just of particular practices, but also of how they are linked together into public logics – and the political implications of those logics. Because these are historical and cultural processes, it is possible to trace the dominance of particular public logics at particular times as well as various forms of contestation and resistance. In fact, as we will argue in the next section of this chapter, we are currently witnessing a transformation not only of public-making practices but also of their dominant public logic.

Reconstituting the public in global governance

What do the public backlash against excessive risk taking leading up to the current financial crisis, the growing discomfort with private security firm involvement in military conflicts, and the emerging debate over the best way of responding to global climate change all have in common? They all point to a renewed debate over the current constitution of the public on both domestic and global levels. We began this chapter with the claim that we were currently witnessing a reconstitution of the public dimension of global governance. We do not intend to provide a comprehensive account of this transformation, either in this chapter or in the book. We do hope, however, through the various contributions to this volume, to provide some broad brush-strokes of the kinds of changes that appear to be ongoing, as well as some of their historical origins.

We interpret the present reconstitution of the public dimension of governance as a moment of disruption – partially in response to the perceived limitations of neoliberal ideas and practices of the public that were prominent in previous years. In the IPE literature, as well as much of the private authority scholarship, the 1990s and early 2000s are seen as an era of privatization – a period that witnessed the hollowing out of the state, the stripping of public powers, and the transfer of capacity and authority to the private sphere at both domestic and global levels.[38] Yet, as we have suggested above, any process of privatization is always partial, dependent on particular public practices and capacities. In fact, at the same time that the private sphere and private actors were gaining greater influence over this period, there was also a significant transformation of the public under way: public sectors were transformed throughout the industrialized world, as public choice theory and new public management came to dominate thinking and practice.[39] The idea, best exemplified by New Zealand, was to not only minimize the size and scope of the public sector, but also to reorganize it so that it more closely resembled the market.[40]

The public logic that came to dominate in this era was that of public goods. The public was assumed to be a largely technical problem of the provision of those goods that the market could not provide alone. Public-defining practices were generally organized within this narrow public-goods logic; thus, for example, questions such as who the public was were defined largely in terms of clients for key public services and what counted as a public issue was defined in minimalist and functionalist terms.[41] Of course, not all public-constituting practices subscribed to the public choice driven logic of public goods. Much of the contestation to this logic was articulated either in the language of civil society and the need for a more robust public sphere, or by critics who pointed to the dangers of the rise of private authority and raised concerns about the decline of public accountability. Yet, until recently, such critical counter-publics have not been particularly successful in redefining the dominant logic of the public at either domestic or global levels.

What has changed? The various contributions to this volume provide somewhat different answers to this question, as well as different understandings of the scope and implications of these changes. What is clear is that the global financial crisis, 9/11, and climate change have all challenged previously taken-for-granted boundaries between the public and private, between the domestic and the international, and between security and economic fields of activity. Each of these crises has forced a redefinition of what counts as a purely domestic issue, as unstable economies, fragile political regimes, terrorist groups, and carbon-hungry development have

---

[38] See, for example, Abrahamsen and Williams 2006; Krahmann 2003 (in the field of security); Cerny 1990; Jessop 1993 (in IPE).
[39] Gore 1993; Hood 1991; Osborne and Gaebler 1992.
[40] Schick 1998.   [41] E.g. Gore 1993.

all refused to stay within national boundaries and have spilled over onto the global scene. At the same time, each of these crises has also forced a rethinking of the previously dominant public logic: while privatized solutions have certainly not disappeared, they have often been scaled back, subject to more public oversight, and to various forms of public consultation.

Does this mean that we are witnessing a shift to an entirely new public logic? It is too early to draw any definitive conclusions. As the various contributions to this collection suggest, however, a measure of caution is definitely warranted. For as Best (Chapter 5) and Helleiner (Chapter 4) both point out, even in those cases in which new kinds of public practices are being introduced – particularly forms of consultation and civil society participation in the security, development, and financial realms – they are often defined in very narrow, instrumentalist terms. The publics consulted are often defined as stakeholders or clients rather than citizens, and the scope of debate is often limited to technical questions. Moreover, where public authority does appear to be growing – in for example, the regulation of certain kinds of derivatives (Helleiner, Chapter 4, this volume) or the provision of particular forms of security (Avant and Haufler, Chapter 3, and Gheciu, Chapter 8, this volume) – it still often takes the form of delegated authority to a market-like process. What we appear to be witnessing at present, therefore, is the emergence of a hybrid of public-goods and public-spheres logics, in which the processes of debate and publicity emphasized in the more critical public-sphere advocates is being adapted to and instrumentalized by the more economistic public-goods logic.

Whatever the ultimate implications of the transformations currently under way, a conception of the public as practices is invaluable in making sense of them. At a time of disruption and contestation it becomes all the more important to be able to disaggregate "the public" and "the private" into the various practices that sustain them. Once we do so, it becomes possible to see the many tensions and complex combinations that make up what might on the surface appear to be relatively stable entities. It also becomes possible to challenge the arguments – put forward by some theorists as well as practitioners – that particular articulations of the public/private are demanded by "objective forces," and that any action that ignores or disrupts those forces can only lead to economic and political disaster.

REFERENCES

Abrahamsen, Rita, and Michael C. Williams. 2006. "Security sector reform: bringing the private in." *Conflict, Security and Development* 6(1): 1–23.
2007. "Securing the city: private security companies and non-state authority in global governance." *International Relations* 21(2): 237–53.

2009. "Security beyond the state: global security assemblages in international politics." *International Political Sociology* 3(1): 1–17.

2011. *Security beyond the State: Private Security in International Politics.* Cambridge: Cambridge University Press.

Adler, Emanuel. 2005. *Communitarian International Relations: The Epistemic Foundations of International Relations.* New York: Routledge.

2008. "The spread of security communities: communities of practice, self-restraint, and NATO's post-Cold War transformation." *European Journal of International Relations* 14(2): 195–230.

Adler, Emanuel, and Vincent Pouliot. 2011. "International practices." *International Theory* 3(1): 1–36.

Amoore, Louise, and Marieke de Goede. 2008. *Risk and the War on Terror.* New York: Routledge.

Archibugi, Daniele, David Held, and Martin Koehler, eds. 1998. *Re-imagining Political Community: Studies in Cosmopolitan Democracy.* Cambridge: Polity Press.

Avant, Deborah. 2005. "Private security companies." *New Political Economy* 10(1): 121–31.

2006. "The implications of marketized security for IR theory: the democratic peace, late state building, and the nature and frequency of conflict." *Perspectives on Politics* 4(3): 507–28.

Avant, Deborah, Martha Finnemore, and Susan Sell, eds. 2010. *Who Governs the Globe?* Cambridge: Cambridge University Press.

Barnett, Michael, and Raymond Duvall, eds. 2005. *Power in Global Governance.* Cambridge: Cambridge University Press.

Best, Jacqueline. 2009. "How to make a bubble: towards a cultural political economy of the financial crisis." *International Political Sociology* 3(4): 461–65.

Best, Jacqueline, and Matthew Paterson, eds. 2010. *Cultural Political Economy.* New York: Routledge.

Bourdieu, Pierre. 1977. *Outline of a Theory of Practice.* Cambridge: Cambridge University Press.

1990. *The Logic of Practice.* Translated by Richard Nice. Stanford, CA: Stanford University Press.

Bourdieu, Pierre, and Loïc Wacquant. 1992. "The purpose of reflexive sociology (The Chicago Workshop)." In *An Invitation to Reflexive Sociology,* edited by Pierre Bourdieu and Loïc J. D. Wacquant, pp. 61–215. Chicago, IL: University of Chicago Press.

Buchanan, James M., and Gordon Tullock. 1962. *The Calculus of Consent: Logical Foundations of Constitutional Democracy.* Ann Arbor, MI: University of Michigan Press.

Buzan, Barry, Ole Waever, and Jaap de Wilde. 1998. *Security: A New Framework for Analysis.* Boulder, CO: Lynne Rienner.

Callon, Michel. 1986. "Some elements of a sociology of translation: domestication of the scallops and the fishermen of St. Brieuc Bay." In *Power, Action, and Belief: A New Sociology of Knowledge?,* edited by John Law, pp. 196–233. New York: Routledge & Kegan Paul.

40   *Jacqueline Best and Alexandra Gheciu*

1998. "Introduction: The embeddness of economic markets in economics." In *The Laws of the Markets*, edited by Michel Callon, pp. 58–68. Oxford: Blackwell.

Carbone, Maurizio. 2007. "Supporting or resisting global public goods? The policy dimension of a contested concept." *Global Governance* 13(2): 179–98.

Cerny, Philip. 1990. *The Competition State*. Cambridge: Polity Press.

Coase, Ronald. 1960. "The problem of social cost." *Journal of Law and Economics* 3: 1–44.

Cooley, Alexander. 2003. "Thinking rationally about hierarchy and global governance." *Review of International Political Economy* 10(4): 672–84.

Cooley, Alexander, and James Ron. 2002. "The NGO scramble: organizational insecurity and the political economy of transnational action." *International Security* 27(1): 5–39.

Coussy, Jean. 2005. "The adventures of a concept: is neo-classical theory suitable for defining global public goods?" *Review of International Political Economy* 12(1): 177–94.

Cutler, Claire A. 2003. *Private Power and Global Authority: Transnational Merchant Law in the Global Political Economy*. Cambridge: Cambridge University Press.

Cutler, Claire A., Virginia Haufler, and Tony Porter, eds. 1999. *Private Authority and International Affairs*. New York: State University of New York Press.

Downs, Anthony. 1957. *An Economic Theory of Democracy*. New York: Harper & Row.

Dreyfus, Hubert. 1991. *Being-in-the-World: A Commentary on Heidegger's Being and Time, Division I*. Cambridge, MA: MIT Press.

Evans, Peter B. 1996. "Introduction: Development strategies across the public–private divide." *World Development* 24(6): 1033–37.

Falk, Richard. 1995. *On Humane Governance: Towards a New Global Politics*. University Park, PA: Pennsylvania State University Press.

Finnemore, Martha, and Kathryn Sikkink. 1998. "International norm dynamics and political change." *International Organization* 52(4): 887–917.

Florini, Ann. 2007. *The Right to Know: Transparency for an Open World*. New York: Columbia University Press.

Foucault, Michel. 1980. *Power/Knowledge: Selected Interviews and Other Writings*. Edited by Colin Gordon. London: Harvester.

Foucault, Michel, Graham Burchell, Colin Gordon, and Peter Miller, 1991. *The Foucault Effect: Studies in Governmentality*. Chicago, IL: University of Chicago Press.

Fraser, Nancy. 2007. "Transnationalizing the public sphere: on the legitimacy and efficacy of public opinion in a post-Westphalian world." *Theory, Culture and Society* 24(4): 7–30.

Germain, Randall D. 2007. "Global finance, risk, and governance." *Global Society* 21(1): 71–94.

Gheciu, Alexandra. 2008. *Securing Civilization? The EU, NATO and the OSCE in the Post-9/11 World*. Oxford: Oxford University Press.

Gore, Al. 1993. *The Gore Report on Reinventing Government: Creating a Government that Works Better and Costs Less, Report of the National Performance Review*. New York: Times Books.

Gowa, Joanne. 1989. "Rational hegemons, excludable goods, and small groups." *World Politics* **41**(April): 307–24.

Habermas, Jürgen. 1974. "The public sphere: an encyclopedia article (1964)." *New German Critique* **3**: 49–55.

1989. *The Structural Transformation of the Public Sphere: An Inquiry into a Category of Bourgeois Society [Strukturwandel der Öffentlichkeit].* Cambridge, MA: MIT Press.

1996. "Three normative models of democracy." In *Democracy and Difference: Contesting the Boundaries of the Political*, edited by Seyla Benhabib, pp. 21–30. Princeton, NJ: Princeton University Press.

Habermas, Jurgen, and William Rehg. 1996. *Between Facts and Norms: Contributions to a Discourse Theory of Law and Democracy [Faktizitat und Geltung].* Cambridge, MA: MIT Press.

Hacking, Ian. 2002. "Making up people." In *Historical Ontology*, by Ian Hacking, pp. 99–114. Cambridge, MA: Harvard University Press.

Hall, Rodney Bruce. 2005. "Private authority." *Harvard International Review* **27**(2): 66.

Hall, Rodney Bruce, and Thomas J. Bierstecker, eds. 2002. *The Emergence of Private Authority in Global Governance.* Cambridge: Cambridge University Press.

Haufler, Virginia. 2007. "The private sector and governance in post-conflict countries." In *Governance in Post-Conflict Societies: Rebuilding Fragile States*, edited by Derick W. Brinkerhoff, pp. 143–60. New York: Routledge.

Heidegger, Martin. 1962. *Being and Time.* Translated by John Macquarrie and Edward Robinson. Malden, MA: Blackwell.

Held, David. 1995. *Democracy and the Global Order.* Cambridge: Cambridge University Press.

Hellman, Joel S., Geraint Jones, and Daniel Kaufmann. 2003. "Seize the state, seize the day: state capture and influence in transition economies." *Journal of Comparative Economics* **31**(4): 751–73.

Hood, Christopher. 1991. "A public management for all seasons?" *Public Administration* **69**(1): 3–19.

Jessop, Bob. 1993. "Towards a Shumpeterian workfare state? Preliminary remarks on post-Fordist political economy." *Studies in Political Economy* **40**(Spring): 7–39.

Johnson, Jim. 1988. "Mixing humans and non-humans together: the sociology of a door-closer." *Social Problems* **35**(3): 298–310.

Kaldor, Mary. 2003. *Global Civil Society: An Answer to War.* Cambridge: Polity Press.

Kamat, Sangeeta. 2004. "The privatization of public interest: theorizing NGO discourse in a neoliberal era." *Review of International Political Economy* **11**(1): 155–76.

Kaul, Inge, Isabelle Grunberg, and Marc A. Stern, eds. 1999. *Global Public Goods: International Cooperation in the Twenty-First Century.* New York: Oxford University Press.

Keohane, Robert O. 1984. *After Hegemony: Cooperation and Discord in the World Political Economy.* Princeton, NJ: Princeton University Press.

King, Michael R., and Timothy J. Sinclair. 2003. "Private actors and public policy: a requiem for the new Basel capital accord." *International Political Science Review/Revue internationale de science politique* 24(3): 345–62.

Klotz, Audie. 2002. "Transnational activism and global transformations: the anti-apartheid and abolitionist experiences." *European Journal of International Relations* 8(1): 49–76.

Krahmann, Elke. 2003. "Conceptualizing security governance." *Cooperation and Conflict* 38(1): 5–26.

Langley, Paul. 2008. *The Everyday Life of Global Finance: Saving and Borrowing in Anglo-America.* Oxford: Oxford University Press.

Latour, Bruno. 1986. "Visualization and cognition." In *Knowledge and Society: Studies in the Sociology of Culture Past and Present,* edited by H. Kuclick, vol. 6, pp. 1–40. Greenwich: JAI Press.

1987. *Science in Action.* Milton Keynes: Open University.

Leander, Anna. 2005. "The market for force and public security: the destabilizing consequences of private military companies." *Journal of Peace Research* 42(5): 605–22.

2006. *Eroding State Authority? Private Military Companies and the Legitimate Use of Force.* Rome: Centro militare di studi strategic:

2008. "Thinking tools." In *Qualitative Methods in International Relations: A Pluralist Guide,* edited by Audie Klotz and Prakash Depaak, pp. 11–28. London: Palgrave Macmillan.

2009. "Securing sovereignty by governing security through markets." In *Sovereignty Games: Instrumentalising state sovereignty in Europe and Beyond,* edited by Rebbecca Adler-Nissen and Thomas Gammeltoft-Hansen, pp. 151–70. London: Palgrave Macmillan.

2011. "The promises, problems and potentials of a Bourdieu-inspired approach to International Relations." *International Political Sociology* 5(3): 294–313.

Long, David, and Frances Woolley. 2009. "Global public goods: critique of a UN discourse." *Global Governance* 15(1): 107–22.

Mattli, Walter, and Ngaire Woods. 2009. "In whose benefit? Explaining regulatory change in global politics." In *The Politics of Global Regulation,* edited by Walter Mattli and Ngaire Woods, pp. 1–43. Princeton, NJ: Princeton University Press.

McMillan, Kevin. 2008. "The emergence of international governance: practices of European politics, 1700–1848." Ph.D. dissertation, Columbia University.

2009. "'The conduct of conduct': great-power management in the Concert of Europe." Presentation, University of Ottawa.

Mügge, Daniel. 2006. "Private–public puzzles: inter-firm competition and transnational private regulation." *New Political Economy* 11(2): 177–200.

Norman, Donald. 1988. *The Design of Everyday Things.* New York: Doubleday.

North, Douglass. 1990. *Institutions, Institutional Change and Economic Performance.* Cambridge: Cambridge University Press.

Olson, Mancur. 1971. *The Logic of Collective Action: Public Goods and the Theory of Groups.* New Haven, CT: Yale University Press.

Osborne, David, and Ted Gaebler. 1992. *Reinventing Government: How the Entrepreneurial Spirit is Transforming the Public Sector.* Reading, MA: Addison-Wesley.

Oye, Kenneth A. 1986. "Explaining cooperation under anarchy: hypotheses and strategies." In *Cooperation under Anarchy*, edited by Kenneth A. Oye, pp. 1–24. Princeton, NJ: Princeton University Press.

Pattberg, Phillip. 2005. "The institutionalization of private governance: how business and nonprofit organizations agree on transnational rules." *Governance* 18(4): 589–610.

Percy, Sarah. 2007. *Regulating the Private Security Industry.* London: Routledge.

Poincignon, Yann. 2005. "Civil aviation and terrorism: the birth of a European air-transport security policy – what is at stake?" *Cultures et Conflits* 56 (Winter).

Polanyi, Karl. 1944. *The Great Transformation: The Political and Economic Origins of Our Time.* Boston: Beacon Press.

Pouliot, Vincent. 2008. "The logic of practicality: a theory of practice of security communities." *International Organization* 62(2): 257–88.

2010. *International Security in Practice: The Politics of NATO–Russia Diplomacy.* Cambridge: Cambridge University Press.

Price, Richard. 1998. "Reversing the gun sights: transnational civil society targets land mines." *International Organization* 52(3): 613–44.

Risse, Thomas. 2000. "'Let's argue!' Communicative action in world politics." *International Organization* 54(1): 1–39.

Ruggie, John Gerard. 2004. "Reconstituting the global public domain: issues, actors, and practices." *European Journal of International Relations* 10(4): 499–531.

Samuelson, Paul. 1954. "The pure theory of public expenditure." *Review of Economics and Statistics* 36(4): 387–89.

Schatzki, Theodore. 1996. *Social Practices: A Wittgensteinian Approach to Human Activity and the Social.* Cambridge: Cambridge University Press.

Schatzki, Theodore, Karin Knorr Cetina, and Eike von Savigny, eds. 2001. *The Practice Turn in Contemporary Theory.* New York: Routledge.

Schick, Allen. 1998. "Why most developing countries should not try New Zealand's reforms." *The World Bank Research Observer* 13(1): 123–31.

Scholte, Jan Aart. 2004. "Civil society and democratically accountable global governance." *Government and Opposition* 39(2): 211–33.

Seabrooke, Leonard, and Eleni Tsingou. 2009. "Power elites and everyday politics in international financial reform." *International Political Sociology* 3(4): 457–61.

Snidal, Duncan. 1985. "The limits of hegemonic stability theory." *International Organization* 39(4): 579–614.

Steffek, Jens. 2010. Public accountability and the public sphere of international governance. *Ethics & International Affairs* 24(1): 45–68.

Stone, Randall W., Branislav L. Slanchev, and Tamar R. London. 2008. "Choosing how to cooperate: a repeated public-goods model of international relations." *International Studies Quarterly* 52(2): 335–62.

Swidler, Ann. 2001. "What anchors cultural practices?" In *The Practice Turn in Contemporary Theory*, edited by Theodore Schatzki, Karin Knorr Cetina, and Eike von Savigny, pp. 74–91. New York: Routledge.

Tarrow, Sidney. 2005. *The New Transnational Activism.* Cambridge: Cambridge University Press.

Taylor, Charles. 1992. *Modernity and the Rise of the Public Sphere*, The Tanner Lectures on Human Values. Stanford, CA: Stanford University.

Thirkell-White, Ben. 2006. "Private authority and legitimacy in the international system." *International Relations* **20**(3): 335–42.

Thompson, John. 1991. "Editor's Introduction." In Pierre Bourdieu, *Language and Symbolic Power*, pp. 1–31. Cambridge: Polity Press.

Van Harten, Gus. 2005. "Private authority and transnational governance: the contours of the international system of investor protection." *Review of International Political Economy* **12**(4): 600–23.

Vogel, David. 2006. "The private regulation of global corporate conduct." Paper presented at the Annual Meeting of the American Political Science Association, Philadelphia, PA.

Wallner, Klaus. 2002. "The provision of public goods in International Relations: a comment on 'goods, games, and institutions'." *International Political Science Review* **23**(4): 393–401.

Walzer, Michael. 1984. "Liberalism and the art of separation." *Political Theory* **12**(3): 315–30.

Whitman, Jim. 2002. "Global governance as the friendly face of unaccountable power." *Security Dialogue* **33**(1): 45–57.

Williams, Michael C. 2007. *Culture and Security: Symbolic Power and the Politics of International Security.* New York: Routledge.

Williamson, Oliver. 1975. *Markets and Hierarchies: Analysis and Antitrust Implications.* New York: Free Press.

Wittgenstein, Ludwig. 1958. *Philosophical Investigations.* Translated by G. E. M. Anscombe, 2nd edn. Oxford: Blackwell.

Woolgar, Steve. 1991. "Configuring the user: the case of usability trials." In *A Sociology of Monsters: Essays on Power, Technology and Domination*, edited by John Law, pp. 57–102. New York: Routledge.

II

Transformations of the public in historical context

3   The dynamics of "private" security strategies and their public consequences: transnational organizations in historical perspective

Deborah Avant and Virginia Haufler

It is commonly accepted that states – assumed to be public authorities – control violence and provide security to their citizens. But over the last twenty years the relationship between states, security, and the public has veered from this conception. A variety of actors – from extractive sector companies to humanitarian aid organizations to private military and security companies (PMSCs) – have generated security for themselves and sometimes others. Looking back through history reveals that this departure is not as unusual as it seems. Transnational organizations seeking to make money or seeking to "help" have secured themselves and their goals for centuries and their actions have been critical to understanding the dynamics of controlling violence and its relationship to what is seen as public.

What "public" means, what should be protected, and what violent practices are considered appropriate have varied over time and place in ways that contest the conventional wisdom. In what follows, we draw from secondary accounts to examine the relationship between Western profit-seeking, helping, and ruling organizations in the management of violence during nineteenth-century imperial expansion, late nineteenth-century modernity, the Cold War, and contemporary global governance. Using examples from these four moments, we illustrate how security practices have had consequences for what counts as public, who is part of the public, and which processes are deemed to be public in the management of violence.[1]

Practices, authority, and relationships

Rather than assuming that states are the dominant actors and the repository for all things public in the management of violence, we ask about

---

[1] What constitutes security has been debated. Traditionalists have argued that it is wrapped up in the management of violence (Nye and Lynn-Jones 1988; Walt 1991) while others have suggested it can be attached to such things economic and environmental well-being (Buzan 1991; Mathews 1989). We do not take a position in this debate but here use the term security as defined more narrowly as the management of violence. See Best and Gheciu (Chapter 2, this volume) for a fuller description of these categories of public practice.

what practices different actors have had in security over time. If public practices are activities that reflect a societal understanding about common concerns, as Best and Gheciu argue (Chapter 2, this volume), then security is the quintessential arena in which to examine whether public practices have indeed changed because security always is assumed to be a common concern. Grounded in concern with contemporary changes, we focus on organizations that travel to other territories – either to make money or to help – and their interaction with rulers and communities. We attend to what choices these organizations make when faced with violence and what their practices tell us about the meaning of the public and the role of the state in security affairs.

We assume a relationship between how an organization gains authority and how we should expect them to behave (Avant, Finnemore, and Sell 2010). We define authority as the ability to induce deference in others. Authority is thus a social relationship, not a commodity.[2] It is created by recognition, even if only tacit or informal, by others. Generating deference (or gaining authority) confers power – having followers allows authorities to exert greater influence than would otherwise be the case. But the basis on which followers defer also constrains the authority. If their actions do not accord with the basis on which their followers defer, the legitimacy of the authority may be questioned and they may lose deference.

There are different bases of authority. In the stories we tell below, for instance, the King of England gains authority on the basis of his claim to be the sovereign – a claim that is tied to his embodiment of a nascent conception of the public. Both missionaries and then NGOs were accorded deference in the West because they represented ideals congruent with accepted norms in Western societies. British chartered companies were delegated authority by the Crown in order to pursue British interests abroad. And contemporary transnational corporations gain authority by virtue of their capacity to effectively provide outcomes (Avant, Finnemore, and Sell 2010).

Many actors rely on more than one source for their authority. Contemporary NGOs, for example, rely not only on their claim to represent ideals but also on their expertise and ability to accomplish goals. Claims to authority on the basis of ideals generate authority among individual contributors and the activist community, while claims to expertise and capacity matter more to donors. When different bases of authority work in tandem, they can lead to a greater amount of deference among a

---

[2] Our definition draws on Barnett and Finnemore 2004 and our analysis here on Avant, Finnemore, and Sell 2010. See also Raz 1990.

wider audience. Many NGOs grew more powerful during the 1990s as their authority increased among activists, donors, and the general public. Different bases of authority can also lead to tensions, though, if the actions accord with one basis of authority but conflict with another. For instance, the compromises necessary for NGOs to be effective, particularly in the midst of violence – competing for donor money, providing services to particular groups and not others – have sometimes been seen to conflict with the ideals they represent (Avant 2004; Cooley and Ron 2002; Stein 2011).

The imperative to retain authority can be a source of behavioral change when the bases of authority conflict, when efficacy is undermined by failure, and when multiple actors seek to become authoritative over the same areas of concern. Tensions among different bases of authority are an important source of change. For instance, when a corporation is delegated authority to address humanitarian concerns but the goals of helping and profiting conflict, the organization must find some way to reconcile these. The organization may need to make new authority claims, cultivate different constituencies, ally with other authorities, or come up with new ideas. A related source of change is failure. In most cases followers defer to authorities not because of their claims alone but because the claims are related to achieving goals. Failure to make progress, particularly when lack of progress generates violence, is a particularly significant source of change. Tensions between different authorities whose work overlaps can be a source of failure, as competition between them undermines their ability to achieve their goals (Avant, Finnemore, and Sell 2010).

Through our examination of who defers to what claims on security issues over time and why, we uncover changes in who is part of the public, what part of managing violence counts as public, and what processes are deemed public. Our main argument is with the conventional wisdom that casts the state as the unchanging representation of the public and exclusive manager of security. By demonstrating changes in the role of the state and the meaning of public, and by establishing the role of non-state actors in these changes, we cast doubt on this widespread assumption.

The trajectory of change we uncover also reveals difficulties with the private authority approach to understanding governance. The separation of actors into the categories of "private" and "public" is not helpful when nominally private organizations act on behalf of the state, or when different types of actors provide protection for the benefit of an entire community and not just a part of it. Once they claim to be pursuing public goals, it becomes problematic to characterize them as "private" actors. Thinking of the public as a set of social practices allows us to more accurately chart the various public logics over time.

We examine the last two centuries to capture a broad sweep of time. Demonstrating the way in which non-state actors have been involved in security historically, and the degree to which states have pursued narrow interests, challenges the assumption that states alone provide security as a matter of common concern. Examining instances in which transnational actors generate security also provides insight into contestations over what is public in (often contested) transnational public spaces. The public is sometimes defined relative to the home society of these organizations, other times to the local society in which they are embedded, and occasionally relative to a transnational public.[3] Our selection of specific instances is meant to be illustrative, not representative, and is largely based on the secondary record, and our reinterpretation of well-known cases comes from a practice-oriented perspective.

As we begin our examination, we see vestiges of the Crown as the embodiment of the body politic, reflecting remnants of sovereignty's origins in the western divine right of kings (Philpott 1995). Practices among Western states at the beginning of the nineteenth century reflected increasing concentration of authority in the hands of the Westphalian state, but only hazy distinctions between public and private. The state and the Crown were not completely distinguishable, which left little logic for differentiating between actions taken for the Crown's personal desires and those that were in the state's interests. What we think of today as "private" actors often were associated with the Crown (e.g. chartered companies) or represented values accepted by the Crown (e.g. missionaries). What constituted state interests or "public" in actions abroad was often the glory or financial gain of the Crown. A loose association between the state and the management of violence was apparent. Thus when royal authorities joined forces with others during this era and delegated authority to act on their behalf abroad, it often included using violence if necessary.

What we understand as the conventional wisdom came into being among Western states at the end of the nineteenth century and reached its height during the Cold War, spreading beyond the West to become taken for granted in many parts of the world (Abrahamson and Williams 2011, 310). During this time the modern state consolidated its authority

---

[3] See Best and Gheciu (Chapter 2, this volume). Critical theory tends to associate the public with a domestic sphere in a Westphalian state-system, but we find some evidence of a transnational public sphere, particularly in the contemporary era; see Fraser 2007; Ruggie 2004.

over violence concomitant with the construction of separate public
and private spheres. By the end of the nineteenth century deference
to rulers as the embodiment of the public by their subjects was gone in
the West. Instead many rulers claimed to be public authorities because
they represented the collective interest of their citizens, which entailed
a monopoly over the management of violence. The management of
violence was seen as public, public was associated with the state, and
states took on responsibility for protecting their citizens both at home
and abroad (Thomson 1994).

During this time, there emerged clearly differentiated roles and behavior for actors on the basis of whether they were designated public (part of
the state) or private (not part of the state) in the security realm. Control
over violence was reserved for state actors and often assumed to be in
the national (public) interest. In Western states, security practices were
embedded within a public sphere dominated by liberal values of deliberation, participation, publicity and transparency (Fraser 2007). Who and
what got protected was determined by who had rights within the domestic system. Both commercial organizations and humanitarians generally
deferred to state authority (the state where they operated, the state from
which they hailed, or rebels seeking control of the state) to protect them
from violence or authorize the use of violence on their behalf.

In the first decade of the post-Cold War era another rearticulation
of security and the public began. The exclusive association of public
with the state, and the state with security, began to break down. The
relationship between security and the public, however, remained and
strengthened in many spaces. As non-state actors adopted security practices deemed relevant to the public they also became subject to demands
that they respect public values – to operate through deliberative, participatory, and transparent processes and to respect the rights of those
affected by their actions. This change has opened space for actors previously labeled "private" to play "public" roles, potentially transforming
the modern relationship between states, security, and the public.
A pattern of discourse that has separated the meaning of the public from
the state has also enabled claims that to be legitimately sovereign, states
must also be responsive to public concerns, expressed in arguments
about the responsibility to protect.[4] By implication, the meaning of
public has begun to shift to what an actor does (respect public norms)
rather than who they are (part of a state or not).

---

[4] See Evans and Sahnoun 2002; also http://www.un.org/en/preventgenocide/adviser/
responsibility.shtml.

In the following sections, we elaborate on this brief summary. By examining who defers to whom, for what ends, and on what basis we shed light on the changing security practices of Western transnational commercial and humanitarian organizations relative to states and the different visions of the public they animate.

Transnational security in historical perspective

In the early nineteenth century, trading companies sought out contact with distant peoples to trade goods and gain access to raw materials. At the same time, missionaries seeking either to serve the needs of their brethren, or convert people who were not Christian, made contact with peoples in far-off lands (Etherington 2005). Though neither chartered companies nor missionaries had inherently violent missions, the pursuit of their goals often caused others to react violently. These organizations adopted different security practices that reflected their constituencies and relations with other authorities. We illustrate our points here by examining transnational missionary and business enterprises based in Britain.

Chartered companies were, as the name implies, authorized by royal charter. The British Crown delegated areas of foreign policy to the company. It did this due to the capacities of these organizations to carry out commercial ventures. Delegated authority plus successful performance gained the deference of those they traded with. If deference waned and violence erupted, though, these companies sometimes raised military forces in their own defense.

Missionary organizations were less clearly authorized by the British government. Instead, missionary groups gained authority from their constituents in Britain due to their work on behalf of religious and humanitarian goals. Reflecting norms prominent in Western societies at the time, they were taking on the "white man's burden," and civilizing barbarous lands.[5] But they also gained deference from those they were attempting to "help" when they successfully carried out their religious and humanitarian works. Their authority among local populations resulted from their capacity to provide valuable services, and links to other Western actors. If deference was not forthcoming, missionaries rarely raised arms but instead allied with others for defense.

---

[5] Rudyard Kipling's poem, "The White Man's Burden" was published in *McClure's Magazine* in 1899 and was seen as justifying cultural "development" of non-Western societies.

Commercial organizations: from chartered monopolies to imperial rule

The precursors to modern corporations were companies founded through the delegation of royal authority via grant or charter, starting in the sixteenth century (Carlos and Nicholas 1988). Companies such as the British East India Company promised profits while simultaneously extending the Crown's reach. Pursuing the Crown's interest was, in some sense, public. By obtaining a Royal Charter, these companies acquired delegated authority and exerted influence over what was considered "public" in Britain, and extended this abroad. Reflecting an association between sovereignty and controlling violence, this delegated authority extended to the raising of military forces when necessary.

Consider the British East India Company, which first began operations in 1601. It had a Royal Charter which awarded it a monopoly on trade with the East, but as a joint-stock company it did not rely solely on royal coffers to support its operations. It was neither public nor private in the modern sense of these terms. Through its Royal Charter, it had authority to operate around the world as a representative of the interests of its shareholders (primarily members of the ruling class). It could pursue its own interests, which were seen as congruent with those of the Crown.

The company's response to hostility (from local communities and colonial competitors) was to raise its own armed forces. It also could call upon British forces to help. Indeed, its ability to rely on the British state for reinforcement was one key to its success relative to the Dutch and other chartered companies (Winius and Vink 1991). After extinguishing its European rivals in India, the company built a local army as an instrument for defense and territorial control, revenue collection, policing, and pacification of local populations (Bowen 2006). In subduing much of India, the Company took advantage of its ambiguous status. It successfully emphasized its sovereign authority (rather than its delegated quality) when it wished to avoid contractual debts to local rulers, but asked for protection by British military forces when it needed to, putting itself clearly under the Crown's wing (McLean 2003).

Over time, it became difficult for the Company to balance relationships with the Crown, the Parliament (which was gaining political influence), its board of directors, and local rulers. By the mid-nineteenth century, all of the Company's bases of authority – its ties to the Crown, its expertise and capacity, and its claims to represent the public interest – were under assault. The financial costs of administering the huge Indian Territory threatened failure, which was a concern for the board of directors and the Crown (Brown 2009; Litvin 2003). The growing power of Parliament relative to the state, and its openness to new voices, allowed for a redefinition of the British public interest. New interests ranged from claims from rival companies wanting a piece of the monopoly, to increasingly vocal outrage from religious groups arguing the government had a responsibility to the welfare of citizens both at home and abroad (Litvin 2003; Bowen 2006).

Parliament reacted by establishing more oversight of the Company, claiming sovereignty for the British Crown over the lands the Company controlled, and opening India to missionaries (Litvin 2003). The Indian Rebellion in 1857 demonstrated the degree to which the Company had lost authority among the local population. Arguing for a national (public) interest in maintaining control over Indian territories, the British government established direct dominion in 1858, took over its military forces, and dissolved the Company in 1874.

The security practices of the British English East Company responded to the violence it encountered as it pursued overseas trade. The Company drew upon its own capacity and called on the British state to support it. These practices incrementally evolved in response to more violence and were taken for granted until they began to fail. The more the Company called upon the state to defend it from violence, the less it was imbued with public authority.

Missionary organizations and imperial expansion

There was an explosion of Christian missionaries and mission societies in the nineteenth century (Etherington 2005), including the London Missionary Society (mixed denominations). These missionaries aimed to help foreigners by saving souls. Their authority in western societies was based on their service to God, and delegated to them by various churches.

Missionary organizations had a less structured relationship with the Crown than chartered companies did. The London Missionary Society's administrative structure at one point, for instance, relied on the work of salaried officials such as the Home Secretary and the Foreign Secretary.[6] But this society could by no means be equated with the British government and received little aid or support from the Crown in its early years. Even those who equate missionary work with imperialism acknowledge that it was often imperialism that followed missionaries rather than the reverse (Dachs 1972).

In addition to seeking converts, missionaries sought to provide humanitarian aid: education, health care, and public works. This array of services, and the links they developed between local communities and

[6] See www.mundus.ac.uk/cats/4/251.htm.

their European supporters, provided a rationale for their authority among local populations. While they offered welfare benefits, they also aimed to transform the societies they ventured into, creating tensions between its bases of authority (Dachs 1972).

Violent reaction by local groups signaled rejection of their presence, their goals, and their authority. In an extreme example, John Williams's work on behalf of the London Missionary Society came to an abrupt end in 1839 when he was killed and eaten by cannibals on the island of Erromango.[7] To avoid such violence, missionaries often entered into agreements with local rulers who wanted access to goods and services, or they only entered territories with stable local rule (Comaroff and Comaroff 1986; Dachs 1972; Simensen 1986). The multiplicity of authorities in Africa meant there were a variety of security associations available to missionaries. For instance, missionaries in South Africa in the late nineteenth century could cooperate with various indigenous rulers, the Boers, the British South Africa Company, or other colonial authorities on the ground, or with the British imperial authorities in London.

The different choices of Joseph Ludorf and John Mackenzie in South Africa demonstrate this variety. In response to a violent land dispute generated by the discovery of diamonds at Hopetown in 1867, Reverend Ludorf urged indigenous local rulers to unite to form an independent confederation of Tswana states as the only way to avoid both Boer oppression and absorption into the British Empire. He saw protecting the Tswana from Boer enslavement, tribal wars, and unscrupulous freebooters as vital to the mission (Comaroff and Comaroff 1986). In contrast, John Mackenzie of the London Missionary Society endorsed imperial rule by the British, since he thought the colonial authorities on the ground were poor choices. Unlike his contemporaries, he saw the ultimate political solution as one where blacks would gain equal rights in a federated, non-racial South Africa (Comaroff and Comaroff 1986). London eventually established a protectorate in Bechuanaland and asked Mackenzie to become the resident Deputy Commander.

Mackenzie's story has led some to argue that missionaries were simply an arm of imperialism (Dachs 1972). This equation, however, misses the fissures within Britain itself, and between imperialists in London and colonists on the ground. It also misses the degree to which Mackenzie saw himself – at least at first – as representative of the black public in southern Africa rather than the white public in London (Comaroff and Comaroff 1986).

---

[7] See www.mundus.ac.uk/cats/4/251.htm.

Pursuing religious and humanitarian quests, missionaries from Britain unsettled the existing order, which led to violence. In the face of violence, they often joined forces with others who had violent capacities. They cast these alliances as consistent with their principles, religious or humanitarian, and thus in keeping with their basis of authority. Over the course of the century, missionaries made arguments that appealed to public notions as we define them in this volume; their civilizing mission was said to hold benefits for both Western and local publics. As alliances with local rulers, colonists, and even the British South Africa Company proved unable to provide these benefits or keep a lid on violence, missionaries such as Mackenzie sought – and thus contributed to – the extension of British imperial rule.

Like the chartered companies, British missionaries entered foreign lands in ways that disrupted existing societies. They sought out associations with others to enhance their security, but drew closer to the British state as other choices became less effective. The failure of both companies and missionaries to cap violence increasingly drew the British government into protecting their foreign investments and their Christian brethren abroad, leading to colonization and imperial rule. By the end of the century, the government was the primary source of security for its British commercial and humanitarian enterprises abroad, reinforcing the model of the state as protector of its citizens (Spruyt 2000; Thomson 1994). While the security practices adopted by chartered firms and missionaries affected common concerns in Africa, their "public" role was fragile and eventually overturned.

Transnational security in the twentieth century

At the turn of the century, Western states consolidated control over violence. Non-state actors increasingly deferred to state authority in the security realm. At the same time a different relationship between rulers and ruled was developing. Sovereignty was no longer synonymous with personal rule by the Crown but, at least in some countries, a function of citizen participation (Bendix 1980). People within a territory were seen less as subjects to be ruled and more as citizens to be represented. With this came a greater rationale for distinguishing public interests from private ones (Elshtain 1981). The state came to be seen as the relevant public actor and control of legitimate violence as one of its key components.

In this context, appropriate behavior for transnational organizations in response to violence was more restricted. While firms could call on the state for protection, raising private armies was not seen as a legitimate activity. In the philanthropic world, humanitarians developed ways to assist others without infringing on the authority of states by remaining neutral. What we now know as the International Committee of the Red Cross developed the principle of "acceptance," under which they could provide help to individuals even in the midst of war so long as they were accepted by all sides. "Purely commercial" and "neutral" became the claims necessary to legitimate the actions of profit seeking and helping organizations – now seen as private actors.

Commercial organizations dependent on states

By the end of the nineteenth century, modern multinational companies came to replace trading companies as the dominant form of overseas enterprise. These companies did not have the official delegation of authority given to the earlier chartered companies. Their authority was based on commercial success and the benefits that might accord to populations. As such, their actions were more restricted. If they met with violence, they called on a state for help – either their home country, or the host state in which they operated. In the early twentieth century the extension of security by Western states to their companies operating in the developing world was not particularly controversial. Over the course of the century, however, such "gunboat diplomacy" became less acceptable and companies relied more on their host states for security (Litvin 2003). The security practices of firms reinforced understandings of the public as associated with the state, even as they redirected their deference from home state to host states.

Security, the public, and corporate behavior intersected most obviously in the exploitation of oil around the globe. Western states endorsed the activities of multinational oil companies as tools for ensuring access to oil – a commodity vital for industrial growth and power (Sampson 1975; Yergin 2008). In return, governments increasingly facilitated access for companies to foreign supplies and, when violence erupted, provided security for oil companies. Though the relationship between states and companies was no less cozy than in the past century, states claimed a monopoly over violence and thus there was a greater division of labor between them.

The struggle between British and American firms over oil in Mexico is illustrative. The British company Aguila gained oil concessions in Mexico in 1910. Aguila developed close links with the Diaz regime, and assisted Diaz when he resigned from office and fled to France in the wake of revolutionary upheaval.[8] There is speculation that Standard

---

[8] General José de la Cruz Porfirio Díaz Mori ruled Mexico with an iron fist beginning in 1877. He resigned and fled in 1911.

Oil, an American firm, may have helped the rebels as a way to get access
to Mexican oil. As the Mexican Revolution unfolded, US and British oil
companies vied for position, and drew in their respective governments
as protectors. American officials believed that British policy in Mexico
directly reflected their oil interests, and pursued policies that laid the
foundation for an "oil war" between the USA and Great Britain after
1918, fostering increasing instability within Mexico (Venn 1986).
This type of dynamic was repeated in other oil-rich areas of the world
throughout the early twentieth century.

After World War II, American multinationals expanded their investments in the developing world, reflecting the increased global power of
the USA. This was also the era when decolonization spread the Western
model of the state. From the end of World War II to the 1980s, leaders of
new states (or the rebel movements that fought them) saw their national
interests differently than did western corporations and nationalized or
expropriated foreign investments (Kobrin 1984; Moran 1973; Truitt
1970). The American state used its military to protect US firms as part
of both Cold War balancing and for the security of American citizens
abroad. The USA sought to maintain its hegemony, protect its national
interests (which included cheap oil), and support US foreign investors.
Local elites who wanted the economic benefits access to foreign investors
brought often shared the perspective of the US government and US
firms (Cardoso and Faletto 1979).

One of the best-known examples comes not from the oil sector,
but from agriculture. In the post-World War II years, the United
Fruit Company (now Chiquita Brands) developed strong ties to the US
government, but protected its foreign investments mainly by allying with
friendly dictators in Central America. The United Fruit Company played
such a dominant role in the politics of many Latin American countries
that they became known as "banana republics." The company professed
to have only commercial interests – it did not create a private army,
acquire territory, or take on administrative functions as the earlier chartered companies had.

The tension between United Fruit's political influence and commercial activities eventually led to changes. In Guatemala, the company
supported an oppressive regime and local elites against a leftist reform
movement. The Guatemalan government valued the ties the company
had with the US government. As the reform movement became more
threatening, the US government and disaffected local military leaders
launched an anti-reform coup in 1954 that benefited company interests.
During the civil war that followed, United Fruit relied on the local
regime for security, with the specter of US intervention always a

possibility. Company security practices were tied to state interests, and an understanding of the public was synonymous with government.

By the 1970s, critics challenged the acceptability of US protection of corporate interests overseas. They argued that the US should not equate corporate concerns with the public interest nor trample on the rights of foreign publics. The relationship between the US intelligence community and US firms in the overthrow of Allende in Chile brought particular outrage, and led to congressional hearings in 1974. Thus began a weakening of the close security ties between the US government and American firms abroad.[9]

Throughout this era, companies declared a policy of staying within commercial bounds. Though their investments and ties with their home countries had political effects, they relied on states to manage violence on their behalf. The authority of states was tied to their sovereign claims, but just what was in the national (or public) interest was subject to pressure from a variety of domestic groups. In the USA, these pressures changed the articulation of the public interest, leading to less acceptance of government practices of providing security to foreign investors. Without state partners, companies had no legitimate claim to violent capacities and often chose to withdraw.

Missionary and humanitarian organizations

In the late nineteenth century, missionaries were joined in "helping" by specifically humanitarian organizations: the International Committee of the Red Cross (ICRC) and its affiliated national Red Cross societies. Its founders were inspired by religious faith similar to missionaries, but their claim to authority was derived from their humanitarian goals – they undertook to deliver humanitarian aid to soldiers wounded in battle, to civilize war.

The ICRC's aims drew humanitarians directly into war zones. Founder Henry Dunant and his colleagues appealed to the warring states and professed neutrality in order to gain safe access to the wounded. They argued it was in the interest of states to have their wounded cared for and that ensuring humane standards of treatment was a basic concern that united all human beings. If medical personnel confined their activities to humanitarian care and pledged to treat wounded soldiers from all sides, they posed no challenge to sovereign authority and could serve

[9] International organizations such as the ILO and OECD developed codes of conduct for multinational corporations in the 1970s, revealing cracks in state–firm relations.

both national and humanitarian interests. The ICRC asked that states accept – and agree not to target – medical personnel on the battlefield. This principle of neutrality reflected the primary role of states in controlling violence, but also distinguished a category of action for private actors to serve humanitarian needs even in the midst of war. Transnational organizations such as the ICRC did not rely on alliances with states nor did they acquire the means to use or repel violence themselves. Instead, they pursued what was called an "acceptance" strategy to establish roles in which private non-combatants were not to be targeted, even when they were on a battlefield. Practices of neutrality reinforced deference to state control of violence and the tie between states and security. By identifying rights to protection rooted outside of the state, it also laid the foundation for challenging the connection between the state and the public.

During the Cold War, many humanitarian organizations built explicitly on this acceptance strategy, including religious organizations such as the London Missionary Society (now the World Council of Churches), secular organizations including diverse NGOs, and United Nations agencies. Following the logic of the ICRC, they deferred to state control of violence but claimed authority on the basis of their worthy goals and their neutrality. Despite this pledged neutrality, many became recipients of donor government aid money as states delegated implementation of programs to NGOs.[10] In unstable areas, humanitarian organizations depended on local governments for security.

Concerns over violence were greatest in areas influenced by superpower rivalry. In Central America, for instance, Honduran camps housed refugees from US-backed regimes in El Salvador and Guatemala, as well as those fleeing the Soviet-backed Sandinista regime in Nicaragua. Despite organizational charters that proclaimed neutrality, many NGOs aided one side over another and relied on that side for protection. Sometimes NGOs were used by governments for express political purposes. When the US Congress banned aid to the Contra guerilla forces in Honduras, President Reagan supported them covertly – one prong of which was mobilization of "private" American organizations in the guise of relief (Terry 2002). Even if they did not intend to, NGOs that assisted one side in a conflict were tainted by their choice. Those NGOs that

---

[10] The Carnegie Corporation published a report in 1966 expressing concern about the future of the independent NGO. "Is the non-governmental organization of the future to be simply an auxiliary of the state, a kind of willing but not very resourceful handmaiden? Or is it to be a strong, independent adjunct that provides government with a type of capability it cannot provide for itself" (Pifer 1966).

supported the Nicaraguan refugees received considerable security protection from the US and the Honduran security forces. Those working with the other side were not protected, and suffered from violence against refugees and aid workers (Terry 2002). When violence became too great or their government patrons could not protect them, NGOs, like companies, withdrew.

Similar to multinational corporations, NGOs during the Cold War depended on governments for protection. Some NGOs were less comfortable than their corporate counterparts relying on this protection. Their commitment to neutrality was sometimes in considerable tension with goals that focused on matters of common concern, and thus could be construed as "public" even though they were not equated with states. Though NGOs were less likely to align themselves with national interests than corporations, they became conduits for government money in their pursuit of broad humanitarian or development goals. This laid the groundwork for what we investigate in the next section: the increasing association of NGOs and global civil society more generally with the "public."

At the beginning of the twentieth century, both commercial and humanitarian transnational actors generally relied on Western states for protection, but increasingly looked to their host states for protection too. Allying with these states (or rebels aiming to be states) was cast as deference to their authority over managing violence. Thus security practices generally reinforced the equation of the state with both the public and with security – an equation that would change by the beginning of the new century.

Transnational security in the contemporary era

Even during the Cold War there were changes affecting state authority and its relationship to the public. Globalization created economic links among peoples and increasing social and political ties. NGOs became prominent advocates for causes of common concern that spanned the borders of states, from opposition to nuclear weapons to the protection of human rights. The end of the Cold War amplified global economic and social connections. Both commercial and non-commercial actors sought to take advantage of the new-found freedom to move beyond the spheres of action defined by the rivalry between the USA and the Soviets. As in the past, however, the extension of commercial and humanitarian activities to new areas sometimes generated violence.

Transnational corporations and NGOs found themselves operating in the midst of violence at the same time as their relationships with states on security issues were increasingly complicated. Part of the complication was a change in attitudes toward states. Rather than assuming congruence between states and the public interest, attention focused on whether states were responsive to their citizens. This is most clearly articulated in the "Responsibility to Protect," a doctrine that imputes state responsibility to protect its people from violence, and an international responsibility to intervene when states fail in this duty (Evans and Sahnoun 2002). At the same time, more attention was focused on the security consequences of non-state behavior. Transnational activists questioned companies' claims to be purely commercial when their investments were associated with repressive local forces. Meanwhile, when opportunistic actors siphoned off humanitarian resources and used them to fund violence, critics also questioned the claim that humanitarians were neutral. As both commercial and humanitarian choices were seen to have political – and sometimes violent – consequences, their security practices were seen to have public import.

Both corporations and NGOs began experimenting with new practices to address violence and they adopted similar approaches. They sought to build relationships with an array of local and international stakeholders, and commit to processes that promised to reduce violence. In approaching security this way, both corporations and humanitarians increasingly associate their behavior with the public. By broadly engaging with many constituents both locally and globally, they reflected developing ideas about what is the public and helped redefine who counts as the public in particular situations. Their actions suggest a conception of the public as defined by what actors do rather than who they are – thus reconstituting what is public as process or action rather than as a particular actor or sphere (Gheciu and Best, Chapter 2, this volume).

Commercial organizations

In the 1990s, governments in the developing world welcomed foreign investors, reflecting a consensus on economic liberalization in the wake of the collapse of the Soviet model. We see the emerging set of corporate security practices this entailed clearly in the extractive sector. As demand for natural resources grew along with the world economy, extractive companies developed new sources that were located in areas beset by violence. They were welcomed for their financial resources, technical expertise, and links to global markets. Sometimes they relied on host governments for security but when host governments were incapable or unwilling, they allied with other local forces or even hired from the growing private security sector to manage force themselves.

Companies encountered increasing criticism for their association with repressive host governments. Observers argued that extractive resources created a "resource curse," leading to repression by local governments, intractable conflicts, and underdevelopement (de Soysa 2000; Karl 1997; Ross 1999). Transnational activists campaigned against companies that were allied with abusive regimes, arguing that they were indirectly complicit with the violent actions of the government (Spar 1998; Zandvliet and Anderson 2009).

Oil companies came under intense scrutiny for their security practices, with Shell Oil in Nigeria gaining particular notoriety. The unequal distribution of oil benefits along with devastating environmental consequences of oil extraction in the Niger Delta led to a "petro-movement" that incited rebellion and violence against the state and oil facilities. In the early 1990s, the Movement for the Survival of the Ogoni People protested the devastation wrought by oil development. The Nigerian dictator Sani Abacha took steps to break up the movement, arrested the leadership, and in 1995 hanged the leaders for their activities (Frynas 1998; Litvin 2003). The result was an international outcry against Shell for not acting against the Abacha regime. In response, Shell undertook a worldwide campaign to engage with stakeholders, both transnationally with activists and locally with the communities where it worked. In 1998 it held regular meetings with key institutional investors to discuss non-financial issues such as human rights and the environment, and in the next year engaged with local communities in ninety-one countries.[11] The company also supported broader multi-stakeholder processes such as the United Nations' Global Compact and the Voluntary Principles on Security and Human Rights.[12] Its efforts to rehabilitate its reputation, however, have not been successful among Nigerians or the wider international community.

Shell's reaction corresponded with the growth of a larger corporate social responsibility movement. Business leaders increasingly recognized the importance of a "social license to operate." (Zandvliet and Anderson 2009). Company claims to be "purely commercial" are not as well received today as they were during the Cold War. To avoid being cast as part of the problem, corporate leaders have tried to adopt new practices and negotiate new relationships that are more responsive to the public (Haufler 2001). This is particularly true in situations where states are unable or unwilling to accomplish what are taken to be public ends.

---

[11] See www.shell.com/home/Framework?siteId=home.   [12] Freeman 2002.

Humanitarian non-governmental organizations

Many NGOs also expanded their areas of operation after the Cold War. Western constituents continued to defer to them based on the values they represented, but they garnered delegated authority from Western states and other donors and began to develop expert authority over the delivery of services. The tension between their traditional neutral stance and their new authority bases became particularly acute in violent areas. Some NGO activities fed into violence even as they sought to address its consequences. Concerns about diversion of resources to support violent actors, NGO vulnerability to manipulation, and the safety of NGO workers led some humanitarians to revisit the acceptance strategy.[13] This revisiting took three main forms: (1) some NGOs reiterated their commitment to acceptance or withdrawal, (2) others endorsed taking sides either to ensure humanitarian space or protect human rights, and (3) some sought to develop practices that would allow NGOs to remain in the field while remaining true to the classic acceptance doctrine (Barnett and Snyder 2009). These approaches have different consequences for NGOs as public actors.

The third approach is interesting for its attempt to smooth over or reconfigure the authority tensions we identify above. These new practices caution against "politicization" or enmity in practice, and recommend that NGOs avoid taking a position as friend or foe. Instead, NGOs should develop a pragmatic plan to ensure their safety that rests on "dialogue with all actors involved in or affecting the outcome of a given situation of conflict..."[14] In the increasingly polarized environment of contemporary conflicts, NGOs sought to avoid either being rejected or instrumentalized.[15] Rejection was often a product of the perceived association between NGO staff and political entities. Instrumentalization occurred when humanitarian aid was siphoned off to support combatants, or when humanitarian language was adopted by militaries and governments in ways that blurred the lines between purely humanitarian and politically motivated actions (Krahenbuhl 2004). Rejection and instrumentalization both threatened to cut to the heart of NGO authority, which is to do good works in a way that is free from the political world of states.

The new security practices prompted by this rethinking were dubbed the "security triangle." They retained acceptance, but added protection

---

[13] Interview with Michael O'Neill, Director of Security, Save the Children, Washington, D.C. August 15, 2006.

[14] Krahenbuhl 2004.

[15] Interview with Michael O'Neill, Director of Security, Save the Children, August 2006.

and deterrence (Martin 1999; Van Brabant 1997). Those who advocated this approach also developed policies of security management to address both global issues and the interaction between an organization and other actors in the field. The ICRC was instrumental in these developments, as were a number of individual NGOs (including World Vision and CARE) and InterAction (a consortium of American NGOs).

Security practices of NGOs increasingly focus on engaging with all actors relevant to violence. They seek to gain the consent of belligerent parties (including government authorities), as well as developing a community stake in programs and increasing working relationships with other interested international actors. Advocates of this approach claim that the mission of an organization needs to be clear and transparent to facilitate both acceptance and a community stake in the project, and NGO personnel need to adjust their behavior to local perceptions (Anderson 1999; Van Brabant 1997).[16] Communication and information sharing is seen as important for ensuring good working relations with other organizations (Schafer and Murphy 2010).

The debate among humanitarians about appropriate security strategies continues today (Nordland 2010). Even among NGOs that adopt security triangle practices there are debates about what strategies to pursue in particular instances. Their practices, however, increasingly transform the meaning of security – associating it more closely with the public, but less closely with the state.

Though there are differences between the security practices of corporations and humanitarians, the language both use is strikingly similar: security for their "missions," engaging "stakeholders," coordinating with others through effective "management," being "transparent." These practices evoke a new conceptualization of the public not defined by who an actor is, but by how they act and whether their activities are in concert with public aims and in accordance with commonly recognized public processes.

Redefining public authority through security practices

This examination of the security practices of non-state organizations reveals the gradual shifting of practices from those that support and reinforce the equation of the state with the public, to patterns that have the potential to transform the public sphere in security affairs. Both humanitarian and business enterprises today seek to integrate local and

[16] Interview with Michael O'Neill, Director of Security, Save the Children, August 2006.

transnational communities into their deliberations, adopting practices of transparency and consultation. By doing so, they redefine the relevant publics from states and citizens in home countries, to people directly affected by their operations. This is captured by the increasing use of the "stakeholder" language in policy arenas. Security practices became a public issue, debated in global policy arenas and subject to an increasing array of international rules, norms, and laws. Both NGOs and companies today are held accountable for their security practices, and in response have adopted new practices that reflect the potential for a transnational public.

At the beginning of the history we examine, there was no distinctive boundary between public and private. Only over time did the state and private actors come to be viewed as operating in separate spheres. By the start of the twenty-first century, the public and private were once again merging – but in a new way, in which the state is no longer equated with the public. This may presage a transformation of the public through the manner in which security is provided – through transparent and accountable processes. What those who provide security do, rather than who they are, is increasingly important for organizations claiming to be acting on behalf of the public.

The interaction between profit-seeking, helping, and ruling organizations has been instrumental in constructing different meanings of the public over time. In the early years of the nineteenth century the violence caused by profit-seeking and helping organizations was an instigator of formal imperialism. As corporations and humanitarians deferred to states and their monopoly role in the management of violence in the twentieth century, they contributed to the solidification of the modern association of states and security. In the contemporary era, the efforts of corporations and NGOs to manage tensions in their respective bases of authority have led each to articulate security practices that support a new meaning of security – one that challenges the modern public/private divide (Avant 2007).

The distinctions between public and private in the security realm are not nearly so settled and uniquely focused on the state as traditional theorizing in international relations would have us think. A private authority approach cannot quite make sense of the trajectory we have described because as profit-seeking and helping organizations have appealed to public principles they have become less clearly "private." Instead, we find it more useful to examine the practices of both public and private in the security realm. We find these practices have shifted over time, and that profit-seeking, helping, and ruling organizations have played different roles at different times in influencing what counts as a public issue, who is part of the public, and what processes are deemed public.

REFERENCES

Abrahamsen, Rita, and Michael C. Williams. 2011. *Security beyond the State: Private Security in International Politics*, Cambridge: Cambridge University Press.

Anderson, Mary B. 1999. *Do no Harm: How Aid Can Support Peace – or War.* Boulder, CO: Lynne Rienner.

Avant, Deborah. 2004. "Conserving nature in the state of nature: the politics of INGO implementation." *Review of International Studies* 30(3): 361–82.

2007. "NGOs, corporations, and security transformation in Africa." *International Relations* 21(2): 143–61.

Avant, Deborah, Martha Finnemore, and Susan Sell, eds. 2010. *Who Governs the Globe?* Cambridge: Cambridge University Press.

Barnett, Michael, and Martha Finnemore. 2004. *Rules for the World: International Organizations in Global Politics.* Ithaca, NY: Cornell University Press.

Barnett, Michael, and Jack Snyder. 2009. "The grand strategies of humanitarianism." In *Humanitarianism in Question: Politics, Power, Ethics,* edited by Michael Barnett and Thomas George Weiss, pp. 143–71 Ithaca, NY: Cornell University Press.

Bendix, Reinhard. 1980. *Kings or People: Power and the Mandate to Rule.* San Francisco, CA: University of California Press.

Bowen, Huw V. 2006. *The Business of Empire: The East India Company and Imperial Britain, 1756–1833.* Cambridge: Cambridge University Press.

Brown, Stephen. 2009. *Merchant Kings: When Companies Ruled the World, 1600–1900.* New York: St. Martin's Press.

Buzan, Barry. 1991. *People, States and Fear: An Agenda for International Security Studies,* 2nd edn. London: Harvester.

Buzan, Barry, Ole Wæver, and Jaap de Wilde. 1998. *Security: A New Framework for Analysis.* Boulder, CO: Lynne Rienner.

Cardoso, Fernando Henrique, and Enzo Faletto. 1979. *Dependency and Development.* Berkeley, CA: University of California Press.

Carlos, Ann M., and Stephen Nicholas. 1988. "Giants of an earlier capitalism: the chartered trading companies as modern multinationals." *Business History Review* 62: 398–419.

Comaroff, Jean, and John Comaroff. 1986. "Christianity and colonialism in South Africa." *American Ethnologist* 13(1): 1–22.

Cooley, Alexander, and James Ron. 2002. "The NGO scramble: organizational insecurity and the political economy of transnational action." *International Security* 27(1): 5–39.

Dachs, Anthony. 1972. "Missionary imperialism: the case of Bechuanaland." *Journal of African History* 13(4): 647–58.

de Soysa, Indra. 2000. "The resource curse: are civil wars driven by rapacity or paucity?" In *Greed and Grievance: Economic Agendas in Civil Wars,* edited by Mats Berdal and David M. Malone, pp. 113–36. Boulder, CO: Lynne Rienner.

Elshtain, Jean Bethke. 1981. *Public Man, Private Woman: Women in Social and Political Thought.* Princeton, NJ: Princeton University Press.

Etherington, Norman. 2005. "Introduction." In *Missions and Empire,* edited by Norman Etherington, pp. 1–18. Oxford: Oxford University Press.

Evans, Gareth, and Mohamed Sahnoun. 2002. "The responsibility to protect." *Foreign Affiars* (November–December): 99–110.

Fraser, Nancy. 2007. "Transnationalization the public sphere: on the legitimacy and efficacy of public opinion in a post-Westphalian world." *Theory, Culture and Society* 24(4): 7–30.

Freeman, Bennett. 2002. "Managing risk and building trust: the challenge of implementing the voluntary principles on security and human rights." Remarks at *Rules of Engagement: How Business Can Be a Force for Peace* conference, The Hague, November 13.

Frynas, George. 1998. "Political instability and business: focus on Shell and Nigeria." *Third World Quarterly* 19(3): 457–87.

Haufler, Virginia. 2001. *A Public Role for the Private Sector: Industry Self-Regulation in the Global Economy*. Washington, D.C.: Carnegie Endowment for International Peace.

2010. "Corporations in zones of conflict: issues, actors, and institutions." In *Who Governs the Globe?*, edited by Deborah Avant, Martha Finnemore, and Susan Sell, pp. 102–30. Cambridge: Cambridge University Press.

Karl, Terry Lynn. 1997. *The Paradox of Plenty: Oil Booms and Petro-States*. San Francisco, CA: University of California Press.

Kobrin, Stephen J. 1984. "Expropriation as an attempt to control foreign firms in LDCs: trends from 1960 to 1979." *International Studies Quarterly* 28(3): 329–48.

Krahenbuhl, Pierre. 2004. "Humanitarian security: a matter of acceptance, perception and behavior." Address given at the *High-Level Humanitarian Forum*, Palais des Nations, Geneva, March 31.

Litvin, Daniel. 2003. *Empires of Profit: Commerce, Conquest, and Corporate Responsibility*. New York: Texere.

Martin, Randolph. 1999. "NGO field security." *Forced Migration Review* 4(1): 4–7.

Mathews, Jessica. 1989. "Redefining security." *Foreign Affairs* 68: 162–77.

McLean, Janet. 2003. "The transnational corporation in history: lessons for today?" *Indiana Law Journal* 79(2): 363–77.

Moran, Theodore. 1973. "Transnational strategies of protection and defense by multinational corporations: spreading the risk and raising the cost for nationalization in natural resources." *International Organization* 27(2): 273–88.

Nordland, Rod. 2010. "Killings of Afghan relief workers stir strategy debate." *The New York Times*, 13 December.

Nye, Joseph, and Sean Lynn-Jones. 1988. "International security studies: a report of a conference on the state of the field." *International Security* 12(4): 5–27.

Ottaway, Marina. 2001. "Corporatism goes global: international organizations, nongovernmental organization networks, and transnational business." *Global Governance* 7: 265–92.

Philpott, Daniel. 1995. "In defense of self-determination." *Ethics* 105: 352–85.

Pifer, Alan. 1966. *Report of the President of the Carnegie Corporation*. New York: Carnegie Corporation.

Raz, Joseph, ed. 1990. *Authority*. New York: New York University Press.

Rogers, Charles, and Brian Sytsma. 1999. *World vision security manual: Safety awareness for aid workers*. Geneva: World Vision.

Ross, Michael L. 1999. "The political economy of the resource curse." *World Politics* 51(2): 297–323.

Ruggie, John Gerard. 2004. "Reconstituting the global public domain: issues, actors, and practices." *European Journal of International Affairs* 10(4): 499–531.

Sampson, Anthony. 1975. *The Seven Sisters: The Great Oil Companies and the World They Shaped*. London: Viking.

Schafer, John, and Pete Murphy. 2010. *Security Collaboration: Best Practice Guide*. Washington, D.C.: InterAction.

Simensen, Jarle. 1986. "Religious change as transaction: the Norwegian mission to Zululand South Africa 1850–1906." *Journal of Religion in Africa* 16(1): 82–100.

Spar, Dobora. 1998. "The spotlight and the bottom line." *Foreign Affairs* 77: 7–12.

Spruyt, Hendrik. 2000. "The end of the empire and the extension of the Westphalian system: the normative basis of the modern state order." *International Studies Review* 2(2): 65–92.

Stein, Janice Gross. 2011. "Background knowledge in the foreground: Conversations about competent practice in 'sacred space.'" In *International Practices*, edited by Emmanuel Adler and Vincent Pouliot, pp. 87–107. Cambridge: Cambridge University Press.

Terry, Fiona. 2002. *Condemned to Repeat: The Paradox of Humanitarian Action*. Ithaca, NY: Cornell University Press.

Thomson, Janice. 1994. *Mercenaries, Pirates, and Sovereigns*. Princeton, NJ: Princeton University Press.

Truitt, J.Frederick. 1970. "Expropriation of foreign investment: summary of the post World War II experience of American and British investors in the less developed countries." *Journal of International Business Studies* 1(1): 21–34.

Van Brabant, Koenraad. 1997. "Security guidelines: no guarantee for security." *Humanitarian Exchange Magazine* 7. www.odihpn.org/humanitarian-exchange-magazine/.

Venn, Fiona. 1986. *Oil Diplomacy in the Twentieth Century*. London: MacMillan.

Walt, Stephen M. 1991. "The renaissance of security studies." *International Security Studies* 35(2): 211–39.

Winius, George D., and Marcus P.M. Vink. 1991. *The Merchant–Warrior Pacified: The VOC (the Dutch East India Company) and its Changing Political Economy in India*. Oxford: Oxford University Press.

Yergin, Daniel. 2008. *The Prize: The Epic Quest for Oil, Money and Power*. New York: Free Press.

Zandvliet, Luc, and Mary Anderson. 2009. *Getting It Right*. Sheffield: Greenleaf Publishing.

4   Out from the shadows: governing over-the-counter derivatives after the 2007–08 financial crisis

Eric Helleiner

Efforts to reform global markets for over-the-counter (OTC) derivatives present a fascinating case for the broader study of the "reconstitution of the public" within global governance in the wake of the 2007–08 global financial crisis. Before the crisis, these markets attracted remarkably little public attention despite their explosive and unregulated growth since the early 1980s. The crisis changed this situation dramatically. Many societal groups and policy-makers suddenly declared that OTC derivative markets were a matter of urgent public concern, and the governance of these markets became a priority item on the public policy agenda within the leading financial powers and at the international level. What arguments have been advanced for this dramatic widening of what counts as "public"? What are the practices being employed to make these markets more public and who is the public that is being appealed to in these initiatives?

To date, political scientists have devoted little attention to these questions. Even before the crisis, the study of the politics of OTC derivatives was considered a rather obscure topic that attracted few researchers. Since the crisis, the issue has received a little more attention, with the tightening of regulation over OTC derivatives sometimes being mentioned in broader analyses of the "return of the state" after the financial meltdown. But we are missing more detailed analyses of the content of regulatory initiatives and their broader significance for scholarly debates about the changing public–private relationship in the global political economy. This chapter aims to begin to fill this gap in the existing literature.

The first section of the chapter briefly explores how the financial crisis gave birth to several distinct narratives about why OTC derivatives should be seen as a public concern. The most politically influential pointed to systemic financial risks emanating from the markets. Also attracting much attention were those highlighting the need to address the abuse of market power by larger dealer banks vis-à-vis other financial market actors. More politically contested were arguments focusing on how unregulated OTC derivatives were strengthening financial interests vis-à-vis public authorities and other societal groups. These latter arguments are reminiscent of arguments that helped generate support for greater public control of international finance at Bretton Woods in the wake of the financial crisis of the early 1930s, but they have had less impact in the current period.

The second section of the chapter analyzes the practices being employed by policy-makers to make OTC derivatives more public. While some involve the tightening of direct state controls over market activity, the publicness of OTC markets is being constructed in more ways than simply through a "return of the state." Indeed, most official attention has been devoted to a quite different strategy of steering market activity through various private institutions – clearing houses, organized trading platforms, and trade repositories – which can act as new sites of governance for making the markets more accountable to public authorities and wider societal actors via liberal practices of transparency, participation, consultation, and information provision. These "public-making" practices are distinct from those in the Bretton Woods era, and they draw on a conception of accountability that is more limited both in its goals and in the "public" that it invokes. This content of post-crisis reforms reflects some enduring features of the politics of OTC derivatives that were apparent in the pre-crisis period, namely the influence of private financial interests and a broader conservative transnational policy community within policy debates concerning this sector of the world economy. As summarized in the conclusion, this analysis contributes to our understandings of the *what* counts as a public issue in global governance, *how* the public is enacted, *who* is empowered to be a public actor, as well as the extent to which communities of practice are being *transformed* in the current era.

Attributing publicness to over-the-counter derivatives: from social silence to the 2007–08 crisis

Derivatives include a wide range of products – futures, forwards, options, and swaps – whose value is derived from the performance of another financial asset or an index of asset values; for example, an investor might buy an option to purchase a particular asset on a given date at a certain price. Although some kinds of derivatives have been traded for centuries on exchanges (e.g. agricultural futures), the rapid growth of derivatives trading after the early 1980s has mostly involved OTC trades – especially swaps and options – negotiated privately between the buyer and seller. By the end of 2008, the total notional size of outstanding OTC derivatives contracts had grown to a staggering $592 trillion, a figure roughly ten times the global GDP (Bank for International Settlements 2009). Of this total, the largest markets involve interest rate derivatives, with currency and credit derivatives next in size, followed by smaller markets for equity and commodity derivatives. The market for credit default swaps (CDS) – a product that promises to compensate the buyer in full for the value of a bond that defaults – grew particularly quickly in the decade before the crisis (Tett 2009a).

Despite the enormous growth of these OTC derivatives markets, they attracted very little public attention before the 2007–08 financial crisis. Indeed, Gillian Tett (2010a) has described the absence of public discussion of the topic during the decade and half or so before 2008 as a remarkable example of Pierre Bourdieu's concept of "social silence." What explained this silence? The few brave scholars who analyzed the politics of OTC derivatives before the recent crisis offered several explanations.

One was the inherent complexity and virtual nature of OTC derivatives which meant that the functioning and consequences of the markets were very difficult to understand to all but those with high technical knowledge. As Edward LiPuma and Benjamin Lee put it,

> The main reason why a market this large has been able to avoid detection and regulation is that derivatives are too complex, too virtual, and apparently too mathematical for either the political community or those who investigate political economy and culture. In a sense, the derivative is the perfect capitalist invention, because it seems to have no concrete form sufficiently legible and visible to allow it to become a sustained subject of conversation in the public sphere. (LiPuma and Lee 2004: 105)

Other analysts highlighted the importance of the hegemony of neoliberal ideas, particularly in elite policymaking circles. In the wake of several financial crises and scandals involving OTC derivatives during the 1990s, public interest in the markets did surface briefly, particularly within the USA. In each case, however, influential policy-makers rejected public action, insisting that the markets were self-regulating and that their untrammeled growth was helping to create a more resilient and stable global financial system. These strongly held beliefs reflected not just a general belief in free markets, but also associated economic theories such as efficient markets hypothesis and other aspects of modern finance theory which predicted that derivatives were dispersing risk and enabling actors to become less vulnerable to risks in useful and efficient ways (Best 2005; Blyth 2003; Mackenzie 2006; Tett 2009a). The influence of these ideas was particularly strong among what Tsingou (2006) calls an exclusive "transnational policy community" of elite technocratic officials, experts, and private financial actors who shaped much of the international policy discourse in this sector before the crisis through their technical expertise.

A final structural factor invoked to explain why OTC derivatives were kept largely out of the public discussion was the power of private financial actors. Particularly opposed to public regulation of the markets were the large dealer banks that dominated the markets through their position as dominant sellers and buyers, and through their control of market information in the opaque markets. Because of its large volume and high margins, OTC derivatives trading was a very significant source of revenue for these firms, making up as much as 40 percent of their total profits (McLean and Nocera 2010: 104). At the brief moments when public debate emerged, these institutions lobbied vociferously and successfully against public regulation at the national and international levels (e.g. Johnson and Kwak 2010; Tett 2009a). They also pre-empted further public discussions through what Morgan (2010) calls "transnational private rule-making." Particularly important were the activities of the International Swaps and Derivatives Association (ISDA) – a powerful transnational industry association dominated by the dealer banks – which created a "master agreement" standardizing contracts and encouraging banks to post collateral against deals.

The 2007–08 global financial crisis ushered in a new political environment for the discussion of OTC derivatives. Very suddenly, the unregulated growth of these markets was deemed by many to be an issue of urgent public concern. By the fall of 2008, a broad-based political consensus had emerged in the major financial powers on this point. The most important signal of this new consensus came at the first G20 leaders' summit in November 2008 when the leaders declared in their final communiqué that the tightening of official regulation over OTC derivatives would be one of their top priorities (G20 2008). The issue remained a priority item at the subsequent G20 leaders' summits when the leaders endorsed a number of very specific regulatory objectives in this area. These goals are presently being met through international initiatives as well as national ones, particularly in the two jurisdictions – the USA and the European Union (EU) – which house the bulk of the world's OTC derivatives trading. The key US legislative initiative has been the July 2010 *Dodd–Frank Wall Street Reform and Consumer Protection Act*, which backs the core G20 goals. The European Commission released draft proposals for EU legislation with similar content initially in September and December 2010. Subsequent negotiations among the Commission, EU Member States, and the European Parliament led to some initial reforms being approved and implemented in 2012.

Although these developments highlighted the new publicness of OTC derivatives very clearly, there were a number of distinct rationales put forward for why these markets needed to be the subject of public concern. Each of these rationales met with differing levels of political support during and in the wake of the financial crisis.

Narratives on the publicness of derivatives

Systemic risks

The most prominent and widely supported narrative pointed to the role of OTC derivatives in contributing to systemic risks in the global financial system. The collapse of Bear Stearns in March 2008 and then Lehman Brothers and American International Group (AIG) in September 2008 highlighted very starkly to policy-makers and the general public how the selling and buying of OTC derivatives – particularly CDS contracts – had become highly concentrated among large US and European financial institutions. It quickly became clear that the collapse of any one of the institutions involved could create a domino effect, bringing down other large institutions that were counterparties to its contracts.

The lack of transparency of the OTC quality of the derivatives market also created enormous uncertainty during the crisis; even the largest institutions lacked knowledge about who held which contracts and with whom. As the financial crisis deepened, this confusion about risk exposure to troubled institutions undermined confidence and market liquidity, heightening panic and fear in the markets. In the words of Andrew Haldane of the Bank of England, market participants were forced to ask "what if Bank B itself has *n* counterparties? And what if each of these *n* counterparties itself has *n* counterparties?" (Haldane 2009: 15) In this context, he noted that the calculation of counterparty risk became "like solving a high-dimension Sudoku puzzle"; it was "not just unknown" but "almost unknowable" (Haldane 2009: 15).

The crisis also demonstrated that the risk management practices of many of the leading players in the OTC CDS markets were flawed. The most dramatic example was AIG, which had emerged as one of the largest issuers of CDS products. It had been selling far more contracts than it had capital to back in the event of widespread defaults. Regulators had failed to recognize its growing systemic significance and the fact that its London division selling CDS had been acting, in Ben Bernanke's words, "like a hedge fund sitting on top of an insurance company" (quoted in Paulson 2009: 236).

The argument that unregulated OTC derivatives contributed to systemic financial risks attracted widespread support. At an elite level, the financial crisis acted as a catalyst for many policy-makers associated with Tsingou's "transnational policy community" to embrace these critiques of unregulated OTC derivatives. Their new attitude was part of an emerging post-crisis, elite-level technocratic consensus around the need for "macroprudential" thinking that focused on mitigating system-wide risks, and was more willing to question free-market thinking (Helleiner and Pagliari 2011). The contribution of OTC derivatives to systemic risks also became politicized to an unprecedented degree among legislative assemblies and societal actors in the USA and Europe because of the severity of the 2007–08 crisis. The massive bailouts of financial institutions were particularly significant in generating broad-based demands for reforms to the governance of the markets, since many of the public funds were used to stabilize CDS trades. Even the large dealer banks that had vociferously opposed regulation in previous years finally accepted the case for governance reform and they set out to shape the debate as much as possible to serve their interests (Weitzman 2008).

Distributional concerns

Concerns about systemic risks were not the only issue that led critics to demand increased public scrutiny of OTC derivatives in the wake of the crisis. Distributional concerns were also prominent in a number of narratives. Many critics argued that the growth of unregulated OTC derivatives was strengthening powerful private financial interests at the expense of public authorities and other societal interests. For example, some argued that the opaque nature of unregulated OTC derivatives markets was facilitating the private evasion of taxes and various kinds of official regulations. Others suggested that powerful speculators were using unattached CDS contracts to engage in short-selling of bonds in ways that were highly destabilizing for the targeted entity whether it was an industrial firm (such as General Motors in 2009) or a government (such as Greece in early 2010). Unregulated speculative activity in OTC commodity derivatives markets was also blamed for contributing to the sharp commodity price volatility during 2008, a phenomenon that had severely impacted not just buyers and sellers of commodities but also the food security of the world's poor.

Many of these criticisms had been leveled at OTC derivatives markets in the past, but they attracted a much wider hearing during and in the wake of the financial crisis because of the broader attention to OTC derivatives markets at this time. In some ways, these distributional arguments were reminiscent of the kinds of critiques of the excessive power of financial interests that provided the rationale for greater public regulation of financial markets in the wake of the Great Depression. At the time of the Bretton Woods conference of 1944, for example, influential policy-makers such as US Treasury Secretary Henry Morgenthau trumpeted their goal of shifting power "from London and New York to the US Treasury," thereby creating "a new concept between nations in international finance." (quoted in Gardner 1980: 76)

The ambitious goals of the Bretton Woods architects led them to endorse controls on speculative cross-border financial flows. In the current era, many of those who critique OTC derivatives on distributional grounds also seek tighter public regulation over financial speculation. Some have called for bans on CDS contracts (or more specifically unattached CDS contracts), while others push for position limits (i.e. ceilings) to be imposed on the number on contracts that speculative traders can hold within OTC commodity derivative markets. These goals have met with some success. The EU, for example, agreed to a form of ban on unattached CDS contracts on sovereign debt in the fall of 2011. In the USA, the Dodd–Frank bill extended position limits on speculators to their trading in OTC commodity derivatives markets, a move that was demanded by a very wide alliance of consumer advocacy groups, international development NGOs, and many producers, distributors, retailers and various end-users in the agricultural, food, and energy sectors (Clapp and Helleiner 2012). Support for position limits was also subsequently expressed by the G20 in their November 2011 summit meeting as part of efforts to mitigate commodity price volatility (G20 2011: 3).

But these initiatives – and their underlying rationales – have often been viewed quite sceptically by elite technocratic officials and experts associated with the pre-crisis transnational policy community identified by Tsingou. While these more conservative figures have come to accept the macroprudential argument that OTC markets may generate systemic risks, they are often less comfortable with the broader political arguments about distributional consequences and the critiques of speculators who they see (in neoclassical economic terms) as useful market makers. Regulatory initiatives of the kind noted above have thus often been driven more by bottom–up political pressures at the domestic level than by initiatives from transgovernmental networks of technocrats. Private financial interests have also fiercely resisted these kinds of direct restrictions on OTC market activity.

Many in the financial industry have been more supportive, however, of initiatives to address systemic risks by steering market activity through new institutions such as clearing houses, organized trading platforms, and trade repositories in ways that are described below. These initiatives have attracted industry support not just because they are less heavy-handed, but also because they address distributional concerns that some in the industry hold. As Daniel Mugge (2006) has noted, initiatives to bring global markets under greater "public" control are often supported by private interests who feel disadvantaged by existing forms of "private" regulation. In the case of OTC derivatives markets, some investor groups on the "buy-side" of the market saw the crisis as an opportunity to push for more transparent markets that were less dominated by the large dealer banks. Financial exchanges also hoped greater official encouragement of organized trading platforms might help them to wrest some of the share of derivatives trading away from the dealer banks (Helleiner 2011).

These kinds of intra-industry distributional concerns have been shared by many elite technocratic officials and experts who recognized that the dealer banks' excessive control of the OTC markets could lead to "market abuse." Indeed, in contrast to the Bretton Woods era, these concerns about distributional issues *within* the financial sector have attracted more attention and had more impact over the direction of official reforms than the broader efforts to restrain the power of financial interests as a whole. This has been particularly true at the international level where the influence of Tsingou's transnational policy community has been more pronounced. When justifying the need for public action on OTC derivatives at their 2009 summit in Pittsburgh, the G20 leaders, for example, invoked only their desire to "improve transparency in the derivatives markets, mitigate systemic risk, and protect against market abuse" (G20 2009: 9). The broader distributional rhetoric of Morgenthau was strikingly absent.

Making over-the-counter derivatives public

If a number of distinct narratives have helped transform OTC derivatives markets into more of an object of public concern, what are the specific practices that policy-makers are using to actually make these markets more "public"? Some involve a straightforward tightening of state regulations over the markets. Two such initiatives have already been mentioned: the banning of specific products (e.g. unattached CDS on sovereign bonds) and the imposition of position limits on market actors. A third has involved the tightening of prudential regulations on institutions that trade OTC derivatives.

But it would be a mistake to argue that the publicness of OTC markets is being constructed primarily through a "return of the state" in these more conventional ways. Most of the attention of policy-makers has in fact been devoted to a more unusual two-step strategy. First, OTC market activity is being steered through three kinds of institutions that can act as central nodes in the markets: clearing houses, organized trading platforms, and trade repositories. Each of these types of institution existed already, but their importance within the markets is now being strengthened. Second, policy-makers are then transforming these entities – most of which are private institutions – into sites of governance that can help make the markets more accountable to public authorities and a wider range of societal actors (especially other market actors). Accountability in this context is being cultivated by liberal practices of transparency, participation, consultation, and information provision.

Despite its importance, the construction of these new sites of governance within OTC derivatives has received no attention to date from scholars of international political economy and global governance. One reason is that the politics of clearing houses, organized trading platforms, and trade depositories have been almost entirely ignored in past scholarship. Even recent pioneering literature in sociology and anthropology that explores the detailed infrastructure of derivatives markets has neglected these institutions, focusing instead on the role of expert knowledge, computer and legal systems, and socio-cultural practices in shaping the markets (e.g. Lepinay 2007; Mackenzie 2006; Riles 2010; Zaloom 2006). For this reason, we need to examine these initiatives in some detail.

Central counterparties

The first important initiative has been to steer more OTC derivatives trading through central counterparties (CCPs). As the G20 leaders put it at their summit in Pittsburgh in September 2009, the goal is for "all standardised OTC derivative contracts" to be "cleared through central counterparties by end-2012 at the latest" (G20 2009: 9).[1] Central counterparties act as an intermediary between sellers and buyers of contracts; once a contract is negotiated, the CCP purchases it from the seller and sells it on the buyer, forcing both to post collateral to cover losses in the event of a collapse of a counterparty. It is hoped that this arrangement will reduce systemic risks by enabling counterparty risks to be managed centrally and by reducing the risk of contagion caused by broader uncertainties about exposures in OTC markets. More generally, as trading is steered through CCPs,

---

[1] They also noted that "non-centrally cleared contracts should be subject to higher capital requirements" (G20 2009: 9).

regulators should be better able to monitor risks in the markets and regulate issues such as margins and capital.

In backing the clearing of OTC derivatives through CCPs, the G20 leaders were endorsing a practice that had already been widespread in some OTC derivatives markets. The London-based LCH. Clearnet, for example, had been clearing inter-dealer interest-rate swaps for almost a decade. But trades of interest-rate swaps involving retail "buy-side" customers, such as asset managers, pension funds, hedge funds, and insurance companies, were largely uncleared before the crisis. So too was trading of other OTC derivatives, such as CDS products. The new public regulatory push for clearing has encouraged many private actors to fill this gap by building new CCPs to capitalize on the new clearing business. The large exchanges have been particularly prominent in the competitive scramble, seeing CCPs as a way to benefit more from the bank-dominated OTC derivatives markets. The goal of challenging the dealer banks' control of the market has also been shared by many institutional investors who hope the development of CCPs – and the accompanying official push for greater standardization of contracts – will bring more transparency and liquidity to the market.

In addition to promoting CCPs, policy-makers have devoted new attention to their governance. One of the consequences of forcing all standardized OTC trades through CCPs is that counterparty risks end up concentrated in the CCP node itself (Singh 2011). As CCPs are transformed into systemically important institutions in OTC derivatives markets, policy-makers have recognized that they must be well managed. Particular concerns have been expressed about the fact that CCPs are profit-maximizing entities which might prompt them to compete for business by lowering margins or other risky practices (e.g. European Commission 2010: 68; Financial Stability Board 2010: 32). Some have also suggested that clearing houses might even be tempted to engage in irresponsible behavior because of an awareness that their new systemic importance will guarantee future bailouts (Podolyako 2010). Indeed, because of these and other concerns, the Bank of England (2010: 10), has suggested that the optimal governance structure is a user-owned, not-for-profit model.

The new focus on CCP governance has been driven not just by these prudential concerns but also distributional ones. Concerns have also been raised about the fact that CCPs owned by exchanges could give preferential treatment to OTC trades done on their own platforms vis-à-vis those traded elsewhere (e.g. Grant 2010b). Others have worried about how powerful dealer banks might control – through ownership or dominance of their management – key rules relating to issues such as access, choice of derivatives to be cleared, and/or collateral levels (e.g. Litan 2010; Story 2010).

The G20 leaders tasked two international standard-setting organizations – the Committee on Payments and Settlements Systems (CPSS) and the International Organization for Securities Commissions (IOSCO) – with developing international standards for the regulation and supervision of CCPs for OTC derivatives.[2] In their April 2012 report, the CPSS and IOSCO advocated governance arrangements that are "clear and transparent," "promote the safety and efficiency" of the CCPs, and "support the stability of the broader financial system, other relevant public interest considerations, and the objectives of relevant stakeholders." The report also noted that CCPs should have "objective, risk-based, and publicly disclosed criteria for participation, which permit fair and open access." It advocated "clear and direct lines of responsibility and accountability" that are disclosed to the public, and urged that "major decisions should be clearly disclosed to relevant stakeholders and, where there is a broad market impact, the public." In addition, the report noted that CCPs "should, at a minimum, disclose basic data on transaction volumes and values" (CPSS–IOSCO 2012: 26, 3, 26, 121).

More specific rules have been debated in the USA and Europe. US regulators have proposed maximum levels of ownership shares of CCPs for members and financial firms, and requirements for independent public directors on CCP boards. To prevent clearing houses from becoming what the head of the US Commodities Futures Trading Commission (CFTC), Gary Gensler, calls "exclusive clubs" (quoted in Rauch 2010), US regulators have also proposed minimum capital requirements for CCP members at $50 million, considerably lower than levels used by many existing CCPs (Stafford 2011). The Dodd–Frank bill also requires CCPs to provide open non-discriminatory access for derivatives mandated for clearing (Norman 2012: 337). The European Commission (2010) has insisted too that CCPs provide "fair access" by accepting contracts from any venue that they are traded (see also Financial Stability Board 2010: 4).

One final governance issue that has arisen is a jurisdictional one. The European Central Bank has suggested that CCPs outside of the Eurozone should not be allowed handle more than 5 percent of any trade in any one euro-denominated instrument (Grant and Barker 2011). Authorities in a number of other countries have also highlighted their

---

[2] In 2004, the CPSS and IOSCO developed "Recommendations for Central Counterparties to CCPs" but these did not fully consider issues raised by CCPs for OTC derivatives at the time.

desire for nationally based CCPs in order to be able to regulate and supervise them, access information from them, and intervene in the event of trouble. At the same time, the emergence of distinct CCPs in many different countries is opposed by many internationally oriented industry actors who fear the efficiencies created by the need to post margins in each place (e.g. Cookson 2010). Some regulators such as Gensler (2010) have also argued that regulators may gain a better and more global view of market risks if one single CCP exists for each product, regardless of location, which is then regulated and supervised by a network of national regulators. Despite these objections, a proliferation of CCPs looks increasingly likely as exchanges in a number of other countries – from Canada and Mexico to Singapore and Hong Kong – are spotting the commercial opportunities associated with clearing and are creating new CCPs (Grant 2011; Norman 2012: 299, 351–54). The jurisdictional issues surrounding regulation and supervision are likely to become only more complicated in the coming years.

Organized trading platforms

Alongside promoting CCPs, the G20 leaders have declared that "all standardized OTC derivatives contracts should be traded on exchanges or electronic trading platforms, where appropriate ... by end-2012 at the latest" (G20 2009: 9). To understand the significance of encouraging trading on these "organized platforms," it is useful to recall how most OTC derivatives have been previously traded. The main sellers of OTC derivatives have been a small number of large dealer banks with extensive information about trading prices and volume because of their central place in the market. In the absence of a centralized market, buyers outside of this circle lack the same information. Regulators have been equally in the dark.

The information gap has been partially filled by specialized firms that have access to collect data primarily from the dealer banks, and sell it on to investors outside of their inner circle. In some markets, this service is provided by a large inter-dealer broker such as the London-based Icap which publishes prices for dollar swaps on Reuters and Bloomberg screens (which are used as a reference point for client deals as well as a benchmark in ISDA-created official derivatives documents) (Mackenzie 2010a). In the CDS market, the British firm Markit (in which the banks are major shareholders) provides a similar service, although it does not provide "live" prices but only average prices calculated at the end of the day from data on price quotes provided by the banks (Litan 2010; Mackenzie 2009a; van Duyn, Mackenzie, and Tett 2009). Because of the market's lack of transparency, questions are inevitably raised about the accuracy of the price information provided by the larger dealers to these firms and whether the dealers may try to manipulate the market through the information they provide (Mackenzie 2009a, 2010a; Tett 2009b). Indeed, in 2008, the US Department of Justice became interested in whether the dealers might be involved in anti-competitive practices vis-à-vis the supply of prices to Markit (Litan 2010; MacKenzie 2009a). In April 2011, the European Commission also launched an investigation into whether Markit may have colluded with banks to dominate the CDS market (Chaffin and Grant 2011).

The official promotion of organized platforms – along with the push for CCPs – is designed to transform this opaque system of pricing in the markets and make trading more transparent. As Tett puts it, policy-makers "want the financial equivalent of democracy: data that is available to all, or produced through open, competitive means" (Telt 2009b). This transformation would both serve prudential purposes, and help reduce market abuse. The Financial Stability Board explains these rationales well:

The OTC derivatives markets are currently relatively opaque due to their privately negotiated, bilateral nature and the limited availability of transaction data such as prices and volumes. In stressed financial circumstances, these characteristics may make OTC derivatives markets less reliable and could lead to increased market and liquidity risks for participants. This opacity also may make valuing transactions more difficult. Because OTC derivatives trading often is not subject to the same level of market surveillance as exchange or electronic platform trading, market abuse may be less likely to be detected. (Financial Stability Board 2010: 10)

Not surprisingly, the dealer banks have been resisting this initiative since their asymmetric control of information in the opaque markets has been a key source of their power and profits in the market. Policy-makers have been very clear, however, about their determination to override their interests in this case. As Gensler has put it, "the only parties that benefit from a lack of transparency are Wall Street dealers. Right now we have a dealer-dominated world, and that nearly drove us off a cliff" (quoted in van Duyn 2010a).

While dealer banks have resisted the push for greater use of organized platforms, many 'buy-side' investors have supported this policy initiative (Mackenzie and van Duyn 2010a). Exchanges in both the USA and Europe have also welcomed the prospect of gaining greater share of the derivatives markets (Helleiner 2011). So too have a number of firms who believe that their existing trading facilities could qualify as "electronic trading platforms" under the rules, such as Icap which has developed electronic trading systems to facilitate trades between the major dealer banks (Grant 2009; Mackenzie 2010b).

Some of the most heated policy debates have in fact centered on the question of defining what will qualify as an electronic trading platform. In the USA, the Dodd–Frank bill mandated trading of standardized OTC derivatives on exchanges or "swap execution facilities" (SEFs).[3] The latter was defined in the legislation as "a facility trading system or platform in which multiple participants have the ability to execute or trade swaps by accepting bids and offers made by other participants that are open to multiple participants in the facility or system."[4] The dealer banks and inter-dealer brokers have lobbied for their existing electronic "request-for-quote" systems to qualify as SEFs, and the CFTC agreed in October 2010 that these systems could qualify. But it insisted that requests for a quote to buy or sell a swap must be sent to at least five market participants in order to end single-dealer platforms where banks set prices directly on a one-on-one basis with individual clients without other clients or dealers knowing the information (Mackenzie 2011; van Duyn 2010c).

As in the case of CCPs, authorities are also setting rules about how organized platforms must be governed. In October 2010, US officials proposed that members of exchanges and SEFs could not have more than a 20 percent share of the ownership of these entities, and that 35 percent of the boards of SEFs be made up of public representatives. Other mechanisms for enhancing the transparency of the governance of exchanges and SEFs to the public are also being considered. Some analysts have also called for rules that would limit dealers' ownership in data service providers such as Markit and would force dealers to "make their data available on equal terms to all vendors or pricing services" (Litan 2010: 36).

Trade repositories

The final node through which public authorities are now steering OTC derivatives markets are trade repositories (TRs). These bodies are centralized registries with electronic databases recording information about who has traded what and with whom in various OTC derivatives markets. The potential usefulness of TRs was highlighted during the 2007–08 crisis. When the crisis began, there was only one TR

---

[3] The EU is using the term "organized trading venues," but has not yet defined them.

[4] See www.sec.gov/about/laws/wallstreetreform-cpa.pdf.

for OTC derivatives in existence: the Trade Information Warehouse (subsequently renamed Warehouse Trust) for CDS contracts. It had been created in late 2006 by the New York-based firm Depository Trust and Clearing Corporation (DTCC) in order to help the financial industry reduce confirmation backlogs in the CDS market.

The DTCC had been seen before the crisis as a rather "sleepy, bureaucratic organization" (Mackenzie 2009b), but it suddenly shot to prominence during the Lehman Brothers crisis. Given the uncertainties about CDS counterparty exposures at the time, the DTCC decided to make public the size of net notional value of the CDS exposure to Lehman Brothers. The figure released was approximately $6 billion, a number that helped to calm market actors, many of whom had feared that exposures were much higher (based on estimates of gross exposures which were believed to be as high as $400 billion) (European Commission 2010: 25 n. 280). The head of the DTCC described this as a "transformative moment" for the firm: "We realized that creating this type of transparency would be an important tool in helping regulators and the public at large better understand the OTC derivatives market" (quoted in Mackenzie 2009b).

This moment was also transformative for public authorities who now recognized the potentially useful role that TRs could play in bringing greater transparency to OTC derivative markets. As part of the post-crisis reforms, the G20 leaders insisted in 2009 that all OTC derivative trades – both of standardized products and non-standardized ones – "should be reported to trade repositories" (G20 2009: 9). Those entities, in turn, would then be required to share detailed information with regulators and aggregate market data to the public. These goals have been reinforced by US and European legislative initiatives. The overall rationale is well explained by the Financial Stability Board:

Regulators currently do not have a practical means of acquiring a full picture of market participants' direct and indirect counterparty credit risk exposures. This incomplete picture of risk exposures makes it difficult for regulators to gauge the concentration of risk-taking activities across markets. During times of dissemination of information in a consistent fashion, trade repositories (TRs) can fulfil an important function as a credible source of data on OTC derivatives transactions for authorities, market participants and the public. (Financial Stability Board 2010: 11)

Public authorities also welcomed the fact that leading market players – including not just the leading G14 banks but also buy-side firms – committed in June 2009 to report all their CDS trades to the DTCC warehouse, ensuring that it now has near-complete information about that market.[5] Further, ISDA has also played a key role of soliciting and adjudicating private sector proposals for new TRs for commodity, interest rate, and equity derivatives according to a framework agreed with leading supervisors (CPSS–IOSCO 2012: 6). The same leading market players – organized through a group called the Operations Steering Committee (see below) – committed to report all their trades to these entities (European Commission 2010).

As in the cases of CCPs and organized platforms, authorities have not just encouraged the creation of these new nodes for OTC markets, but also set rules for their governance. In April 2012, the CPSS and IOSCO set out global standards in this area that outlined similar provisions as for CCPs. They also noted that "a TR should ensure that it effectively identifies and manages conflicts of interests that may arise between its public role as a centralised data repository and its own commercial interests, particularly if it offers service other than recordkeeping." The CPSS–IOSCO report also set standards for information disclosure:

at a minimum, a TR should provide aggregate data on open positions and transaction volumes and values and categorized data (for example, aggregated breakdowns of trading counterparties, reference entities, or currency breakdowns of products), as available and appropriate, to the public. Relevant authorities should have access to additional data recorded in a TR, including participant-level data, that is relevant to their respective regulatory mandates and legal responsibilities. (CPSS–IOSCO 2012: 28, 124)

The issue of the release of information to authorities had been particularly controversial. The DTCC began publishing aggregate data on CDS trades on its website in November 2008, but it did not initially reveal information regarding specific trading counterparties to authorities without the traders' consent. Under pressure from US and European regulators, it finally agreed in March 2010 to give regulators "unfettered access" to this information (van Duyn 2010b). Regulators were driven at this time by their desire for more information about CDS trades in Greek sovereign debt, trades that were blamed by some for contributing to Greece's financial difficulties at the time (Oakley et al. 2010). The G20 leaders subsequently endorsed the Financial Stability Board's recommendation that "market regulators, central banks, prudential supervisors and resolution authorities must have effective and practical access to the data collected by trade repositories that they require to carry out their respective regulatory mandates" (Financial Stability Board 2010: 6).

---

[5] See www.ny.frb.org/newsevents/news/markets/2009/ma090602.html.

The Greek episode also highlighted jurisdictional issues. Their dependence for information on the US-based DTCC during the Greek crisis frustrated many European policy-makers and left them wanting a European-based TR over which they had jurisdiction (e.g. Tait and Grant 2010). Others, however, including DTCC itself and many in the industry, feared that the proliferation of TRs might be inefficient and fragment data. They preferred to see one single global repository for each asset class that would enable a truly global view of the market and risks therein. To make their preferred solution more acceptable politically, the DTCC made it clear that they would share information with European regulators on the same terms as US regulators (Donahue 2010). The DTCC also noted that it was working with an international group of regulators to develop global rules on when information can be requested and disclosed. In September 2010, US and European regulators also issued a joint statement backing international cooperation that facilitates "global access to all data on derivatives that is maintained by trade repositories" (Gensler and Barnier 2010). Reinforcing this commitment, the CPSS–IOSCO report of April 2012 noted that "all relevant authorities should mutually support each other's access to trade data in which they have a material interest in furtherance of their regulatory, supervisory, and oversight responsibilities, regardless of the particular organizational form or geographic location of a TR" (CPSS–IOSCO 2012: 136).

Who is the public?

The "publicness" of OTC derivatives markets is thus being constructed in a manner that involves much more than simply "bringing the state back in." Policy-makers are devoting most of their energy to a two-step strategy involving: (1) a strengthening of the nodal position of key private institutions within the marketplace – CCPs, organized platforms, and TRs – and (2) a transformation of the governance of these institutions into entities that are more accountable to the public. But who exactly is the "public" that is being invoked and constituted by this strategy?

In one sense, this strategy is designed to serve a kind of "global public" (Germain 2004, 2010) by addressing prudential concerns about worldwide systemic risks emanating from OTC markets. This global focus is apparent from the very extensive international coordination involved in implementing this strategy. Coordination is taking place not just through the G20 process and international regulatory bodies such as the Financial Stability Board, the CPSS, and IOSCO. Also significant are two new bodies devoted solely to this issue: the OTC Derivatives Supervisors

Group (ODSG) and OTC Derivatives Regulators' Forum (ODRF).[6] As legislative proposals have been developed and implemented in the USA and EU, coordination has also been extensive at a bilateral level between these two political jurisdictions (e.g. Grant 2010b).

The intensity of this cooperation is driven partly by a sense of shared vulnerability to systemic risks in these globally integrated markets. But it also reflects competitive concerns. In the past, the very mobile nature of the derivatives business has forced national officials to be highly conscious of how any unilateral regulatory initiatives might undermine the international competitiveness of their markets and firms involved in derivatives trading. This concern was particularly strong among US and British officials whose countries housed a very large share of global OTC derivatives trading and who saw financial services as one of their countries' leading sectors (Coleman 2003). By tightening regulations in a coordinated fashion, policy-makers are hoping to contain competitive pressures and ensure that their countries' actions do not simply divert business to another with lighter regulation (Stafford 2011).

The way in which a "global public" is being constructed through these initiatives bears some similarity to the Bretton Woods moment. At that time, efforts to bring international finance under greater public control were driven by a sense of internationally shared vulnerability to the Great Depression and new conceptions of a post-war multilateral political community. Both then and now, the global nature of the "public" being constructed should not, of course, be overstated since international cooperation was/is often designed to serve primarily the national community. In the current era, we have also noted the ongoing jurisdictional controversies about whether regulation and supervision of entities such as CCPs and TRs should be done on a territorial basis or not (see also Helleiner 2014).

In another sense, there is discontinuity with the Bretton Woods period. The Bretton Woods negotiators set out to design an international financial order that was meant explicitly to serve a wide conception of society, rather than just the private financiers who had dominated the pre-1931 financial world. The wartime context of the conference only reinforced this inclusive vision. As US Treasury Secretary Henry Morgenthau put it at the end of the conference: "We must offer this [the Bretton Woods agreements] to the men in the armies and on the sea and

---

[6] The former had its origins in an official grouping created in 2005 of the supervisors of the major OTC derivatives dealers, while the latter was created in September 2009 as a forum for national regulators of the main derivatives markets and representatives of the CPSS and IOSCO. See www.otcdrf.org/

in the air. We must offer them some hope that there is something to look forward to a little better than in the past and I like to think that Bretton Woods is the hope in somewhat concrete form" (US Government 1948: 1126). It is also worth noting that the Bretton Woods agreements were designed to serve much more than narrow economic interests. As Harry Dexter White put it in an early draft of the Bretton Woods proposals, the goal was to go "far beyond usual commercial considerations and considerations of economic self-interest" in order to link the operations of international finance to the "the ideal of freedom" and "a bill of rights of the peoples of the United Nations" (quoted in Oliver 1975: 319).

Today, the conception of the "public" is much narrower. To be sure, policy-makers have in mind the needs of society as a whole when addressing systemic risks. But these needs are expressed primarily only in this limited prudential sense. When broader political issues relating to fairness and participation in governance are addressed, policy-makers' vision of the "public" usually narrows to include only the participants in the markets themselves. For example, the controversies surrounding the fair access to, and ownership of, CCPs are driven primarily by distributional issues *within* the financial community. Only in a few international policy initiatives, such as effort to constrain volatile world food prices through commodity derivatives regulation, has the possibility been opened to discuss the "global public interest" in wider political terms.

The perception that policy-makers often have a narrow notion of the public they are serving is reinforced by their patterns of consultation. In developing and implementing the initiatives outlined above, policy-makers have engaged in continuous and extensive consultation with the private financial sector, often delegating key reforms to private actors and industry associations. This pattern partly reflects their reliance on the expertise of the private sector as well as their need to smooth the implementation of reforms by securing the "buy-in" of the large private players in the markets who retain enormous clout even in the wake of the crisis (Litan 2010; Morgan 2010: 39–40).

Policy-makers' willingness to partner with, and delegate to, the private sector marks a continuity with the pre-crisis period, when policy-makers often worked closely with ISDA and the major dealer banks to encourage changes to the infrastructure of the markets. The one change has been that public authorities have made active efforts to engage with more representatives from the 'buy-side' of the market who have often been more supportive of the goals of public authorities, as we have seen. In addition to pushing ISDA to include more voices from the buy-side, officials have worked closely with a new private sector body called the Operations Steering Committee (OSC) which includes not just G14 dealer banks but also representatives of investors, as well as three trade associations (ISDA, the Managed Funds Association, and Securities Industry and Financial Markets Association).[7]

Policy-makers have devoted much less time to the task of engaging with, and cultivating input from, other societal interests. The relatively limited engagement with wider societal interests in the reform process is not just the fault of policy-makers. The complexity and virtual nature of derivatives markets continues – as it did before the crisis – to create barriers to entry in debates to all but those with high technical knowledge. There have been a few notable exceptions such as the broad-based mobilization within the USA around commodity derivatives regulation. But if that experience is not replicated in other areas and on a more international scale, the prospects for a broader conception of the "global public" to be constituted in debates surrounding OTC derivatives will remain dim.

Conclusion

What is the broader significance of this episode for scholarly debates about the reconstitution of the public in global governance? Four points stand out. First, the episode provides particularly dramatic evidence of the socially constructed nature of the public/private divide in global governance. From being a poster child for private transnational authority before the crisis, the governance of OTC derivatives suddenly became an issue of public concern during and in the wake of the financial crisis. Several distinct narratives generated this transformation, some more politically influential than others. But taken together, they showed very effectively how the question of "*what* is public" is subject to constant renegotiation.

Second, the question of *how* the public is enacted has also been answered in an unusual way in this instance. The publicness of OTC derivatives in the wake of the financial crisis is being constituted through much more than simply the return of the state. Policy-makers have set

---

[7] For the official encouragement of ISDA to provide better representation for investors, see Mackenzie, Bullock, and Tett 2009. The buy-side interests represented in the OSC are: AllianceBernstein, BlackRock, BlueMountain Capital Management, Citadel Investment Group, D.E. Shaw & Co., DW Investment Management, Goldman Sachs Asset Management, Pacific Investment Management Company, and Wellington Management Company. The OSC evolved from another group called the Senior Oversight Group which the major dealer banks had established in 2005 to work with US authorities in strengthening the operational infrastructure of the OTC derivative markets. Its membership widened beyond the dealer banks in December 2007 when it was named the Operations Management Group; it was then renamed the OSC in 2009.

out to create what one market analyst calls a brand new "ecosystem" for OTC derivatives in which market activity is steered through CCPs, organized platforms and TRs (Brian Daly, quoted in Grant 2010a). The governance of these new nodal institutions is, in turn, being reformed in ways that make the markets more accountable to public authorities and wider societal actors. This accountability is being cultivated through practices associated with the liberal public sphere such as transparency, participation, consultation, and information provision.

Third, the episode raises important questions about *who* the public is. When invoking the "public interest" in discussions of the need to mitigate systemic risks, policy-makers appeared to invoke a conception of a kind of "global public." But in their patterns of engagement with societal actors and when discussing distributional issues, they often seem to have a narrower "public" in mind: that of the private financial community. The episode thus suggests that the content of both the distinct narratives and the specific practices that generate "publicness" in turn influences the very identity of the public being constituted by these practices.

Finally, the public-making practices in post-crisis OTC politics provide an example of both transformative and limited change in communities of practice. They certainly have transformed the "social silence" surrounding OTC derivatives during the decade and a half leading up to the 2007–08 global financial crisis. But when compared to the Bretton Woods precedent, the constitution of the public in international finance today seems much more limited. Contemporary narratives invoking a public interest in global financial markets have rested less on critiques of the power of private financial actors and more on concerns about systemic risk and distributional issues *within* the financial community. The practices for making markets more public have also relied less on direct regulation by the state, drawing more on a conception of accountability that is more limited both in its goals and in the "public" that it invokes. These features of contemporary reforms clearly reflect the enduring influence of some aspects of the politics of OTC derivatives that were apparent in the pre-crisis period, particularly the power of private financial interests and a broader conservative transnational policy community. But to explain these unique features of our age more fully, we need a more detailed understanding of the contemporary politics of derivatives. Although the world of OTC derivatives has become more public, there is still much more work to be done to bring it out from the shadows within the scholarly world.

REFERENCES

Bank for International Settlements. 2009. *OTC Derivatives Market Activity for the Second Half of 2008*. Basel: BIS.

Bank of England. 2010. *Financial Stability Report*, no. 28. www.bankofengland.co.uk/

Best, Jacqueline. 2005. *The Limits of Transparency*. Ithaca, NY: Cornell University Press.

Blyth, Mark. 2003. "The political power of financial ideas." In *Monetary Orders*, edited by Jonathan Kirshner, pp. 239–59. Ithaca, NY: Cornell University Press.

Chaffin, Joshua, and Jeremy Grant. 2011. "Brussels launches probe into swaps." *Financial Times*, April 29.

Clapp, Jennifer, and Eric Helleiner. 2012. "Troubled futures? The global food crisis and the politics of agricultural derivatives regulation." *Review of International Political Economy* 19(2): 181–207.

CPSS–IOSCO. 2012. *Principles for Financial Market Infrastructure*. Basel and Madrid: BIS and IOSCO.

Coleman, William. 2003. "Governing global finance: financial derivatives, liberal states and transformative capacity." In *States in the Global Economy*, edited by Linda Weiss, pp. 271–92. Cambridge: Cambridge University Press.

Cookson, Robert. 2010. "Asian regulators launch reforms for OTC derivatives." *Financial Times*, February 25.

Donahue, Donald. 2010. "Consensus is crucial for global OTC ground rules." *Financial Times*, May 4.

European Commission. 2010. *Impact Assessment: Accompanying Document to the Proposal for a Regulation of the European Parliament and of the Council on OTC Derivatives, Central Counterparties and Trade Repositories*, SEC (2010) 1058/2. Brussels: European Commission.

Financial Stability Board. 2010. *Implementing OTC Derivatives Market Reforms*. Basel: FSB.

Financial Times. 2011. "Derivatives reform threatened by lack of harmony." *Financial Times*, March 25.

Gardner, Richard. 1980. *Sterling–Dollar Diplomacy in Current Perspective*. New York: Columbia University Press.

Gensler, Gary. 2010. "OTC derivatives reform." Remarks to European Parliament, Economic and Monetary Affairs Committee, Brussels March 16. www.cftc.gov/

Gensler, Gary, and Michel Barnier. 2010. "Joint statement," by CFTC Chairman Gary Gensler and European Commissioner Michel Barnier on the financial reform agenda. September 28. www.cftc.gov/

Germain, Randall. 2004. "Globalizing accountability within the international organization of credit: financial governance and the public sphere." *Global Society* 18(3): 217–42.

2010. *Global Politics and Financial Governance*. Basingstoke: Palgrave Macmillan.

Grant, Jeremy. 2009. "Icap welcomes Geithner initiative." *Financial Times*, May 19.

2010a. "Market structures face test of trust". *Financial Times*, November 3.
2010b. "Aiming for a united front on derivatives." *Financial Times*, September 16.
2011. "Dealers warn against spread of derivatives clearing houses". *Financial Times*, April 14.
Grant, Jeremy, and Alex Barker. 2011. "ECB preference for Eurozone clearers raises ire in London." *Financial Times*, November 24.
G20. 2008. *Declaration of the Summit on Financial Markets and the World Economy*. www.g20.org/Documents/g20_summit_declaration.pdf.
2009. *Leaders' Statement: The Pittsburgh Summit*, September 24–25. www.g20. org/Documents/
2010. *The G20 Toronto Summit Declaration*, June 26–27. www.g20.org/ Documents/
2011. *Communiqué: G20 Leaders Summit – Cannes*, November 3–4. www.g20. org/Documents/
Haldane, Andrew. 2009. "Rethinking the financial network." Speech delivered at the Financial Student Association, Amsterdam. April.
Helleiner, Eric. 2011. "Reining in the market: global governance and the regulation of OTC derivatives." In *Governing the Global Economy*, edited by D.H. Claes and C.H. Knutsen, pp. 131–49 New York: Routledge.
2014 "Towards cooperative decentralization? The post-crisis governance of global OTC derivatives." In *Transnational Financial Regulation After the Crisis*, edited by Tony Porter. New York: Routledge.
Helleiner, Eric, and Stefano Pagliari. 2011. "The end of an era in international financial regulation? A post-crisis research agenda." *International Organization* 65(1): 169–200.
Johnson, Simon, and James Kwak. 2010. *Thirteen Bankers*. New York: Pantheon.
Lépinay, Vincent-Antonin. 2007, "Decoding finance: articulation and liquidity around a trading room." In *Do Economists Make Markets?*, edited by Donald MacKenzie, Fabian Muniesa, and Lucia Siu, pp. 87–127. Princeton, NJ: Princeton University Press.
LiPuma, Edward, and Benjamin Lee. 2004. *Financial Derivatives and the Globalization of Risk*. Durham, NC: Duke University Press.
Litan, Robert. 2010. *The derivatives dealers' club and derivatives market reform*. Initiative on Business and Public Policy at Brookings, April 7. Washington: Brookings Institute.
Mackenzie, Donald. 2006. *An Engine not a Camera*. Cambridge, MA: MIT Press.
Mackenzie, Michael. 2009a. "DoJ's antitrust missile could have explosive consequences." *Financial Times*, July 18.
2009b. "DTCC paves way for all roads to lead to its warehouse." *Financial Times*, July 1.
2010a. "Frozen in time." *Financial Times*. June 16.
2010b. "Rate swap traders wait for no man." *Financial Times*, October 20.
2011. "Key move over OTC swaps trading." *Financial Times*. January 7
Mackenzie, Michael and Aline van Duyn. 2010. "US swap trading reforms hit obstacle." *Financial Times*, December 10.

Mackenzie, Michael, Nicole Bullock and Gillian Tett. 2009. "Big Bang arrives for credit default swaps industry." *Financial Times*, April 8.
McLean, Bethany, and Joe Nocera. 2010. *All the Devils Are Here: The Hidden History of the Financial Crisis.* New York: Portfolio.
Morgan, Glen. 2010. "Legitimacy in financial markets: credit default swaps in the current crisis." *Socio-Economic Review* 8(1): 17–45.
Mugge, Daniel. 2006. "Private–public puzzles: interfirm competition and transnational private regulation." *New Political Economy* 11(2): 177–200.
Norman, Peter. 2012. *The Risk Controllers.* Chichester: John Wiley.
Oakley, David, Nikki Tait, Stephanie Kirchgaessner, and Henny Sender. 2010. "Regulators probe euro trades." *Financial Times*, March 4.
Oliver, Robert. 1975. *International Economic Cooperation and the World Bank.* New York: Macmillan.
Paulson, Hank. 2009. *On the Brink.* New York: Business Press.
Podolyako, Ilya. 2010. "Central clearing and systemic risk." http:// baselinescenario.com/
Rauch, Joe. 2010. "ICE Trust pulls credit default swap application." *Reuters*, December 23. www.reuters.com/
Riles, Annelise. 2010. "Collateral expertise: legal knowledge in the global financial markets." *Current Anthropology* 51(6): 795–818.
Singh, Manmohan. 2011. *Making OTC Derivatives Safe: A Fresh Look*, IMF Working Papers No. 11/66. Washington, D.C.: International Monetary Fund.
Stafford, Philip. 2011. "Domestic pressures weaken US/EU consensus." *Financial Times*, January 10.
Story, Louise. 2010. "A secretive banking elite rules trading in derivatives." *New York Times*, December 12.
Tait, Nikki, and Jeremy Grant. 2010. "EU seeks 'unfettered access' to US data on OTC trades." *Financial Times*, April 28.
Tett, Gillian. 2009a. *Fool's Gold.* New York: Free Press.
2009b. "How Markit turned from a camera into an engine." *Financial Times*, July 17.
2010a. "Silos and silences." *Financial Stability Review* 14: 121–30.
2010b. "Derivatives body needs to undergo a radical rethink." *Financial Times*, August 27.
Tsingou, Eleni. 2006. "The governance of OTC derivatives markets." In *The Political Economy of Financial Market Regulation,* edited by Peter Mooslechner, Helene Schuberth, and Beat Weber, pp. 168–90 Cheltenham: Edward Elgar.
US Government. 1948. *Proceedings and Documents of the United Nations Monetary and Financial Conference, Bretton Woods, New Hampshire, July 1–22, 1944,* vol. 1. Washington, D.C.: US Government Printing Office.
van Duyn, Aline. 2010a. "CFTC urges end to derivatives secrecy." *Financial Times*, March 10.
2010b. "Tighter OTC derivatives rules loom." *Financial Times*, March 25.
2010c. "New rules aim to bring trading of derivatives more into public view." *Financial Times*, December 17.

van Duyn, Aline, Michael Mackenzie, and Gillian Tett. 2009. "Regulators put CDS pricing in focus." *Financial Times*, July 24.

Weitzman, Hal. 2008. "Banks back mandatory clearing." *Financial Times*, November 20.

Zaloom, Caitlin. 2006. *Out of the Pits*. Chicago, IL: University of Chicago Press.

III

Reconstituting the global public today

5   The "demand side" of good governance: the return of the public in World Bank policy

Jacqueline Best

In the last half-century we have developed a better understanding of what helps governments function effectively and achieve economic progress. In the development community, we have a phrase for it. We call it good governance. It is essentially the combination of transparent and accountable institutions, strong skills and competence, and a fundamental willingness to do the right thing. Those are the things that enable a government to deliver services to its people efficiently.

Speech by World Bank President Paul Wolfowitz, April 2006

In its insistence that good governance is central to economic development, the World Bank has put "the public" back on the development agenda once more. Over the past decade and a half, a whole range of public processes ranging from budget development to public sector management and civil society engagement have appeared on the organization's radar. Does this mean that the state is back in international development theory and practice, after several decades of languishing as insignificant and downright dangerous? Yes and no. There is no doubt that staff and management at the World Bank are more interested in the potentially positive role of the state than in the 1980s, when state–market relations were viewed in largely zero-sum terms. Yet, a closer look at the kinds of policy practices being developed in the context of the good governance agenda reveals that the kind of public that the World Bank and other international financial institutions (IFIs) and donors are seeking to engage through their policies is a much more complex thing than the state alone. They are seeking to define a new kind of public, in which a multitude of different kinds of public actors (state, private sector, civil society) are engaged in a range of public processes, providing certain public goods.

This chapter draws in part on Chapter 6 of my recent book: Best 2014. I benefited from some excellent research assistance by Marie Langevin and Kailey Cannon in researching and writing this chapter, as well as helpful feedback from the other contributors to this volume, particularly Alexandra Gheciu. The research for this chapter was made possible by a grant from the Social Sciences and Humanities Research Council of Canada, as well as the support of the Faculty of Social Sciences at the University of Ottawa.

This trend towards a more dynamic public has become more pronounced over the last few years, as the World Bank has sought to foster the "demand side" of good governance. Having spent the better part of a decade trying to improve the *supply* of better governance practices, World Bank staff are now focusing more attention on the *demand* for them. In the simplest terms, this means encouraging poor people, civil society groups, parliaments, and market actors to demand better governance. In other words, this new development strategy seeks to exercise an indirect and productive form of power to create new kinds of public actors, processes, and goods: to foster the formation of public groups, to encourage them to engage in particular kinds of public speech, and to hope through those means to create a more responsive and accountable public sector.

As Best and Gheciu discuss in the framing chapter of this volume, the public generally takes one of three classic forms in global governance literature: as a form of authority in decline in the context of the rise of private authority; as global public goods needed when the market fails; or as a global public sphere of debating individuals who seek to hold the state accountable. Each of these concepts of the public is present in World Bank rhetoric and practice on good governance: we can find a continued interest in shifting the provision of public services to the market, a tendency to frame good governance in public choice terms as a public good, and efforts to encourage processes, such as participation and transparency, that we would normally associate with the public sphere.

On one level, what we are witnessing is the emergence of a hybrid public logic (see Best and Gheciu, Chapter 2, this volume), which combines all three classic forms of the public in new ways. Yet such a characterization oversimplifies the processes under way. The new practices that the World Bank is engaging in are more intent on re-engaging public actors than we would expect if the shift were driven by the rise of private authority. And while the Bank leaders represent these initiatives as fostering new kinds of public goods, they do so by drawing on moral as well as public choice conceptions of the common good. Moreover, the new public processes that they are promoting are far thinner and more instrumentalized than those that we would traditionally associate with the public sphere.

In fact, the kind of public that is emerging is far more than the sum of these three traditional forms. It is defined above all by its refusal to remain contained in any one space or sphere. Who counts as a public actor depends less on where they are situated, and more on what kinds of *practices* they are engaged in. Are they fostering transparency? Are they engaging in consultations about publicly necessary services? Are they demanding better services, whether provided by the state, the non-profit sector, or the market? If so, they are at least in some measure to be defined as public actors. This is therefore a more fluid kind of public that is defined by the kinds of relations that are built between actors, practices, and goods and the kinds of claims about their publicness made by them or on their behalf. It is therefore an example of the public as practice, as defined by Best and Gheciu in the framing chapter to this volume.

I begin this chapter by taking a closer look at the evolution of the good governance agenda at the World Bank. I will then examine the kinds of public that these new policies seek to constitute, focusing in particular on three central dynamics at work: the organization's efforts to define good governance as a public good; its efforts to engage new kinds of public actors in the production of good governance; and its attempts to foster particular kinds of public processes as a means of achieving that goal. These are all examples of public practice, I will suggest.

What is at stake in this new kind of public practice? I will tackle this question by considering the forms of indirect and productive power and authority involved in these efforts to foster new kinds of publics. Drawing on the concepts developed in Best and Gheciu's framing chapter, I will suggest that the World Bank's practices are both transformative – in their efforts to reconstitute the public in new ways – and reinforcing – in their tendency to fortify the Bank's own institutional authority. Yet these efforts have not been entirely successful to date, suggesting that there are limits to recent efforts to constitute a new kind of public. I will conclude by reflecting on the broader implications of these changing practices both for our understanding of the role of the public in global governance more generally and for the evolving character of political life.

The evolution of good governance

Over the past two decades, it has come to seem quite natural that IFIs and donors would make good governance and limits on corruption part of their development programs. Governance is also front and centre in many donor assistance programs, including the Department for International Development in the UK (DFID 2006), USAID (2011) and the Millennium Challenge Corporation (Danilovich 2007; MCC 2008) in the United States. Yet when the issue of governance was first introduced at the World Bank, it was the subject of considerable internal debate. In some ways, nothing has changed since then: the pursuit of good governance continues to encounter opposition. Nonetheless, good governance and anti-corruption efforts have also become normalized into IFI practices.

How did we get to this point? Given that IFIs are legally mandated to stay clear from political intervention of any kind, the very fact that the World Bank now spends considerable energy giving advice and imposing conditions on civil service reform, reforming legal systems, and encouraging civil society organizations to play a role in these processes requires some kind of explanation.

Some of the initial impetus for the policy shift came from assessments of the limits of development efforts in Africa during the 1980s; it was this insight that first put the issue explicitly on the agenda of the World Bank. Another major underlying factor was the end of the Cold War and the experience with transitional economies in Eastern Europe and the former Soviet Union, where it quickly became clear that economic reform without institutional change was a recipe for disaster. These experiences also helped to foster the increasing influence of new institutionalist economics, as many development practitioners became less satisfied with narrowly neoclassical approaches to their task. Over time, significant pressure for the change also came from donors who faced a combination of "aid fatigue" from voters and increasing pressure to cut back government spending. They spearheaded the new emphasis on "aid effectiveness" and ultimately focused on domestic governance as one of the solutions to what had been ailing development assistance.

It is possible to define two broad phases in the evolution of the governance agenda at the World Bank: the first phase, from 1989 to 1998, was very much an extension of the neoliberal agenda, and saw governance defined primarily in public choice terms, as an effort to avoid rent-seeking by creating a leaner, more effective government. The second phase, dating roughly from 1999 onwards, saw a broadening of the theoretical justification for good governance to include institutionalism and more emphasis on the "demand side" of governance, through transparency and participation.

The term "good governance" first appeared as a central theme in the Bank's 1989 report on long-term development in sub-Saharan Africa (World Bank 1989: xii).[1] The report's authors sought to explain the persistent failure of development efforts in the region over the previous decades. They argued that the principal source was not external – in

---

[1] The actual history of Bank interest in what eventually became known as good governance dates back further, to the late 1970s (Miller-Adams 1999; Weaver 2008), while the attention to the role of the state in economic development of course has a much longer history, dating back to early development economics of the 1940s and 1950s.

declining terms of trade, for example – but was internal, based in a failure of investment that had its roots in bad public management (World Bank 1989: 3). This "crisis of governance" they argued must therefore be addressed before economic progress could be expected (World Bank 1989: 60). Although the report did place some responsibility for failure on the Bank's inability to recognize the institutional basis of economic development, it also implied that the ultimate blame rested with poor countries' governments and argued that the solution was to create a leaner and more effective state (World Bank 1989: 4–5).

Within the next few years, the governance agenda began to command greater attention within the institution. Bank reports on governance in the early 1990s began to flesh out a particular vision of what good governance was, and to identify the steps needed to promote it (World Bank 1991, 1992, 1994). Throughout these early governance documents, the relationship between state and market is defined in terms of public choice theory, which views political and social interactions through the lens of economic theory, treating key players as self-interested and individualistic agents. Perhaps the most pervasive argument made at this time is the claim that rent-seeking is the central problem of governance (World Bank 1991: ii–iii, 4–6; 1992: 7–9; 1994: 15–16, 32). Rent-seeking is a public choice concept that suggests that the state's ability to make decisions about resource allocation – for example the building of a dam in a particular location – encourages the unproductive use of resources (legally or illegally) by those who would benefit from the decision being made one way or another (Krueger 1974). The most often touted solution to rent-seeking is to reduce the scope of state decision-making by shifting greater responsibility to the market – a classic example of the kinds of trend towards privatization discussed in the private authority literature.

By the mid-1990s, the governance agenda was having a concrete impact on Bank operations: the volume of governance-related lending was significant and increasing, with as many as 68 percent of lending operations containing some kind of governance dimension (World Bank 1994: xv). Yet, even as the idea of governance began to take hold within the institution, it was a fraught issue. The Bank's General Counsel, Ibrahim Shihata, was asked to provide a legal opinion on whether the institution's mandate allowed it to address questions of governance. Shihata's opinion sought to define narrowly the scope of the Bank's involvement in governance to those questions that had a direct impact on economic development (Shihata 1990).[2]

---

[2] For an interesting discussion of this opinion, see Thomas 2007: 733.

It was not until James Wolfensohn took the helm of the Bank in 1995 that the issue of governance – and the related problem of corruption – took center stage, and the governance agenda entered its second phase at the Bank. In a famous speech at the Annual Meetings in 1996, Wolfensohn called for an end to the "cancer of corruption" that he argued was eroding development efforts around the world (World Bank 1996). Over time, Wolfensohn significantly transformed the character of the governance agenda at the Bank. It was during his tenure that the 2000–01 World Development Report, *Attacking Poverty*, and the 2002 *Building Institutions for Markets* were released (World Bank 2001, 2002b).

As the good governance agenda entered this second phase, the theoretical justification for good governance changed somewhat: while public-choice theory remained influential, it was supplemented by more emphasis on institutionalist economics.[3] This shift is significant because although an institutionalist approach remains consistent with much neoclassical economic theory, it does place considerable emphasis on the problems of market failure – instances in which the state must step in because markets are unable to allocate resources effectively. Together, new institutionalist economics and public-choice theory provided a basis for a public-goods justification of the importance of good governance, as I will discuss further below.

Under Wolfensohn, the Bank staff also began to place more emphasis on the importance of public participation and voice in the process of governance. Although the idea of public voice is a theme that carries through from the earliest Bank governance strategies, by 2000 the idea that governance reform should be driven by the "demand" of public and private actors had become a defining feature of the governance agenda (World Bank 2000, 2002a).

When Paul Wolfowitz took over as Bank President in 2005, he continued this emphasis on the demand side of good governance, integrating it into his governance and corruption (GAC) strategy, which remains the principal framing document for governance activities at the Bank today (World Bank 2007a). As one World Bank staff member put it:

A lot of Wolfowitz's enthusiasm for governance and anti-corruption has given a real boost to an interest in citizen participation, because – we can have a discussion about neoconservatism and Strauss and some very interesting

---

[3] Classic institutionalist texts here include: Coase 1937; North 1990; Williamson 1985. Douglass North, in particular, is cited in a number of Bank documents as an inspiration for governance policy, particularly from the 2002 World Development Report on institutions (World Bank 2002b) onwards, in which the first footnote cites North, Williamson, and Coase on institutions (Bank 2002b: 5 n.1)

philosophical ideas – but a central neoconservative idea is let's support human rights, citizen rights and grassroots democracy... The [World Bank] President loves this stuff.[4]

As I will discuss further below, this demand-based framing of good governance represents an important step in the Bank's efforts to bring the public back into development policy by defining good governance as a new kind of public good, by mobilizing a broader set of public actors, and by integrating a range of new public practices into its policies.

Redefining the public good

"If you want to make poverty history you have to make corruption history." That is why for the World Bank group, corruption and governance are such important subjects. Yes they are *moral issues* and the *moral dimension* has got to be kept in mind, but from our perspective they are development issues, they are poverty issues.[5]

As this brief history indicates, the idea of good governance has been hotly contested, in large measure because it significantly expands the scope of IFI policies into far more explicitly political terrain. In order for good governance to become accepted, it was necessary for its advocates to establish just why it was an essential part of development policy. One of the chief ways in which they have done so is by arguing that good governance is a public good, a discursive practice that works to constitute a new kind of public – not unlike the efforts to narrate derivatives as a public concern that Helleiner describes (Chapter 4, this volume). What is particularly interesting about the World Bank's efforts is the way in which the good governance agenda hinges on a peculiar combination of moral and technical claims about why good governance constitutes a public good.

As Wolfowitz's statement above makes clear, the Bank's GAC agenda derives some of its legitimacy from the moral assumptions that underpin the concepts. The term "good governance" carries clear normative assumptions: it tells us that the objective of the policy is good (as opposed to bad) governance; that it is possible to distinguish between the two forms; and that the pursuit of the better kind of governance is in the public interest. Moreover, as Mlada Bukovansky has argued in her appropriately titled paper, "Corruption is bad," the concept of corruption has long carried a powerful set of moral assumptions (Bukovansky 2002). Both IMF and Bank leaders have made strong moral claims for the importance of the good governance agenda.[6] Not only, we are told,

---

[4] Interview with senior World Bank staff member, May 10, 2011.
[5] Speech by World Bank President Paul Wolfowitz, March 2007 (emphasis added).
[6] See Best 2005, 2006.

are these new policies good for the economic prospects of those living in countries reliant on Bank assistance, but they also foster global economic growth and stability.

This normative framing of governance supplements the institution's more traditional (and still dominant) technocratic conceptions of the public good. The two are not in fact as far apart as one might imagine: part of the power of economics is its appeal to universality – to the universal laws that govern human behavior, whatever the time or place. As Wolfowitz's above statement makes clear, the Bank cannot rely too explicitly on its moral claims about good governance, given its commitment to technical neutrality: hence the technical argument for governance as a public good becomes essential. As one Bank staff member put it, echoing Wolfowitz, "a technocratic approach leads you to a set of prescriptions which are squarely in the realm of what are usually discussed in ethical and normative terms. We come at it from a positive angle but end up in what appears to be a normative position."[7]

In defining good governance as a public good, World Bank staff have drawn on both public choice and new institutionalist theory. The Bank's 1991 report suggests: "Governments play a key role in providing two sets of public goods: the rules to make markets work efficiently, and, more problematically, correcting for market failure" (World Bank 1991: ii). For the report's authors, the correction of market failure is problematic because it leaves scope for rent-seeking and more overt forms of corruption. Not only must the state provide public goods, it must do so in such a way that minimizes opportunities for abuse: hence the need for good governance policies as an antidote for government activism. The public-choice theory of principal–agent dynamics, which assumes that actors cannot be trusted to pursue anything other than their own self-interest, thus becomes a central framework for understanding the dynamics of political accountability (World Bank 2004: ch. 3). For example, those collecting taxes (the agents) on behalf of the public (the principal), need incentives and checks to ensure that they do in fact act in the interests of the public rather than for their own enrichment (World Bank 1991: 3).[8] This is an approach that treats governance problems as the logical outcome of rational agents pursuing their own self-interest.

---

[7] Interview with a senior World Bank staff member, May 10, 2007. Of course, this "positive" angle carries within it a particular set of normative assumptions rooted in the presumed universality of its methodological individualism. For an analysis of the moral assumptions implicit in different kinds of economic theory, see Best and Widmaier 2006.

[8] Classic public-choice texts on principal–agent dilemmas include: Coase 1937; Kiewiet and McCubbins 1991; Niskanen 1971; Williamson 1975

Through the lens of public-choice theory, good governance becomes a particular kind of public good that is needed because of the perverse outcomes of human self-interest and the difficulties of collective action.

Redefining public actors

The World Bank's increased engagement in public-constituting practices is not limited to its efforts to define governance as a public good. The organization's good governance policies also seek to define and constitute new kinds of actors capable of achieving that public good – actors that include a more "efficient" and "responsive" state and a more engaged group of non-state actors. Such practices are simultaneously discursive and material: they seek to conceptualize and define state, market, and civil society actors in particular ways, goals that they achieve through concrete techniques, including processes for empowering citizens and for keeping errant government bureaucrats in check. These public practices are therefore performative: they seek to produce the very thing that they define.

One of the most striking aspects of the changes taking place in IMF and World Bank policies and pronouncements over the past decade has been their renewed interest in the state after several decades of denigrating its developmental role. Yet that renewed attention has consistently retained a certain skepticism about the state, and a belief that its role should remain secondary to that of the market:

Markets discipline participants more effectively than public sector accountability mechanisms generally can. Enlarging the scope and improving the functioning of markets strengthens competitive forces in the economy and curtails opportunities for monopoly profits, thereby eliminating the bribes public officials may be offered (or may extort) to secure them (IMF and World Bank 1996: 3).

In 1997, the World Bank published its landmark document on the return of the state, *The State in a Changing World*. This report, like those before it, took great care to differentiate its approach from earlier state-led development efforts in the 1950s and 1960s, arguing that, today, developing country states can only become effective if they first focus on the fundamentals and pare down the role of the state by shifting some of its "burdens" to the private sector and to local communities (World Bank 1997: 3). The report then goes on to note:

But reducing or diluting the state's role cannot be the end of the reform story. Even with more selectivity and greater reliance on the citizenry and on private firms, meeting the broad range of citizens' collective needs more effectively will still mean making the state's central institutions work better. (World Bank 1997: 3).

The new and improved state will not only be leaner, but will also be "effective" and "efficient." The Bank defines an effective state as one that has the capacity to undertake certain necessary functions; to do so, it must be able to "undertake and promote collective action efficiently" (World Bank 1997: 3). These bases for assessing a state are clearly drawn from economics, in which efficiency is defined in terms of an effective cost–output ratio. This kind of market-based approach to the state is clearest in the earliest Bank documents, but it also appears in the later institutionalist-inspired governance strategies in which there is a call to bring market-style competition to bear on state institutions, at the same time as the state comes to play a greater role in setting clear rules for the market (Stiglitz 1998; World Bank 2002b). The most recent Bank strategy on GAC also explicitly warns against "excessive regulation," arguing for reforms that "clarify the role of the state, reduce excessive regulatory burdens, and promote competition" (World Bank 2007a: ii, iv).

These policies seek to engage state functionaries in a renewed role in development, but it is one that is narrowly defined and carefully limited through interaction with other actors. How does one avoid the potential for corrupting "public officials" noted in the quotation above (IMF and World Bank 1996: 3)? By ensuring that they are kept in check by active and empowered citizens and other non-state actors. The Bank's emphasis on a broader kind of public can be seen as far back as the early 1990s, when their role is defined as ensuring the "micro-accountability" of the state (World Bank 1991). From the late 1990s on, they are understood as a source of "demand" for good governance (DFGG) (World Bank 1997, 2007a). Rather than emphasizing only the "supply side" of governance (through World Bank and IMF imposed reforms), the idea is that non-state actors will combine to form the "demand side" of the good governance strategy.

There is of course a long history of the World Bank's interest in using market actors and forces as a check on government action – that is part of the logic underpinning decades of privatization. The logic behind these new initiatives is somewhat different, however: there is a genuine attempt in the demand-side initiative to encourage not just market agents, but also citizens to press for better governance. What is particularly interesting in fact is the way in which the differences among these actors become blurred. Thus, the 'DFGG' website notes:

Demand for Good Governance (DFGG), or "demand-side" activities are made up of development approaches that focus on *citizens* as the ultimate stakeholders for better governance. With this focus, they strengthen the capacity of *civil society*, the *media, parliament, local communities*, and the *private sector* to hold authorities accountable for better development results. (World Bank 2011a)

This slippage between citizens and other kinds of actors is even more explicit in the 2004 World Development Report, which provides part of the analytic framework for this approach. The report, entitled *Making Services Work for Poor People*, emphasizes the role of "citizen/clients": individuals who are both clients of the providers of basic services, such as water or health care, and citizens of a particular state responsible for the provision of those services (World Bank 2004: 6, 49). For the authors of this report, it is the hybrid identity of the poor – as economic actors who are recipients of services and as political subjects – that motivates and justifies their efforts to demand accountability. Their identity as public actors is linked to their role as private consumers – an identity, I will suggest below, that effectively limits the scope of their participation.

The conception of public actors contained in the 2004 World Development Report is thus more narrowly defined in public choice terms than the one underpinning the wider DFGG strategy. Yet both identify as public actors a wide range of different groups and individuals, and blur the line between those who would traditionally be seen as public and private. Moreover, they go further and refuse to identify these actors with a coherently defined public or private sphere. As the documentation for the Cambodian DFGG project makes clear, those responsible for this project view public actors in terms of their practices, not their formal identity:

A state-run broadcasting cooperation involved with disseminating information about public programs and their budgets, and providing feedback of citizens to public officials is as much a "demand side" actor as civil society and the private media promoting demand... What matters for strengthening DFGG under this project is therefore *what an institution does rather than where it is situated*. (World Bank 2007b: 3, emphasis in original)[9]

Whether you count as a public actor therefore depends on what you do – and whether or not those practices can be counted as public.[10]

Redefining public processes

What kinds of processes count as public – and entitle someone to be defined as a public actor? The processes the World Bank staff identify in their "demand-side" strategy should be familiar to anyone who has examined theories of the public sphere. As discussed in the framing

---

[9] This point is taken up again and reinforced in the 2008 stocktaking report on DFGG: Chase and Anjum 2008: 10.
[10] Deborah Avant and Virginia Haufler make a similar point about contemporary transnational actors (Chapter 3, this volume).

chapter to this volume, as well as in Matthew Paterson's contribution (Chapter 7), both Habermas and Arendt have defined the public sphere as a site in which individuals engage in publicity (typically through a free press) and debate. World Bank staff have identified several related practices as key to supporting demand for good governance: transparency and the dissemination of *information*, consultation and *participation*, and ongoing *monitoring* and evaluation. These are all examples of public practices that combine a set of liberal ideas about what counts as public together with specific material techniques necessary for enacting them.

Both classical and contemporary conceptions of public practice emphasize the importance of *information* as the foundation of public action: before individuals can hold state actors accountable, they need to know what they are doing. In economic theory, moreover, information is seen as vital for market actors to make informed decisions. Hence the Bank's emphasis on government transparency, which they define as its disclosure of relevant information (World Bank 2009). Some versions of the demand side of good governance are based on what one World Bank staff member has called a *"Deus ex machina* theory of political change based on demand by civil society: the assumption is that if only they had a copy of the [government] budget then they would rise up and demand change."[11] Over time, however, the demand for a good governance framework has relied less on such *deus ex machina* and has placed increased emphasis on actively promoting demand: such efforts go beyond requiring the disclosure of information about government activities and include practices of active "information dissemination" and "demystification" – to ensure that this information is readily accessible to "the ordinary public" (World Bank 2009, 2011b). In concrete terms, such practices might include "initiatives such as freedom of information, awareness campaigns, rights education, and media programs that 'promote' demand" (World Bank 2007b: 2).

In the place of the classical idea of public debate, the World Bank has instead focused on increasing a range of other forms of engagement, loosely organized around the ideas of "voice," and *participation*. These practices take a number of forms, ranging from more collective forms of mobilization (which are defined as part of the promotion of demand) to more localized and institutionalized forms of interaction, designed to provide feedback to government decision-makers and service providers about public concerns. One of the most commonly cited examples of this kind of strategy for increasing the public's voice is that of "citizen report

---

[11] Interview with senior World Bank staff member, May 11, 2007.

cards"; in Bangalore, India, for example, "Citizens are asked to rate service access and quality and to report on corruption and general grievances about public services" (World Bank 2004: 88). The publication of report card results puts pressure on government actors to reform those services deemed least satisfactory.

These public practices do share some similarities with the forms of debate and deliberation articulated in more traditional conceptions of the public sphere. There are clear parallels with Habermas' definition of the public sphere as "a realm of our social life in which something approaching public opinion can be formed" (Habermas 1974). Yet it is not at all clear that these forms of consultation constitute the kind of deliberative activity that both Habermas and Arendt are talking about: the emphasis is on participation and consultation, rather than on deliberation and debate, and therefore constitutes a much thinner version of public activity.[12] While such thin public practices could potentially spill over into thicker more genuinely political activities, this possibility is constrained by the tendency to frame civil society actors as consumers of services first and foremost. Narrowly economic forms of consultation such as obtaining customer feedback thus come to redefine and constrain activities that might have produced more political kinds of engagement.

This slippage between political and economic forms of public practice is particularly apparent in the 2004 World Development Report discussed above. The goal of the report is evident from its title, *Making Services Work for Poor People*: finding ways of improving services for poor people, including basic health care, education, and water provision. The report's authors suggest that for this to happen, the poor must become more active in demanding improvements. One of the ways of fostering this kind of demand is through the increased voice of the poor as citizens – what the report describes as the "long route" to accountability – using the various participatory practices described above. Yet there exists another route to ensuring accountability – the "short route" which traditionally goes through the market, in which the poor, as clients, hold service providers more directly accountable by taking their business elsewhere if they are unsatisfied (World Bank 2004: 6).

The report's authors ultimately recommend a combination of long and short routes to accountability, proposing a hybrid form of service delivery. The report sets out to demonstrate "why pure public sector provision often fails – and why pure privatization is not the answer" (World Bank 2004: 46, 54). Their alternatives combine public and

---

[12] See Helleiner (Chapter 4, this volume) for a similar assessment of the kind of public being engaged and created by recent efforts to regulate derivatives.

private practices and actors in various ways, depending on the circumstances on the ground. Whatever the particular form service provision takes, they suggest that it can be viewed through the framework of principal–agent dynamics, in which both democratic and market forms of accountability are seen through the same lens.

The final set of public processes that the World Bank has proposed as a part of its demand for good governance initiative are all organized around the central role of *monitoring*. The goal is not simply to engage public actors' attention early on in the formulation of policies, but rather to create mechanisms through which they can monitor, evaluate, and report on government policies on an ongoing basis (World Bank 2007b, 2011b). For this to happen, it is necessary to gather information about the effects of those policies, to assess them against predefined indicators, and to communicate them to the public. These can include "Doing Business Indicators," a Bank initiative that scores countries on how easy it is to set up a business, complaints mechanisms, media investigations, and 'citizen report cards' (Chase and Anjum 2008: 14, 19). Through these monitoring practices, it is hoped that public actors will become actively engaged in a service management process that places increasing emphasis on targets and testing. Transparency, participation, and monitoring thus come together, as information on service performance is transmitted to encourage public actors to "voice" their views, producing data that is in turn used to improve service delivery.[13]

Reconstituting power and authority

Why do these changes in the kinds of public constituted by the World Bank and other development actors matter? Although there are many possible answers to this question, I will focus here the implications of these new public practices for the character of power and authority in global governance. Engaging in new public-constituting practices, whether defining the public good, engaging new public actors, or fostering new public processes, all involve power relations. The IMF and World Bank have always relied on a wide range of forms of authority, from the more coercive power of conditional lending to the informal power of technical advice and assistance. As Barnett and Finnemore suggest, international organizations like the IMF and World Bank use productive power through their capacity to define and categorize objects

---

[13] This shift is part of a much broader turn to results-based management at the World Bank and more generally in the global governance of development. I discuss this phenomenon in more detail in Best 2014.

of governance in order to give them real meaning and presence (Barnett and Finnemore 1999, 2004). The idea of good governance is a classic example of a term whose invention has had significant performative effects by making possible a range of practices and interventions that would not have been possible before. The term can be seen as an extension of earlier such categories like "sound economics" which have been used for much longer. Yet whereas past calls for sound economics tended to define state and market actions in largely negative terms, as a matter of deregulating and liberalizing, the category of good governance seeks to define far more explicitly – and positively – what counts as a public good, a public actor, and a public process.

As the governance agenda has begun to focus more on the demand side, Bank staff have argued for the importance of actively *promoting* demand. In the proposed Cambodian project, for example, they plan to support not only state institutions, such as the national radio station, but also non-state actors with the hope of increasing their capacity to mobilize public pressure (World Bank 2007b). If all of these individuals and groups are to play their part in this demand-based strategy, they need to become more active and skilled public actors. Moreover, it is not simply this broader range of public actors that the World Bank seeks to engage and reshape through its demand-side strategy: its ultimate object remains the government itself. The DFGG approach not only hopes to promote and mediate demand through various consultation mechanisms but ultimately to foster more responsive government agencies and service providers. To achieve this end, DFGG advocates argue for the import-ance of restructuring the public service around performance incentives that link rewards to government actors' achievement of results. Ultim-ately, the good governance agenda is an ambitious one that seeks to transform the cultures of several different publics – fostering more active and reflexive actors in government, civil society, and the market.

What is notable about the forms of authority that the World Bank seeks to exercise in this context is how indirect they are. The aim of changing government policy is to be achieved not directly – by stipulating changes as a condition for a loan, for example – but by creating the conditions in which others will demand those changes. This is a circuitous, provisional form of authority that relies on the power of information and indirect incentives to achieve its ends.[14] Not only is the form of this strategy therefore unusual, but its goal is also novel: the attention to public demand together with the emphasis on transparency, accountability,

---

[14] The rise of a more provisional form of authority and style of governance is one of the central themes of my recent book: Best 2014.

and monitoring make it quite clear that the objective is to create what Mitchell Dean, drawing on Peter Miller (1992), has described as reflexive government:

> The imperative of reflexive government is to render governmental institutions and mechanisms... efficient, accountable, transparent and democratic by the employment of technologies of performance such as the various forms of auditing and the financial instruments of accounting, by the devolution of budgets, and by the establishment of calculating individuals and calculable spaces. (Dean 1999)

World Bank actions are therefore quite ambitious. But do they involve a significant transformation in how global development is practiced? As Best and Gheciu discussed in the framing chapter for this collection, practices can either work to *reinforce* an existing community, often by supporting ongoing background assumptions and habits, or they can work to *transform* it by unsettling taken-for-granted norms and activities. In this case, the Bank staff's practices can be understood as both reinforcing and transformative. There is little doubt that the Bank seeks to redefine what counts as a public good and as a public actor, extending its authority into new more political terrain; such efforts work at local as well as global levels, transforming communities of development practice in important ways. Yet these policies are also designed to re-establish existing hierarchies of development practice – above all reinforcing the World Bank's own place as the central authority.

Contested publics

The evolution of good governance strategies and the Bank's efforts to reinforce its global authority are only part of the story, however. For there has been significant resistance to these changes – both within and outside the organizations – as well as signs of the limits of these new strategies.

If, as I argued at the beginning of this chapter, and as is argued in the framing chapter for this volume, the kind of public that is re-emerging in these policies is always linked to a set of claims that this (good, actor, process) *is* public, then we would also expect such claims to be challenged sometimes. In the final pages of this chapter, I will briefly outline some of these challenges and consider their implications for our understanding of the kind of public that the World Bank is seeking to define. I will focus on three specific challenges: the ongoing contestation over whether good governance is in fact a universal public good; the persistence of divisions within the organization in defining public actors and processes; and the limits that the strategy has faced when being put into practice.

While the Bank has always sought to define good governance as a universal public good – as a set of universally applicable principles or best practices that are broadly applicable in any specific development context – there has, over time, been growing ambivalence among staff and state representatives about the appropriateness of such universalist claims. This discomfort became particularly pronounced with the arrival of Wolfowitz in 2005, and his increased emphasis on corruption as the centerpiece of the good governance agenda. This more recent GAC strategy produced a return to the kind of Executive Board resistance that characterized the earliest discussions of governance at the Bank (Conable 1991). This time, the attack was led by the United Kingdom representatives, among others, who raised concerns about the likelihood that the poor would suffer from having aid cut because their leaders were corrupt, and the dangers of applying the policy without attending to the complexities of local context (Thornton 2006).

At around the same time, a debate erupted about the possibility of objectively measuring good governance. Under Wolfowitz's leadership, the Bank began to put increasing emphasis on the development of quantitative governance indicators (World Bank 2007a: ix, 34–35). Although the World Bank Institute – a semi-autonomous think-tank within the institution – had developed a range of governance indicators, the Executive Board rejected attempts to integrate them into the Bank's lending operations. At the heart of this debate was a lack of faith in the possibility of aggregating a range of diverse and locally specific forms of data into a series of universal metrics of just how "good" the governance of any country is. As one senior World Bank staff member put it (probably not representing the mainstream view):

Governance indicators are subjective and atheoretical. We have no good indicators despite what others here would assert. To the extent that they're used to allocate resources or to punish countries, those who are on the short end of the stick are screaming mad.[15]

In addition to these rather public differences of opinion on the Bank's Board about the good governance agenda, there remain subtler divisions among the different departments of the organization. As I discussed above, there are several different approaches to good governance at the Bank, which become particularly evident in later demand-side strategy documents. Although the World Development Report's focus on accountability and the DFGG emphasis on mobilizing demand are closely connected (with the World Development Report's accountability

---

[15] Interview with senior World Bank staff member, May 11, 2007.

triangle appearing in most DFGG documents), they each define public good, actors and processes somewhat differently: above all, the World Development Report approach is more strongly defined by public-choice theory and more clearly instrumentalizes political activity.

This lack of a singular coherent conception of demand for good governance at the World Bank is not surprising: the organization is notoriously complex, with an institutional structure that makes it common for different sectors, regions, and thematic departments to act with some autonomy. There are several agencies responsible for pursuing the demand-side agenda, including the Social Development Department and sectoral governance and corruption teams within the Human Development and Infrastructure sectors. The Social Development Department has historically been more interested in participatory approaches to development than other divisions within the Bank; in this case as well, the DFGG strategies and projects have been generally developed by those working from this part of the Bank, whereas the 2004 World Development Report's more public-choice-based focus on accountability in service provision carries over into the Human Development sector's work on education, health, and social protection. Even within a single organization, we can find a variety of conceptions of the public at work.

This lack of coherence also helps to explain one other important limitation in the Bank's efforts to emphasize the demand side of good governance: the fact that the efforts to translate discursive claims into concrete actions have been less than successful to date. There have been two recent reviews of demand-side policies – neither of them particularly positive. The Quality Assurance Group's 2009 review found that demand-side initiatives had received less attention than fiduciary or political economy initiatives and concluded that "a great majority of the projects have little or no DFGG mechanisms in place" (World Bank 2009, 2011c). A draft stocktaking report by the Social Development Department provides some insight into why there has been so little take-up of the demand-side practices on the ground. As the report's authors bluntly put it, "even though the governance agenda is everyone's business, it is in fact no one's business" (Chase and Anjum 2008: 9). The report suggests that while demand-side initiatives are present in a wide range of Bank operations and activities, they are fragmented and uncoordinated. There are few incentives for integrating participatory mechanisms in particular, since they can slow down the disbursement of funds (Chase and Anjum 2008: 35–36).[16]

---

[16] The primary incentive operating at the World Bank has for a very long time been to move money out the door.

How much of a limit do these challenges pose to the good governance agenda? To date they have been relatively minor, yet they point towards both technical and political tensions in the good governance strategy's efforts to re-engage the public through its demand-side approach. The difficulties of accurately quantifying good governance pose serious challenges to an organization that relies for its authority on its capacity to translate the world into numbers, while the failure to operationalize demand-side policies could ultimately reduce the strategy to little more than rhetoric. Moreover, those developing country representatives who have argued most strenuously against efforts to develop universal indicators remind us of the fact that responsible governance cannot be easily aggregated precisely because it is contextual, and that what is often labeled as "good governance" is often derived from particular Western values. Although the World Bank's evolving good governance agenda involves some quite ambitious efforts to reconstitute a new kind of active, engaged public and a responsive, reflexive state, its future remains uncertain.

Conclusion: a new kind of public

I began this chapter with the question of whether we are witnessing a return of the public in the governance of global economic development. Like many of the other chapters in this book, my answer is a qualified yes. Yes, the public is playing a more important role now in global governance than in the recent past, but it is taking an unfamiliar form. Theoretical approaches that focus on the decline of *public authority*, the centrality of *public goods*, and the rise of the *public sphere* all provide some clues to the kind of public involved in the Bank's good governance programs. But they also miss some of the most importance features of this emergent public.

Echoing some of the literature on *private authority*, this study has revealed that we do see a continued focus on redistributing some of the state's authority among different actors, whether in civil society or the private sector. Yet even as authority is spread to more sites, there is still far more emphasis on fostering a more active role by the state and other public actors than was the case in the 1980s when the mantra of privatization was at its peak. Moreover the form that authority takes is not as formalized, direct, or as closely tied to the private realm as studies on private authority tend to suggest. Actors are deemed to have authority to speak for the public based on what they do, rather than where they are – in state institutions, the private sector or civil society.

One of the ways in which World Bank staff have explained and justified the need for a more robust public has been through the logic of *public goods*: if they are less sanguine about the market as a panacea for all basic development needs, it is largely because they have begun to take more seriously the challenges of market failure. Many of the policies contained in the good governance agenda, from the emphasis on transparency and institution building to the insistence on increasing accountability, can be explained in terms of an economistic conception of public goods. Yet the idea of the common good that is contained in many of these policies is ultimately thicker than these narrowly economistic conceptions assume, relying on moral as well as technical claims. Moreover, the kinds of practices that the Bank seeks to encourage, particularly through its demand for good governance programs, require more than individual self-interested behavior to make them possible.

What DFGG initiatives in particular are calling for is a more collective and activist form of public action that bears more resemblance to the kinds of public process normally associated with the *public sphere*. Yet here again, not all of the elements of the public sphere seem to apply: the actors and institutions involved can be part of the state, civil society, or private sphere; the links of accountability being fostered can just as easily connect a client to a service provider (public or private) as a citizen to a state department; and the kinds of practices involved, such as consultation, participation, and monitoring, are thinner and more instrumental than we would normally expect from genuine public debate and contestation.

The kinds of public that the World Bank seeks to foster through its good governance programs cannot therefore be reduced to any of these more traditional forms. What is emerging is a hybrid public: one that is characterized not by bounded and coherent spaces but rather by the kinds of actions that individuals engage in and the ways that they define them. Many of the chapters in this book have pointed to similar phenomena in the governance of derivatives (Helleiner: Chapter 4), climate change (Paterson: Chapter 7 and Bernstein: Chapter 6), and security (Avant and Haufler: Chapter 3 and Gheciu: Chapter 8), pointing to the way that practices and processes such as transparency, participation, and monitoring have become increasingly integrated in governance strategies and justified in terms of their (various) public attributes. A push for transparency can be justified as necessary for better market discipline (private authority), as a way of increasing government agents' accountability (public goods), or as essential to a vibrant civil society (public sphere). Moreover the actors involved in creating and responding to that transparency can be state officials or departments, NGOs, poor individuals, business groups, or activists. It is through the act of engaging in this practice that they become public actors involved in creating a public good.

This is a more dynamic and fluid kind of public insofar as what is done and how that action is justified are more important than whether someone sits on one side or another of some imagined public/private dividing line.

As this chapter has already suggested, how we define and practice the public always has normative implications. In this case, the very combination of different kinds of public logics – the more technical, economistic public-goods approach, and the more moral and political public-sphere approach – has potentially important consequences. Although the technical logic remains the predominant one, it is supplemented by a broader, thicker conception of the public, enhancing the basis of institutions' claims to legitimacy. In the case of the World Bank and other IFIs, this thicker conception of the public – as voice and participation as well as functional goods – provides a more robust foundation for expanding the institutions' mandates to include increasingly contested and politically charged areas in their programs. At the same time, the combination of normative and technical conceptions remains somewhat perverse – for just as the normative claims help to thicken the thin appeal of economic theory, those normative claims' increasing dependence on economic logic also has the effect of thinning and instrumentalizing their political character (Abrahamsen 2000). Public actors and processes are now admitted to be a part of the logic of economic development in a way that they had not been for quite some time. Yet the kind of public *politics* that appears in this particular conception of good governance is an impoverished one indeed.

REFERENCES

Abrahamsen, Rita. 2000. *Disciplining Democracy: Development Discourse and Good Governance in Africa*. London: Zed Books.
Barnett, Michael, and Martha Finnemore. 1999. "The politics, power, and pathologies of international organizations." *International Organization* 53(4): 699–732.
    2004. *Rules for the World: International Organizations in Global Politics*. Ithaca, NY: Cornell University Press.
Best, Jacqueline. 2005. "The moral politics of IMF reforms: universal economics, particular ethics." *Perspectives on Global Development and Technology* 4(3–4): 357–78.
    2006. "Coopting cosmopolitanism? The International Monetary Fund's new global ethics." *Global Society* 20(3): 307–27.
    2014. *Governing Failure: Provisional Expertise and the Transformation of Global Development Finance*. Cambridge: Cambridge University Press.
Best, Jacqueline, and Wesley Widmaier. 2006. "Micro- or macro- moralities? International economic discourses and policy possibilities." *Review of International Political Economy* 13(4): 609–31.

Bukovansky, Mlada. 2002. *Corruption is Bad: Normative Dimensions of the Anti-Corruption Movement*, ANU Department of International Relations Working Paper No. WP2002/5. Canberra: Australian National University.

Chase, Robert S., and Anushay Anjum. 2008. *Final Draft: Demand for Good Governance Stocktaking Report*. Washington, D.C.: World Bank.

CIDA. 2011. *Governance*. Canadian International Development Agency. www. acdi-cida.gc.ca/

Coase, Ronald. 1937. "The nature of the firm." *Economica* 4(3): 386–405.

Conable, Barber. 1991. *Memorandum to Bank Managers, Subject: Managing Development: The Governance Dimension*. Washington, D.C.: World Bank.

Danilovich, John. 2007. "Remarks by MCC CEO, Ambassador John Danilovich, at Brown University's Center for Latin American Studies." www.mcc.gov/

Dean, Mitchell. 1999. *Governmentality: Power and Rule in Modern Society*. Thousand Oaks, CA: Sage.

DFID. 2006. *Eliminating World Poverty: Making Governance Work for the Poor*. www.dfid.gov.uk/

Habermas, Jürgen. 1974. "The public sphere: an encyclopedia article." *New German Critique* 3(1): 49–55.

IMF and World Bank. 1996. *Helping Countries Combat Corruption and Improve Governance: A Joint World Bank/IMF Issues Paper Prepared for the Development Committee*, EB/CW/DC/97/3. www.worldbank.org/

Kiewiet, D. Roderick, and Mathew McCubbins. 1991. *The Logic of Delegation: Congressional Parties and the Appropriations Process*. Chicago, IL: University of Chicago Press.

Krueger, Anne. 1974. "The political economy of the rent-seeking society." *American Economic Review* 64(3): 291–303.

MCC. 2008. *MCC: Indicators Home 2008*. www.mcc.gov/

Miller, Peter. 1992. "Accounting and objectivity: the invention of calculating selves and calculable spaces." *Annals of Scholarship* 9(1): 61–86.

Miller-Adams, Michelle. 1999. *The World Bank: New Agendas*. London: Routledge.

Niskanen, William. 1971. *Bureaucracy and Representative Government*. Chicago, IL: Aldine.

North, Douglass. 1990. *Institutions, Institutional Change and Economic Performance*. Cambridge: Cambridge University Press.

Shihata, Ibrahim. 1990. *Issues of "Governance" in Borrowing Members: The Extent of their Relevance under the Bank's Articles of Agreement*. Washington, D.C.: World Bank.

Stiglitz, Joseph. 1998. "More instruments and broader goals: moving towards the post-Washington consensus." *WIDER Annual Lecture*, January 7, at Helsinki.

Thomas, M.A. 2007. "The governance bank." *International Affairs* 83: 729–45.

Thornton, Philip. 2006. "Benn beat World Bank chief over corruption policy." *The Independent*, September 19.

USAID. 2011. *Democracy and Governance*. www.usaid.gov/

Weaver, Catherine. 2008. *The Hypocrisy Trap: The World Bank and the Poverty of Reform*. Princeton, NJ: Princeton University Press.

2010. "The meaning of development: constructing the World Bank's good governance agenda," In *Constructing the International Economy*, edited by Rawi Abdelal, Mark Blyth, and Craig Parsons, pp. 17–67. Ithaca, NY: Cornell University Press.

Williamson, Oliver. 1975. *Markets and Hierarchies: Analysis and Antitrust Implications*. New York: Free Press.

1985. *The Economic Institutions of Capitalism*. New York: Free Press.

World Bank. 1989. *Sub-Saharan Africa: From Crisis to Sustainable Growth – A Long-Term Perspective Study*. Washington, D.C.: World Bank.

1991. *Managing Development: The Governance Dimension*. Washington, D.C.: World Bank.

1992. *Governance and Development*. Washington, D.C.: World Bank.

1994. *Governance: The World Bank's Experience*. Washington, D.C.: World Bank.

1996. "World Bank president outlines a new agenda: describes a Bank 'on the move.'" *World Bank*, October 1, 1996. http://go.worldbank.org/

1997. *World Development Report 1997: The State in a Changing World*. Washington, D.C.: World Bank.

2000. *Reforming Public Institutions and Strengthening Governance: A World Bank Strategy*. Washington, D.C.: World Bank.

2001. *World Development Report 2000/01: Attacking Poverty*. Washington, D.C.: World Bank.

2002a. *Reforming Public Institutions and Strengthening Governance: A World Bank Strategy – Implementation Update*. Washington, D.C.: World Bank.

2002b. *World Development Report 2002: Building Institutions for Markets*. Washington, D.C: World Bank.

2004. *World development report 2004: Making Services Work for Poor People*. Washington, D.C.: World Bank.

2007a. *Strengthening World Bank Group Engagement on Governance and Anticorruption*. Washington, D.C.: World Bank.

2007b. *The Cambodian Demand for Good Governance (DFGG) Project: An Updated Storyline*. Washington, D.C.: World Bank.

2009. *QAG Report: Governance and Anticorruption in Lending Operations: A Benchmarking and Learning Review*. Washington, D.C.: World Bank.

2011a. *Demand for Good Governance: Social Development*. Washington, D.C.: World Bank.

2011b. *Governance and Anticorruption: DFGG Analytical Framework*. Washington, D.C.: World Bank.

2011c. *TAP (Transparency, Accountability and Participation) Framework*. Washington, D.C.: World Bank.

6 The publicness of non-state global environmental and social governance

Steven Bernstein

This chapter examines how practices of "publicness" increasingly render ostensibly "private" transnational governance as public in the social and environmental issue areas. These governance efforts – a term used here self-consciously to refer to attempts to establish transnational political authority – have arisen as intergovernmental processes, have failed to deliver authoritative and effective rules where demand for such rules is high (e.g. in labor practices, forestry, or the social and environmental effects of commodity trade) or where multilateral rules exist but are limited in their effect (e.g. climate change). Prominent examples of these non-state governance systems include producer certification and product-labeling systems that consist of third-party auditing, and, in climate change, the proliferation of voluntary carbon markets, and the monitoring and standard-setting bodies that interact with them.

Their constitution as public governance arises, in the first instance, from their goal to pursue public ends or, in Best and Gheciu's terminology, a common concern – in this case, environmental and social regulation, or sustainable ecological and social practices more generally. Explicitly "private" forms of governance, i.e. those that involve self-regulation or coordination within an industry, club goods, or technical services for a defined membership such as business associations, are not public since their goal is to provide a rule, good, or service for the private benefit of its members or a target group. The pursuit of common concerns, however, is not sufficient to render a form of authority or governance public. Two other conditions must be met. First, the authority to pursue that public goal must be publicly recognized. Second, that recognition demands political legitimacy, which when addressed to public ends requires practices of "publicness," elaborated below.

Following this volume's Introduction, I draw on theoretical insights from the "practice turn" in international relations (IR) theory to identify practices – or "competent performances" – of publicness that constitute transnational public authority (Adler and Pouliot 2011). International relations scholars have drawn on a variety of social theorists in defining practices, but Adler and Pouliot's emphasis on practices as performative is especially helpful in understanding the production of public authority as well as their transformative potential. As Best and Gheciu put it, practices seek to create things they describe.

These practices – ranging from democratic participatory or deliberative processes to practices that define legitimate international standards under trade agreements – in turn can only be understood by attention to institutional and productive forms of power that circumscribe and produce them. In this sense, I follow Best and Gheciu's approbation to embrace a "cultural" conception of the public that acknowledges its historicity and the role of power and practices in reproducing and redefining the public/private boundary. Practices do not simply occur by effect or habit, however; they are conscious and can be strategic. The transnational governance institutions addressed in this chapter purposefully tap into broader norms that define and empower public authority and into practices required for an actor to be recognized as such. In engaging in such practices, these non-state institutions also participate in redefining the old divisions of public and private.

The argument proceeds as follows. First, I discuss the limits of the public/private distinction for analyses of global governance because, if understood as political authority, governance always rests on some degree of "publicness." Second, I draw on Adler and Pouliot's (2011) concept of international practices to show its relevance for understanding how practices of publicness can render private or marketplace authority public. Third, I develop an explanation of where practices of publicness come from in the transnational social and environmental issue area: the interaction of international social structure and "communities of practice," mediated by institutional and productive power. I then apply this framework to one set of the most relevant examples of transnational non-state governance systems vying for political authority, members of the International Social and Environmental Accreditation and Labelling (ISEAL) Alliance, an umbrella organization created to develop agreement on "best practices" for its members, and to gain credibility and legitimacy for its members' standards (ISEAL Alliance 2010a).

Limits of the public/private distinction in global governance

At its core, global governance concerns efforts to create political authority beyond the state. If one accepts that claim (defended below), the language of public and private as distinctive forms of global governance offers limited analytic traction since publicness is constitutive of "political" authority.[1] Governance, on this understanding, is constitutionally a public practice. The question of whether authority is public or private rests not on its domain (e.g. state or market), but in whether there is a claim to a right to rule. Only public authorities can invoke this right, which requires political legitimacy, or the acceptance and justification of shared rule by a community (Bernstein 2004; Bernstein and Coleman 2009). As this definition suggests, political authority always has some element of publicness – since it is rooted in community – whether or not authority resides in, or is directly delegated from, states as opposed to non-state institutions or actors. If "private" simply demarcated marketplace interactions or practices relatively autonomous from the public authority of states, then the public/private distinction might still be analytically useful for identifying different realms of human activity, although even in that case one may still ask if the market can truly be understood as solely a realm of private action.[2] If public and private are understood instead, however, in terms of their everyday usage as governance versus private activity beyond the scope of governance, then the "publicness" of non-state governance in the social and environmental issue area belies the analytic utility of this distinction. Following Best and Gheciu's admonishment, this understanding avoids the reification of public and private actors as given, as is common in the private-authority literature, since the boundary here is not based on the ascriptive status of the actor but rather on their practices.

This blurring of the public/private distinction makes delineating the boundary in advance over which an entity becomes public difficult to define. For example, the provision of a "club" good that delivers benefits to its members can also aim to serve a broader public interest, as in some instances of the multilateral "clubs" Robert Keohane and Joseph Nye identified as the dominant form of multilateralism until it came under challenge in the latter part of the twentieth century (Keohane and Nye 2001; also Potoski and Prakash 2005). Paterson's (Chapter 7, this volume) delineation of the "private" as the realm of activity in which "the interests of individuals, or specific collectivities (families, firms, unions, etc.) are what count" can thus blur when those concerns have broader implications for society at large. Under this condition, the strict

---

[1] I do not mean there is no private authority or power. I mean only that such authority or power is not properly understood as *political* authority or governance subject to the need for *political* legitimacy.

[2] While not the topic of this chapter, many scholars, following Polanyi's (1944) classic work, understand markets to be socially embedded and the unregulated market a myth. Others point to the social consequences of market activity from which it can only be separated artificially.

boundary of a social realm in which "individuals can *deprive* either other individuals, or the collectivity at large, from intervention" comes under question (Paterson, Chapter 7, this volume). Thus, one might look for signs of publicness by asking: to what degree does the reach of a governance system's provisions demand wider legitimacy and accountability beyond its immediate constituency?

A good starting point for delineating the public/private authority boundary, then, is to ask whether there is political authority and where it is located. In the case of intergovernmental institutions, the answer is clear: where states bind themselves to rules to address collective problems, the political authority of the institutions created resides in the recognized public authority of states or is delegated by agreement to the intergovernmental institution. In the case of transnational non-state institutions, a much smaller subset involved in global environmental and social issues can be rightfully labeled non-state global governance.

Governance and political authority

The move to narrow the understanding of "governance" to institutions that claim the functional equivalent of political authority corrects an opposite tendency that dates back to Rosenau and Czempiel's (1992) landmark volume on *Governance without Government*. Unfortunately, their minimalist understanding of political authority led others to see governance anywhere there appeared to be "purposeful order" (Benedict 2004: 6232). Thus global governance could be located in an enormous range of mechanisms and means to regulate, manage, promote, control, or simply engage in transnational activities or provision of services. What precisely makes these activities governance as opposed to coordinated activities across borders gets lost in this formulation.

Rosenau later provided a useful corrective (Rosneau 1995). Stripped of its dependency on centralized state power, governance, he says, consists of two elements: purposeful steering of actors towards collective or shared goals or values and authoritativeness in the sense of consisting of "systems of rule" (Rosenau 1995: 14–15). At the same time, one should not set the bar so high as to suggest that political authority must always require a monopoly on authority, universal, or general-purpose jurisdiction within a defined territory, or the equivalent of state sovereignty.

On the first count, global governance frequently interacts with other rules, whether international or transnational, in the form of overlapping, nested, or intersecting regimes. It also may interact with domestic rules because many global institutions explicitly link to national laws, regulations, or standards. Nonetheless, non-monopolistic forms of authority can still be authoritative for those who "sign on" or consent. The test is whether a sense of obligation and recognition of the authority follows that consent or whether it may be easily or arbitrarily withdrawn.

Global governance also need not be territorially based or geographically universal. It might apply to a transnational marketplace sector or to a profession (such as accountants in the case of the International Accounting Standards Board [IASB] or the forest sector in the case of the Forest Stewardship Council [FSC]), or exist regionally or in pockets. As long as its political authority is recognized, a governing institution or mechanism can still count as global in the sense of transcending the state. Moreover, global governance is never characterized by universal or general-purpose jurisdiction, like states owing to formal anarchy in the sovereign-state system. The scope of governance varies considerably across institutions of global governance. Some are narrow and issue-specific, while others (the UN Security Council, for example) have a broader, albeit still limited, scope.

Thus, global governance worth its name ought more to resemble government than most writings acknowledge, but not be so narrow a category as to dismiss the meaningful political authorities that exist in transnational and global spaces. Most definitions of political authority provide room for this middle ground. According to Max Weber, political authority exists when there is a good "probability that a command, with a given specific content will be obeyed by a group of persons" (Weber 1978: 55). Authority relationships are those in which an actor or institution makes a *claim* to have a right to govern (Uphoff 1989). They *authorize* particular "governors" (Avant, Finnemore, and Sell 2010) to make, interpret, and enforce rules. Hence, the governance label should be limited to institutions that create, implement, and/or adjudicating rules or normative standards, or where their decisions create an obligation to obey. Moreover, Weber also understood that the location of a monopoly on legitimate force (i.e. the right to rule) in the modern state is a historical construction (Weber 1978: 54–56). At the same time, Weber understood political authority as a specific category: "legitimate" authority, which is constitutive, I would argue, of public authority. Authority that lacks legitimacy is coercive, not political, and illegitimate authority cannot be public since it would not be collectively recognized.

Political legitimacy

Political authority thus requires *political* legitimacy. It concerns situations in which a community is subject to decisions by an authority that claims to have a right to be obeyed, and actors inter-subjectively hold the belief that the claim is justified and appropriate. It reflects the "worthiness of a political order to be recognized" (Habermas 1979: 178, 182) or "a more general support for a [governance institution], which makes subjects willing to substitute the regime's decisions for their own evaluation of a situation" (Bodansky 1999: 602). This idea of substitution is important because it directs attention to the difference between voluntary and authoritative institutions. If actors – whether states, firms, or NGOs – evaluate with each decision whether to maintain or withdraw support, governance or authority in any meaningful sense of the word is absent.

Legitimacy is also the glue that links authority and power. It not only can justify power, thereby increasing the likelihood commands will be obeyed absent coercion (Claude 1966: 368; Hurd 2007), but can also reinforce or reflect underlying power relationships. This linkage is particularly important for the question here of why particular practices produce political legitimacy.

The most relevant types of power for this question are "institutional" and "productive."[3] Institutional power operates indirectly in the form of rules or laws or the empowering of particular actors such as technical experts. The idea of productive power resonates with Michel Foucault's notion of "governmentality," or the idea that "disciplines" or "epistemes" – the background knowledge that passes "the command structure into the very constitution of the individual" (Foucault 1991) – extend into sites of authority, thereby empowering and legitimating them (Barnett and Duvall 2005: 20–22; Douglas 1999: 138).

In terms of community, legitimacy rests on shared acceptance of rules and rule by affected groups, who constitute the community that grants legitimacy, and on the justificatory norms they recognize. The community's coherence or incoherence matters, since incoherence or strong normative contestation among groups within a legitimating community make establishing clear requirements for legitimacy difficult. Thus, defining who is a member of the relevant community, on what basis community identification must rest, and to what degree norms of appropriateness must be shared to achieve legitimacy all become central analytic concerns.

The importance of community also means that what legitimization of transnational political authority requires cannot be known a priori. Taking practice seriously entails recognizing that legitimacy requirements evolve, in the interaction of affected communities and social

---

[3] These conceptions come from Barnett and Duvall's (2005) fourfold typology of power in global governance.

structures. For example, state consent is no longer fully sufficient for legitimacy in global governance, even in multilateral settings, with the advent of a growing normative consensus on the need for greater global democracy. As Christopher Hobson observes, "The now widespread agreement over the normative desirability and political legitimacy of democracy is noticeably different from the historically dominant understanding that regarded it as a dangerous and unstable form of rule which inevitably led to anarchy or despotism" (Hobson 2009: 632).

On this reading, as transnational authority evolves, it interacts historically with expectations generated both by the web of norms and institutions of the evolving "global public domain" (Ruggie 2004) or social structure as well as expectations (not completely divorced from those web of norms) of the communities of practice and broader audiences which must recognize that authority. Focusing on socially constructed understandings and the practices that constitute them is a promising avenue to understand how actors' performances produce their own public authority, or at least attempt to do so.

Public authority and publicness

The foregoing discussion highlights that political authority has a public character. Thus, attempts to create political authority transnationally or globally require practices that produce at least two characteristics of "publicness" in addition to the demand for political legitimacy. First, "governance is defined by the 'public' nature of its goals" or "concerned with conducting the 'public's business'" (Andonova *et al.* 2009: 55, quoting Ruggie 2004: 504). The pursuit of aims, or the provision of goods, which benefit "common concerns" (Best and Gheciu, Chapter 2, this volume) is generally understood as a constitutive feature of political authority.

Second, there must be an element of publicity or opportunities for the public to engage in political discourse and ideally deliberation, if not the creation of a full blown "public sphere" in which to deliberate and provide reasons in order to guard against coercion or manipulation (Chambers 2004; Germain 2010). This idea has its roots in the political thought of Hannah Arendt, and has been elaborated most thoroughly in Habermas' political writings (Arendt 1958). A focus on *practices* of political authority, however, following Best and Gheciu's caution against relying on naturalism to understand the performance of political authority in particular spatial or historical contexts, allows for an analysis of the ways in which it might be transformed as it transnationalizes, complicating the boundaries between public and private.

Such a view of public authority also resonates with arguments of interactional legal theorists who emphasize that the bindingness of legal rules – their ability to influence conduct and promote compliance – comes not simply from consent, but from a series of practices that, in the contemporary period, mirror those identified by deliberative democracy theorists, including treatment of parties as equals, the need to give reasons and opportunities to present arguments, and transparency to affected actors (Brunnée and Toope 2010). For Germain (2010), demand for these practices is driven in part by the shift of institutions formerly hidden from view to widespread public consciousness (see also Devetak and Higgot 1999). Whether or not there has been a material change in how institutions of "global governance" such as the IMF, World Bank, or International Organization for Standardization (ISO) affect the "public" under increasing globalization, those effects have become more visible. This element of publicity is not, therefore, simply a requirement of legitimacy of public authority in the abstract: it may precede or increase demands for legitimacy, or the public nature of authority, *because* it makes visible what may have been formerly hidden from view.

The irony is that transnational social and environmental governance systems' focus on regulating firms and supply chains, and not states, has created high demand for publicity from the outset, while intergovernmental organizations with greater authority and scope are only now beginning to face similar demands. Their new legitimacy problems stem from disjunctures between their expert-driven policies and decision-making processes and their shifting view of their social constituency of legitimation (Best 2007; Seabrooke 2007). Thus, while there might be an active argument about the degree to which global financial regulation must live up to these new demands – compare Germain's (2010) emphasis on the need for a global public sphere with Pauly's (1997) view that the legitimacy of financial markets rests primarily with practices of sovereign states – there is virtually no such debate in the case of transnational social and environmental institutions.

One important reason for this difference is that the examples of ISEAL members analyzed below are explicitly autonomous from state authority, not delegated, so legitimacy demands are naturally high in order to generate authority. In contrast, expert-based authority can at least potentially suffice in intergovernmental organizations, empowered by its delegation from the already legitimate political authority of states. The authority has an administrative character (and would be understood by Weber as bureaucratic, legal–rational), in much the same way as national bureaucracies or courts gain authority because of the rule-bound nature of their operation, the delegation of their administrative competence from the political realm, and the specialized or technical knowledge of their officials. Thus, owing to their overt political as opposed to bureaucratic basis of authority, the third characteristic of "publicness" is the need to generate political legitimacy, as discussed above. Before elaborating on the production of legitimacy, I outline the approach to practices that informs that analysis.

Practices and their transformative capacity

Adler and Pouliot define practices as "competent performances" or "socially meaningful patterns of action" that "act out and possibly reify background knowledge and discourse in and on the material world" (Adler and Pouliot 2011: 1). One need not ascribe extraordinary transformative power to practices to see how a focus on them can be useful in concretizing otherwise abstract ideas like political authority or private and public. Actors who claim authority engage in "practices" that solidify these categories and reinforce, undermine, or transform these abstract understandings. Performed competently, public authorities in the state have produced and reproduced their authoritative relationship with their constituent publics for over 350 years. Performed incompetently, their authority becomes questioned, as it has both in particular circumstances throughout the sovereign-state period or more generally in periods of systemic transformation. Similarly other actors, whether new states or actors that claim authority for common concerns, are expected to perform competently as public authorities as their claims to be authoritative for public aims increases. In so doing, they may shift our understanding of the legitimate bases of public authority.

These performances occur in a context or social structure though. In Adler and Pouliot's words, practice creates "one coherent structure, by pointing out the patterned nature of deeds in socially organized contexts … and as such, are articulated into specific types of action and are socially developed through learning and training" (Adler and Pouliot 2011: 5). Practices are "general classes of action," not the actions themselves, that are socially structured and reiterated, thus producing social meaning. Practices "have effects." Like all practices, those that render authority public are consciously performed, and patterned, and must be competent from the perspective of relevant audiences who "tend to interpret its performance along similar standards." Thus, "social recognition" is a "fundamental aspect of practice: its (in)competence is never inherent but attributed in and through social relations" (Adler and Pouliot 2011: 7).

Finally, Adler and Pouliot elaborate on Wenger's "community of practice" concept, defined as a "configuration of a domain of knowledge that constitutes like-mindedness, a community of people that 'creates the social fabric of learning,' and a shared practice that embodies 'the knowledge the community develops, shares, and maintains'" (Adler and Pouliot 2011: 18, quoting Wenger *et al.* 2002: 28–29). While shared practices define such a community, which is made up of concrete actors and institutions that engage in, reproduce, and sometimes change those practices, such a community is not a closed system. Practices are produced in a wider social context of meaning, or social structure that produces expectations around public authority in the issue area.

Governing practices can be transformative in the sense of empowering actors that in other contexts might be considered private into public authorities, subject to similar legitimacy demands as pre-constituted public authorities like governments. As will be shown below, however, in the area of environmental and social regulation, that transformation is incomplete and contested. One source of contestation concerns different interpretations of whether practices do, or should, faithfully reproduce democratic or deliberative practices in transnational spaces, or if, as critics maintain, the inability to adequately engage with the proper community of legitimation means they are transforming and legitimizing a proxy set of practices that cannot escape from market rationality.

There are also tensions between reinforcing and transformative elements of these practices. For example, practices that legitimate public authority transnationally are less transformations of the rules of the game – as Best and Gheciu (Chapter 2, this volume) would describe it – and more a transformation of the domain in which the public is practiced. To the degree they elevate private interests of market actors as legitimate public concerns, however, the transformation would be more profound, though largely unintended at least by ISEAL members themselves. While the incorporation of collective goals of economic prosperity would not entail a transformation of public practices, the empowering of individual corporate actors to place their corporate interests on par with individuals or groups in society – even if conceived of transnationally – would be a significant transformation of public authority. The core argument here, though, is that normative pressures of public legitimation are likely to hold the second tendency in check to the degree they seek what broad communities of legitimation would demand of public authorities. This too, however, has transformative implications. While it may not transform notions of public authority, these practices, drawing on transnational and international norms that legitimate authority, help to transform acceptable practices of standard setting by making them more visible to affected constituencies. In so doing, they increase requirements for their legitimation compared to earlier eras when standard-setting went largely unnoticed or was deemed acceptable if within industry bodies followed their own internal procedures, technical advice, or were satisfied it helped them solve coordination problems. One can see the transformation, for example, in the way the ISO and WTO have had to change their practices of standard-setting in the social and environmental realm, and the way industry-sponsored standardization processes are starting to resemble those of ISEAL members (involving more stakeholders, engaging increased accountability mechanisms in the form of third-party auditing, etc.) as these practices evolve (Bernstein and Cashore 2007; Dingwerth and Pattberg 2009). These practices also hold enormous potential to transform actors previously defined as private, defining firms as actors with public responsibilities in an explicit way that subjects them collectively to new forms of regulation, though this transformation is far from complete in the sectors ISEAL members are attempting to govern.

A final ambiguity in the transformative/reinforcing dichotomy concerns the practical question of whether, in the case of ISEAL members, their ultimate goal to socially and environmentally re-embed markets can be achieved without collaborating with states, thus reinforcing practices that associate public authority primarily with state forms of governance (e.g. Lister 2011).

Explaining the demand for practices of publicness in transnational governance

Practices of publicness that produce political authority result from an interaction of the community of actors affected by the regulatory institution (i.e. the public who grant legitimacy) with broader institutionalized norms – or social structure – that prevails in the relevant issue area. These interactions create different legitimacy requirements across different issue areas and forms of governance, and thereby define practices of public authority.

Social structure

Social structure is composed of global norms and institutions. It serves a constitutive function by defining what appropriate authority is, where it can be located, and on what basis it can be justified. It also serves a regulative function by prescribing and proscribing the boundaries of governance activities (see Barnett and Coleman 2005; Finnemore 1996; Meyer *et al.* 1997; Reus-Smit 1999; Ruggie 1998: 22–25).

Social structural norms can be found not only in specific declarations or principles that apply to the sector, product, or process in question (for example, the Statement of Forest Principles or Convention on Biodiversity in the case of forestry or International Labor Organization [ILO] conventions in the case of labor), but also include broadly accepted norms of global governance. These norms may be embodied in the "hard" law of international treaties as well as legalized trade rules, since attempts to regulate across borders must navigate WTO rules or be subject to possible dispute. Norms may also be found in "soft" declaratory international law (Abbott and Snidal 2000; Kirton and Trebilcock 2004), action programs, or statements of leaders.

In the case of governance institutions in the environmental arena, three specific elements of social structure are most relevant. First, the deep structure of the system remains norms that have legitimated the sovereign authority of states (Ruggie 1998: 20), although there is nothing immutable about states as the sole repository of authority (Cutler *et al.* 1999; Grande and Pauly 2005; Hall and Biersteker 2002; Hurd 2008; Reus-Smit 1999). Thus, delegated state authority is only one possible foundation for non-state institutional legitimacy, especially when relevant communities demand governance after states have failed to act.

Norms defining the prevailing international political economy of an issue comprise a second relevant element of social structure. Elsewhere (Bernstein 2001) I have characterized this element of social structure as "liberal environmentalism," which predicates environmental protection on support for liberalized markets, deregulation, and working with markets and the private sector, including the use of market-based policy instruments, to achieve policy goals.

Third, since the end of the Cold War, a growing normative consensus has emerged on the need to "democratize" global governance. These norms include demands for improved public accountability of international institutions to states and/or broader affected publics (e.g. Held and Koenig-Archibugi 2005; Payne and Samhat 2004), as well as "stakeholder democracy" which calls for "collaboration" and truer "deliberation" among states, business, and civil society (Bäckstrand 2006). Such normative pressure is especially prevalent in international environmental and sustainable development institutions, treaties, and declaratory law, which have been on the forefront of promoting increased public participation and transparency at all levels of governance since the 1972 Stockholm Conference on the Human Environment (Mori 2004).

These norms have been reinforced in countless declarations and treaties, most generally in the 1992 Rio Declaration Principle 10, which states that environmental issues are best handled with participation from all "concerned citizens at the relevant level."

These elements operate in part through social structure's discursive and disciplining role. For example, while there may be no formal hierarchy of international laws, some institutions play a dominant role in legitimating and de-legitimating practices. For instance, in the case of ISEAL members who aim to set standards, the WTO, especially the Technical Barriers to Trade (TBT) agreement, defines requirements to be recognized as a legitimate standard-setting body.

Community

New modes and sites of governance throw traditional notions of the international community into question because they increasingly target or affect non-state, sub-state, transnational, or local actors and communities. The result is a mixing of international and "global" communities from which justification and acceptance of rule stems (Clark 2007). Environmental institutions, by their very nature, experience a legitimacy challenge because their "realm of political action" extends beyond the conduct of states, thus so too must their view of their "social constituency of legitimation" (Seabrooke 2007). An appropriate research strategy, then, is to identify political communities wherever they form, whether in professional or technical networks, relevant marketplaces, transnational, or local civil society, or the traditionally demarcated "international society" of diplomats and officials, and ask on what basis legitimacy within those communities rests.

Establishing the boundaries of the relevant communities is an empirical and interpretive endeavor, and unlikely to be without controversy. It poses a particularly significant challenge for non-state governance, which may target non-state as well as state actors for regulation, and which often depends on a diverse group of actors to support or promote it (Black 2008: 147). As a first cut, the relevant community consists of rule-makers and those over whom authority is claimed, or targets of rules, i.e. the "community of practice." In this case, that community is actively reproduced through participation in the ISEAL alliance and is both subject and object of wider social structures around global environmental and social governance.

Even when a particular member of a community of practice, however, seeks legitimacy from fellow members (say, in the case of certification institutions, from participating firms and the sponsoring NGOs), its rules may have implications for a wider community (say, a broader group of transnational and local NGOs and non-participating sectoral actors, standard-setting organizations, or states in the case of certification systems). This complexity forces attention to how different audiences of states, global civil society, or marketplace actors may share or differ in criteria or weightings of the elements of legitimacy that justify political domination. Many global civil society organizations highly value practices of accountability, participation, transparency, and equity, while business actors may value efficiency, the rule of law, and fairness in the marketplace. Moreover, discourses of rights, global environmental stewardship, or traditional knowledge may play different legitimating roles in different local contexts.

Case application: the ISEAL Alliance

Out of the vast array of non-state attempts to socially and environmentally regulate the global marketplace, a small subset has arisen in the last twenty years that can be rightfully labeled non-state global governance. These mechanisms – usually in the form of producer certification and product labeling systems that include third-party auditing – are remarkable for their similarity to state-based regulatory and legal systems (Meidinger 2007).

The best examples of these non-state governance systems in the social and environmental area are members of the ISEAL Alliance, an umbrella organization created to develop agreement on "best practices" for its members, and to gain credibility and legitimacy for its members' standards (ISEAL 2010a). Its thirteen full members (it also has associate members who must show a commitment to move toward full membership, which entails adherence to its codes of good practice) include: Fairtrade International, which aims to improve conditions for workers and poor or marginalized producers in developing countries through certifying commodities including coffee, cocoa, and sugar; the Forest Stewardship Council (FSC), which aims to combat global forest deterioration; the International Organic Accreditation Service (IOAS), which accredits and assesses services to certification bodies working in organic agriculture; the Marine Stewardship Council (MSC), which combats fisheries depletion; and the Rainforest Alliance, which has developed certification systems for a wide variety of agricultural products from tropical countries to promote sustainable agriculture and biodiversity. Collectively, their standards cover an increasing range of sectors, including agriculture, mining, climate finance, fishing, manufacturing, textiles, and forestry. While actual uptake in each sector remains limited, ranging from about 2 percent to 15 percent of production, they have a strong regulatory relationship with firms that sign on to them.[4]

Members aim to be *authoritative* in the sense of creating rules with a sufficient "pull toward compliance" (Franck 1990: 24) and regulatory capacity to back up those binding obligations on firms that sign on with enforceable rules. Institutionally they are notable for establishing their own governing systems that typically include representation from corporations, civil society, and affected local communities, but not governments (Cashore 2002). Although they work with markets and the private sector, they also engage directly or indirectly with NGOs in active campaigns to manipulate the market through targeting high-profile firms and, sometimes, boycotts. They also work with governments and international organizations to promote their standards in an effort to create legitimate authority independent, and often in the absence, of intergovernmental agreements. Scholars in law, political science, and business have variously labeled them "transnational regulatory systems," (Meidinger 2007) "non-state market driven" (NSMD) governance systems (Cashore 2002), and "civil regulation" (Vogel 2008). The goal for many of these governance systems is not simply to create niche markets that apply their standards, but to promote their standards as appropriate and legitimate across an entire market sector. In this regard, a major new thrust of ISEAL's work is to scale up the impact and adoption of its member organizations' standards. As the document outlining this strategy puts it: "With 10% or more of global production certified in key sectors such as forestry, fisheries and key agricultural commodities, sustainability standards have the potential to transform global markets" (ISEAL and AccountAbility 2011: 3).

Twenty years ago these initiatives might have been automatically characterized as the privatization of global governance or marketization, because at the time the prevailing model tended to be either industry self-regulation, such as the case of Responsible Care in the chemical industry, or the ISO model of developing standards through participation of national standard-setting bodies, where industry experts and technical experts dominate decision-making. Pioneering writing on ostensibly "private" governance focused on how it appeared to replace public domestic and international governance or characterized it as delegated authority with little accountability but increasing power and responsibility (e.g. Cutler, Porter, and Haufler 1999), a trend noted with concern as popular pressure for increased environmental standards and these

---

[4] These figures are largely self-reported, taken from each system's website in 2012 and are available from the author.

types of organizations initially filled that gap (see Clapp 1998; Falkner 2003; Newell 2008; Paterson 2009). But, as Best and Ghuciu observe (Chapter 2, this volume) that characterization misses a potentially more profound transformation of the public/private divide under way.

The newer breed of initiatives reflected in ISEAL membership can be seen as a "response to the perceived limitations of neoliberal ideas and practices of the public that were prominent in previous years" (Best and Gheciu, Chapter 2, this volume). Indeed, their attempts to produce new sites of public rather than private authority can reconstitute the public via institutionalizing "public" practices of governance that exceed those of even democratic states in terms of access to participation, transparency, and accountability. These practices can also be seen as attempts to re-embed the market in social and environmental purposes, though trans-nationally as opposed to necessarily through the state, reflecting these broader public concerns. Moreover, there is evidence that these practices – many of which were first adopted transnationally by initiatives that are now ISEAL members – are transforming requirements for social and environmental standard setting more broadly (Bernstein and Cashore 2007; Dingwerth and Pattberg 2009).

Of particular interest are ISEAL members that are certification systems. These systems use global supply chains to recognize, track, and label products and services from environmentally and socially responsible businesses, and have third-party auditing processes in place to ensure compliance. Their governing arrangements usually include stakeholders as well as representation from the targeted firms, owners, service pro-viders, or producers. Moreover, their goals are to transform markets, to establish authority independently of sovereign states (even if they increasingly engage with states and other international public authorities), and to develop dynamic and adaptive governance mechanisms.

To identify the relevant practices that produce "publicness" and political authority, I apply the theoretical argument put forward above on the interaction of social structure and communities of practice.

Legitimating practices in non-state environmental governance: social structure

Sovereignty norms work in ironic ways in this case. On the one hand, non-state governance systems have bypassed sovereignty concerns that have been a major impediment to intergovernmental agreement on social and environmental issues, because they target firms instead of states. Their relative autonomy from intergovernmental processes also allows them to tap into emerging environmental and social norms more quickly – themselves often stemming from public processes. On the other hand, ISEAL members are disadvantaged in gaining legitimacy because they have no pre-existing basis in public authority. The problem is particularly acute among constituencies in the global South, who often view these mechanisms as reflecting Northern interests (Joshi 2004). Apart from Fairtrade International and the Sustainable Agriculture Network, which exclusively target Southern producers, this problem is reflected in significantly lower Southern adoption rates of ISEAL member standards. That concern combines with broader democratization trends in social structure to create higher requirements, relative to intergovernmental institutions, of access and participation, transparency, accountability, and deliberation directly among stakeholders in order to successfully gain public authority. In addition, legitimacy requires that ISEAL members actively ensure developing country and/or small producers have the capacity and information to participate in decisions that affect them.

Institutional power and productive power are at work here as well. Non-state environmental and social governance operates in an institutional context of hierarchy, with dominant economic institutions and norms setting the rules through which ISEAL members must navigate. Power is most concretely manifested in WTO agreements, especially the Technical Barriers to Trade (TBT) agreement, which define conditions for recognition as legitimate standard-setting bodies (for a detailed analysis see Bernstein and Hannah 2008). Key requirements – found in TBT Annex 3 and the non-binding Annex 4 of the TBT Committee's Second Triennial Review (2000) – include: adhere to the Most-Favored Nation and National Treatment principles; avoid unnecessary barriers to trade; encourage consensus decision-making; promote transparency through regular publication of work programs; promptly publish standards once adopted; provide opportunities for all interested parties to comment on proposed standards; and encourage multi-stakeholder participation at every stage of standard development. They also encourage international harmonization of standards. These guidelines also include special provisions for participation of developing country governments and stakeholders in standardization bodies and technical assistance to prevent unnecessary obstacles to trade for developing countries. They also say standardization bodies should be open to membership from all relevant bodies of WTO members, which suggests that non-state standard-setters may face increased pressure to open themselves up to government participation.

As evidence of the WTO's power, ISEAL's flagship document, the *Code of Good Practice for Setting Social and Environmental Standards* (ISEAL 2010a) – to which all full members must adhere – asks members to incorporate the above TBT provisions, as well as *ISO/IEC Guide 59:*

Code of Good Practice for Standardization (ISO 1994), which covers similar ground. ISEAL's code goes further than either in its emphasis on performance and process standards.

The Code also goes beyond these documents with additional criteria aimed specifically at social and environmental standard-setting. Some of these criteria are technical, reflecting practices of efficiency and performance of central importance to its credibility and legitimacy among marketplace actors in the community of practice. These criteria include knowledge of its standards, fulfilling technical requirements, and engaging with technical arguments over trade rules. Others aim to augment the provisions in TBT Annex 3 and Second Triennial Review Annex 4 for the participation of developing countries. For example, the Code explicitly requires multi-stakeholder consultations and Section 7.2 requires that all interested parties "be provided with meaningful opportunities to contribute to the elaboration of a standard." Section 7.4 also requires that ISEAL members give special consideration to disadvantaged groups, such as developing country stakeholders and small and medium-sized enterprises, and seek a balance of stakeholder interests among sectors, geographical regions, and gender. Specific recommendations include funding to participate in meetings, measures to improve technical cooperation and capacity-building, and mechanisms that facilitate the spread of information.

The Code and its requirements are also clearly part of a legitimation strategy. The requirements tap into expectations within the international trading system, evolving international norms on democracy, and specific practices of participation, transparency, and accountability, as well as evolving international environmental and social norms from which the basic purposes of ISEAL member systems are constituted. There is also a power dynamic at play because ISEAL member systems at once tap into norms that encourage market mechanisms and promote liberalized trade (i.e. liberal environmentalism), while also trying to navigate concerns of environmental and social groups about the power of the marketplace or marketplace actors to shape governance in ways that may be difficult to reconcile with some environmental or social goals. This dynamic reflects the embeddedness of practices in social structure.

There is also evidence that interaction among non-state governance systems – in which ISEAL plays a role – has led to diffusion and mutual reinforcement of these legitimacy requirements, consistent with social structural constraints (Dingwerth and Pattberg 2009; Meidinger 2008). These increased requirements also reflect demands from its core constituencies of legitimation. In the absence of an official process or body that determines which standards are authoritative, member systems are engaged in a multi-pronged strategy to conform to every possible relevant international rule to increase their legitimacy and uptake, and the chances their standards would survive a trade challenge. ISEAL also recently introduced a *Code of Good Practice for Assessing the Impact of Social and Environmental Standards* in 2010. It establishes a process through which member systems can measure and evaluate the effectiveness of their standards, address poor performance, and further enhance their accountability mechanisms (ISEAL 2010b).

Notably, these codes reflect a bottom–up process of members who engage in these practices, and are themselves an attempt to reflect and enhance those standards across its members. Many commentators have pointed to the Forest Stewardship Council (FSC) as the prototypical example of the attempt to develop and implement democratic practices. As described by Meidinger: "all of the procedural devices and institutional *practices* [my emphasis] of aggregative and deliberative democracy exist within [the FSC]" (Meidinger 2008: 523). The FSC's global "general assembly" is made up of economic, environmental, and social chambers, each with equal voting power, and each subdivided into "northern" and "southern" subchambers, also with equal voting power (regardless of membership numbers). In addition, votes on major policies require a two-thirds majority, thus ensuring strong consensus on major decisions, while also allowing local input and variation on regional standards. The MSC has adopted a similar decision-making structure.

The undertaking of these practices, however, is not perfect, nor is that the argument here. Questions are often raised about who gets to participate, especially in regard to developing countries, as well as competing claims among sometimes competing standard-setters – including many who are not ISEAL members – on who better represents core constituencies, a problem that besets transnational labor regulations standards in particular (Franzen 2011). The point here is that engaging in these practices competently is central to gaining public authority and the scaling up of that authority across a sector, which requires broad recognition of its authority.

Legitimating practices in non-state environmental and social governance: community

Authority granted to ISEAL member systems emanates from the market's supply chain, in interaction with civil society. These interactions occur both globally and locally, especially because particular governance systems frequently have regional standard-setting processes in addition to the general standard (Cashore 2002). Moreover, these systems depend upon, and encourage, community participation in decision-making and the development of standards in locations where certification is taking place.

Community support is vitally important for legitimacy since non-state governance systems claim authority directly in the marketplace. The relevant community includes producers (or other market players along the supply chain), consumers, environmental and labor activists, and affected local communities. States are also interested actors, though generally not actively engaged in granting legitimacy. Since many non-state governance systems increasingly aim to make their standards acceptable to states, however, their importance is likely to increase. This creates a complicated picture of what legitimacy requires, and suggests difficulty in achieving it.

Moreover, the relevant political community intersects, but is not coterminal, with the community of practice, and will vary across governance systems. For example, in the case of forestry, membership will include forest landowners, forest management companies, producers of forest products, purchasers of those products further down the supply chain, retailers, consumers, and members of communities where certification occurs. In the case of Fair Trade coffee, relevant audiences include coffee brokers, communities who subscribe to fair trade, coffee retailers, and individual coffee consumers.

A central element of normative contestation is between business and environmental NGO understandings of what legitimacy requires. Business stakeholders often see trade-offs between market and environmental and social goals. Moreover, their core interests lead them to heavily weigh "output legitimacy," efficiency, or gaining advantage in the marketplace when evaluating whether to join or accept as legitimate a regulatory system it is not legislated to follow (Cashore, Auld, and Newsom 2004). Governments and NGOs are also frequently initially driven by pragmatic concerns to turn to non-state governance systems as second-best solutions, after failures in intergovernmental forums, consistent with neoliberal norms and trade rules (Bartley 2007). Environmental and social NGOs' evaluations of legitimacy are, however, deeply rooted in their conceptions of appropriate environmental and social practices. They will generally not accept a system that appears lax on performance criteria, producing on-the-ground improvements in environmental or social integrity, or in monitoring (Bartley 2007; Sasser 2002). Evidence from a recent survey of stakeholders in ISEAL member systems, however, does show a strong consensus among businesses and NGOs on the priority and importance of goals of inclusiveness and participation for stakeholders, as well as independent auditing to verify compliance (ISEAL 2007).

The support of both market actors and civil society (including local communities) is nonetheless essential for ongoing political legitimacy. Thus, ISEAL's latest initiative is to develop a set of "Credibility Standards" to guide all future standard-setting. The thirteen draft principles reflect these tensions, as do survey results that show differences between firms and NGO stakeholders. The draft principles are broken down into two categories: "Performance" (effectiveness, rigor, impartiality, efficiency, accuracy, coordination, and relevance), which is generally more important to business; and "Uptake" (engagement, accountability, transparency, truthfulness, capacity, and accessibility), generally more important to NGOs. Defining these principles involves multiple consultations and channels of input in a process that is as much about learning among stakeholders as generating an overlapping consensus. This is an example of more general evidence that institutionalized practices of learning, dialogical, and deliberative processes are essential to produce sufficient coherence in practices to produce political authority (see for example Meidinger 2008).

Learning has clearly had effects outside ISEAL as well. The high legitimacy bar reflects in part a response to known critiques that Northern business interests dominated decision-making in established standard setters like ISO, that entered into this area through its 14000 series environmental management standards, and explain ISO's decision to move more closely to a multi-stakeholder model for its Corporate Social Responsibility Standard, ISO 26000 (Clapp 1998; Knight 2008). ISO learned from ISEAL members and its experience with ISO 14000 that its regular practices for technical standard-setting no longer sufficed to create authority in the social and environmental realms. It also relied less on its technical expertise for its legitimacy claim and more on its claim that it had experience in developing standards in related areas (Wood 2008).

A similar dynamic may be unfolding in the case of climate change where competition among standard-setters is leading to some emulation of practices to produce political authority. Many of these are in response to legitimacy problems in the offset – largely private – carbon markets, where individuals or firms can purchase carbon credits to offset their emissions. The board of the Voluntary Carbon Standard (VCS), for example, contains representatives from key market players, as well as NGOs and business lobbies (see Paterson, Chapter 7, this volume). As Paterson notes, "while the representation is business dominated, it represents a broad variety of business interests, and the attempt to branch out to a broader range of interests is indicative of the desire to respond to the legitimacy crisis of 'privatised' governance." We also see the example of external standards arising that bring in broader sets of values than existing standards more closely associated with fulfilling internal market functions and not perceived as responding to the wider public concern. The Gold Standard (a certification system for carbon offsets to ensure credibility and adherence to broader sustainable development goals) is a case in point. Since it explicitly presents itself as vying for public authority and in pursuit of broader (public) social and environmental aims as opposed to functional governance of private markets, it more explicitly engages in practices that resemble those of ISEAL members to try to gain public authority. As Paterson describes, its consultation process and board are the most broadly representative in the ecology of carbon market regulation.

Conclusions

To the degree the above analysis is persuasive, the ostensible public/ private divide in global politics no longer applies to a division between state and non-state governance. Rather, the question is whether governance understood as public authority has been produced as opposed to a form of non-governance (i.e. lacking in legitimate political authority) or non-public authority (i.e. authority for private ends). What constitutes political authority is a set of practices recognized by a community of practice to produce legitimate public authority.

I focused here on initiatives of social and environmental global governance to flesh out this argument. First, I showed that there are a limited number of such initiatives that properly qualify as global governance. Second, I showed that they both reflect the practices of political authority in the "social structure" in which they operate as well as consciously engage in those practices to produce public authority. In addition, they are part of, and seek legitimacy from, communities of practice engaged with and affected by the environmental and social practices they wish to regulate and influence. I also provided a framework to explain where those practices come from and how they evolve. Members of the ISEAL Alliance, who gain membership by adhering to its code of good practices, arguably provide the best examples of non-state public authorities in the social and environmental issue areas.

The analysis also raises at least one additional empirical and one additional normative question worth highlighting related to the themes of this volume. First, normatively, how well can these new forms of governance fully achieve their public ambition? In practice, it can be difficult to achieve publicity for these initiatives and their operation beyond elites or those with specialized knowledge who are active on the particular concerns at stake in these governance systems. Their standards are still less well known, for example, than ISO standards, even among "thought leaders" in global businesses supportive of corporate social responsibility surveyed in 2010 (ISEAL 2011). While ISEAL is actively trying to address this concern (ISEAL and AccountAbility 2011), it remains normatively problematic if these practices empower political authority that may remain largely unknown to most members of society, even if the governance system is more open in theory than most national governments. The risk is that the corresponding reconstitution of public authority legitimizes the slicing up of a divisible transnational "public" – made up in practice of elites engaged in particular issues or market sectors – in the absence of a globally constituted public. In other words, it could be argued that only a pre-constituted public that empowers and legitimizes governors with general jurisdiction over it, including areas in which that public may not be particularly engaged, can generate the requisite political authority. This is a normative debate that is difficult to resolve here – but one could imagine counter-arguments concerning whether already constituted political communities are better "in practice" in engaging relevant publics. This dilemma for non-state public authorities points back to the argument made earlier that the legitimacy bar for issue specific forms of public authority may always be higher than already constituted general-purpose and universal jurisdiction forms of governance such as the state.

This normative dilemma points to an empirical question of whether a role for public authorities can be completely avoided, no matter how legitimate a non-state governing system or how much political authority it generates among those it targets for regulation. In this context, it is not surprising that ISEAL members increasingly interact with governments and other established public authorities, often in various configurations of co-regulation, as they attempt to increase their range of authority in a sector (fisheries, forests) or across a set of practices (e.g. labor practices, carbon markets transactions) they are trying govern. To take one of the most well-established examples, forest certification, one recent study of Canada, the United States, and Sweden found those governments: "have adopted increasingly direct approaches towards certification, including endorsing certification standards, establishing legislation to enable certification implementation, adopting certification on public land and mandating certification" (Lister 2011: 201).

Notably, while the state and non-state authorities may co-regulate or build on each other's legitimacy, their practices reinforce the autonomous public authority of each rather than moving toward a hierarchical relationship. Each must generate its own political authority and legitimacy, even if the way they interact can reinforce legitimacy for each (endorsement by governments shore up the legitimacy of certification systems while certification systems may demand adherence to domestic laws and regulations and increase legitimacy for domestic policies). More work needs to be done, however, on whether this is a virtuous circle or one that is more likely to lead to contestation and potentially undermine public authority. While ISEAL aims to create a virtuous circle, "the greatest dilemma faced by governments relates to stimulating and supporting private certification systems while ensuring the reliability and accountability of the sustainability claims made by existing certification systems" (Vermeulen *et al.* 2010: 63). This finding comes from one of the few studies that directly engaged stakeholders on their perceptions on the role of government. While they did not see a strong need for governments in order to produce legitimacy or credibility, they did see a role for broader checks on credibility and legitimacy, singling out ISEAL as a promising player in this role (Vermeulen *et al.* 2010: 64).

REFERENCES

Abbott, Kenneth W. and Duncan Snidal. 2000. "Hard and soft law in international governance." *International Organization* 54(3): 421–56.
Adler, Emanuel. 2005. *Communitarian International Relations: The Epistemic Foundations of International Relations*. New York: Routledge.
Adler, Emanuel and Vincent Pouliot. 2011. "International practices." *International Theory* 3(1): 1–36.
Andonova, Liliana B., Michele M. Betsill, and Harriet Bulkeley. 2009. "Transnational climate governance." *Global Environmental Politics* 9(2): 52–73.
Arendt, Hannah. 1958. *On the Human Condition*, Chicago, IL: University of Chicago Press.
Avant, Deborah, Martha Finnemore, and Susan Sell, eds. 2010. *Who Governs the Globe?* Cambridge: Cambridge University Press.
Bäckstrand, Karin. 2006. "Democratizing global environmental governance? Stakeholder democracy after the world summit on sustainable development." *European Journal of International Relations* 12(4): 467–98.
Barnett, Michael, and Liv Coleman. 2005. "Designing police: Interpol and the study of change in international organizations." *International Studies Quarterly* 49(4): 593–619.
Barnett, Michael, and Raymond Duvall, eds. 2005. *Power and Global Governance.* Cambridge: Cambridge University Press.
Bartley, Timothy. 2007. "Institutional emergence in an era of globalization: the rise of transnational private regulation of labor and environmental conditions." *American Journal of Sociology* 113(2): 297–351.
Benedict, Kennette. 2004. Global governance." In *International Encyclopedia of the Social and Behavioral Sciences*, edited by Paul Baltes and Neil Smelser, pp. 6232–37. Amsterdam: Pergamon.

Bernstein, Steven. 2001. *The Compromise of Liberal Environmentalism*. New York: Columbia University Press.

2004. *The Elusive Basis of Legitimacy in Global Governance: Three Conceptions*. Hamilton: Institute for Globalization and the Human Condition, McMaster University.

2011. "Legitimacy in intergovernmental and non-state global governance." *Review of International Political Economy* 18(1): 17–51.

Bernstein, Steven, and Benjamin Cashore. 2007. "Can non-state global governance be legitimate? A theoretical framework." *Regulation and Governance* 1(4): 347–71.

Bernstein, Steven, and William D. Coleman, eds. 2009. *Unsettled Legitimacy: Political Community, Power, and Authority in a Global Era*. Vancouver: University of British Columbia Press.

Bernstein, Steven, and Erin Hannah. 2008. "Non-state global standard setting and the WTO: legitimacy and the need for regulatory space." *Journal of International Economic Law* 11(3): 575–608.

Best, Jacqueline. 2007. "Legitimacy dilemmas: the IMF's pursuit of country ownership." *Third World Quarterly* 28(3): 469–88.

Black, Julia. 2008. "Constructing and contesting legitimacy and accountability in polycentric regulatory regimes." *Regulation and Governance* 2(2): 137–64.

Bodansky, Daniel. 1999. "The legitimacy of international governance: a coming challenge for international environmental law?" *American Journal of International Law* 93(3): 596–624.

Brunnée, Jutta, and Stephen Toope. 2010. *Legitimacy and Legality in International Law: An Interactional Account*. Cambridge: Cambridge University Press.

Cashore, Benjamin. 2002. "Legitimacy and the privatization of environmental governance: how non-state market-driven (NSMD) governance systems gain rule-making authority." *Governance* 15(4): 502–29.

Cashore, Benjamin, Graeme Auld, and Deanna Newsom. 2004. *Governing through Markets: Forest Certification and the Emergence of Non-State Authority*. New Haven, CT: Yale University Press.

Chambers, Simone. 2004. "Behind closed doors: publicity, secrecy and the quality of deliberation." *Journal of Political Philosophy* 12(4): 389–410.

Clapp, Jennifer. 1998. "The privatization of global environmental governance: ISO 14000 and the developing world." *Global Governance* 4(3): 295–316.

Clark, Ian. 2007. *International Legitimacy and World Society*. Oxford: Oxford University Press.

Claude, Inis L. Jr. 1966. "Collective legitimization as a political function of the United Nations." *International Organization* 20(3): 367–79.

Connolly, William. 1984. Introduction: Legitimacy and modernity." In *Legitimacy and the State*, edited by William Connolly, pp. 1–19. Oxford: Basil Blackwell.

Cutler, A. Claire, Virginia Haufler, and Tony Porter, eds. 1999. *Private Authority and International Affairs*. Albany, NY: State University of New York Press.

Devetak, Richard, and Richard Higgott. 1999. "Justice unbound? Globalization, states, and the transformation of the social bond." *International Affairs* 75(3): 483–98.

Dingwerth, Klaus, and Philipp Pattberg. 2009. "World politics and organizational fields: the case of transnational sustainability governance." *European Journal of International Relations* 15(4): 707–44.

Douglas, Ian R. 1999. Globalization as governance: toward an archaeology of contemporary political reason." In *Globalization and Governance*, edited by Aseem Prakash and Jeffrey A. Hart, pp. 134–60. New York: Routledge.

Dunoff, Jeffrey. 2006. "Constitutional conceits: the WTO's 'constitution' and the discipline of international law." *European Journal of International Law* 17(3): 647–75.

Falkner, Robert. 2003. "Private environmental governance and international relations: exploring the links." *Global Environmental Politics* 3(2): 72–87.

FAO. 2003. *Environmental and Social Standards, Certification and Labeling for Cash Crops*. Rome: FAO.

Finnemore, Martha. 1996. *National Interests in International Society*. Ithaca, NY: Cornell University Press.

Foucault, Michel. 1991. "Governmentality." In *The Foucault Effect: Studies in Governmentality*, edited by Graham Burchell, Colin Gordon, and Peter Miller, pp. 87–104. London: Harvester Wheatsheaf.

Franck, Thomas M. 1990. *The Power of Legitimacy among Nations*. Oxford: Oxford University Press.

Franzen, Luc. 2011. "Why do private governance organizations not converge? A political–institutional analysis of transnational labor standards regulation." *Governance* 24(2): 359–87.

Germain, Randall. 2010. "Financial governance and transnational deliberative democracy." *Review of International Studies* 36(2): 493–509.

Grande, Edgar, and Louis W. Pauly. 2005. *Complex Sovereignty: Reconstituting Political Authority in the Twenty-First Century*. Toronto: University of Toronto Press.

Habermas, Jürgen. 1979. *Communication and the Evolution of Society*. Translated by Thomas McCarthy. Boston, MA: Beacon Press.

Hall, Rodney Bruce, and Thomas J. Biersteker, eds. 2002. *The Emergence of Private Authority in Global Governance*. Cambridge: Cambridge University Press.

Held, David, and Mathias Koenig-Archibugi, eds. 2005. *Global Governance and Public Accountability*. Oxford: Wiley-Blackwell.

Hobson, Christopher. 2009. "Beyond the end of history: the need for a 'radical historicisation' of democracy in international relations." *Millennium – Journal of International Studies* 37(3): 631–57.

Howse, Robert, and Kalypso Nicolaïdis. 2001. Legitimacy and global governance: why constitutionalizing the WTO is a step too far." In *Efficiency, Equity and legitimacy: The Multilateral Trading System at the Millennium*, edited by Roger B. Porter, Pierre Sauve, Arvind Subramanian, and Americo Beviglia-Zampetti, pp. 227–52. Washington, D.C.: Brookings Institution Press.

Hurd, Ian. 2008. *After Anarchy: Legitimacy and Power in the UN Security Council*. Princeton, NJ: Princeton University Press.

ISEAL. 2005. Stakeholder Consultation Practices in Standards Development, R044, Public Version 1. http://portals.wi.wur.nl/files/

2007. *Factors Contributing to the Credibility of Social and Environmental Standards: ISEAL Survey Results Summary*. www.isealalliance.org/
2010a. *ISEAL Code of Good Practice for Setting Social and Environmental Standards*, P005, Public Version 5. www.isealalliance.org/
2010b. *ISEAL Code of Good Practice for Assessing the Impacts of Social and Environmental Standards Systems*, P041, Public Version 1.0. www.isealalliance.org/
ISEAL and AccountAbility. 2011. *Scaling-up Strategy: A Strategy for Scaling Up the Impacts of Voluntary Standards*. www.isealalliance.org/
ISO. 1994. *ISO/IEC Guide 59: 1994 Code of Good Practice for Standardization*. Geneva: ISO.
Joshi, Manoj. 2004. "Are eco-labels consistent with world trade organization agreements?" *Journal of World Trade* 38(1): 69–92.
Keohane, Robert O., and Joseph S. Nye, Jr. 2001. The club model of multilateral cooperation and problems of democratic legitimacy." In *Efficiency, Equity and Legitimacy: The Multilateral Trading System at the Millennium*, edited by Roger B. Porter, Pierre Sauve, Arvind Subramanian, and Americo Beviglia-Zampetti, pp. 264–294. Washington, D.C.: Brookings Institution Press.
Kirton, John, and Michael Trebilcock, eds. 2004. *Hard Choices, Soft Law: Combining Trade, Environment, and Social Cohesion in Global Governance*. Farnham: Ashgate.
Knight, Sam. 2008. "Everyone needs standards." *Prospect Magazine* 144, March 28. www.prospectmagazine.co.uk/
Levin, Kelly, Benjamin Cashore, and Jonathon Koppell. 2009. "Can non-state certification systems bolster state-centered efforts to promote sustainable development through the Clean Development Mechanism?" *Wake Forest Law Review* 44: 777–98.
Lister, Jane. 2011. *Corporate Social Responsibility and the State*. Vancouver: University of British Columbia Press.
Meidinger, Errol. 2007. Beyond Westphalia: competitive legalization in emerging transnational regulatory systems." In *Law and Legalization in Transnational Relations*, edited by Christian Brütsch and Dirk Lehmkuhl, pp. 121–43. New York: Routledge.
2008. "Competitive supragovernmental regulation: how could it be democratic?" *Chicago Journal of International Law* 8(2): 513–34.
Meyer, John, John Boli, Francisco O. Ramirez, and George M. Thomas. 1997. "World society and the nation–state."*American Journal of Sociology* 103(1): 144–81.
Mori, Satoko. 2004. Institutionalization of NGO involvement in policy functions for global environmental governance." In *Emerging Forces in Global Environmental Governance*, edited by Norichika Kanie and Peter M. Haas, pp. 157–75. Tokyo: UN University Press.
Newell, Peter. 2008. "The political economy of global environmental governance." *Review of International Studies* 34(3): 507–29.
Paterson, Matthew. 2009. "Legitimation and accumulation in climate change governance." *New Political Economy* 15(3): 345–68.

Pauly, Louis W. 1997. *Who Elected the Bankers?* Ithaca, NY: Cornell University Press.

Payne, Roger A., and Nayef H. Samhat. 2004. *Democratizing Global Politics.* Albany, NY: State University of New York Press.

Polanyi, Karl. 1944. *The Great Transformation: The Political and Economic Origins of our Time.* New York: Farrar & Rinehart. (Reprinted 1957, Boston, MA: Beacon Press.)

Porter, Tony, and Karsten Ronit, eds. 2010. *The Challenges of Global Business Authority: Democratic Renewal, Stalemate or Decay?* Albany, NY: State University of New York Press.

Potoski, Matthew, and Aseem Prakash. 2005. "Green clubs and voluntary governance: ISO 14001 and firms' regulatory compliance." *American Journal of Political Science* 49(2): 235–48.

Reus-Smit, Christian. 1999. *The Moral Purpose of the State: Culture, Social Identity and Institutional Rationality in International Relations.* Princeton, NJ: Princeton University Press.

   2011. "Obligation through practice." *International Theory* 3(2): 339–47.

Risse, Thomas. 2000. "'Let's argue!' Communicative action in world politics." *International Organization* 54(1): 1–40.

Rosenau, James. 1995. "Governance in the twenty-first century." *Global Governance* 1(1): 13–43.

Rosenau, James, and Ernst-Otto Czempiel, eds. 1992. *Governance without Government: Order and Change in World Politics.* Cambridge: Cambridge University Press.

Ruggie, John G. 1998. *Constructing the World Polity.* New York: Routledge.

   2004. "Reconstituting the global public domain: issues, actors and practices." *European Journal of International Relations* 10(4): 499–531.

Sasser, Erica. 2002. "The certification solution: NGO promotion of private, voluntary self-regulation." Paper presented at the *74th Annual Meeting of the Canadian Political Science Association,* Toronto, Canada, May 29–31.

Scholte, Jan Aart, ed. 2011. *Building Global Democracy: Civil Society and Accountable Global Governance.* Cambridge: Cambridge University Press.

Seabrooke, Leonard. 2007. "Legitimacy gaps in the world economy: explaining the sources of the IMF's legitimacy crisis." *International Politics* 44(2): 250–68.

Upham, Frank. 2002. *Mythmaking in the Rule of Law Orthodoxy,* Working Paper No. 30. Washington, D.C.: Carnegie Endowment for International Peace.

Uphoff, Norman. 1989. "Power, authority and legitimacy: taking Max Weber at his word by using resource-exchange analysis." *Polity* 22(2): 295–322.

Vermeulen, Walter J.V., Yukina Uitenboogaart, J. Metselaar, and M.T.J. Kok. 2010. *Roles of Governments in Multi-Actor Sustainable Supply Chain Governance Systems and the Effectiveness of their Interventions: An Exploratory Study.* The Hague/Bilthoven: Netherlands Environmental Assessment Agency (PBL).

Vogel, David. 2008. "Private global business regulation." *Annual Review of Political Science* 11: 261–82.

Wara, Michael, and David G. Victor. 2008. *A Realistic Policy on International Carbon Off-Sets*, Program on Energy and Sustainable Development Working Paper No.74. Palo Alto, CA: Stanford University.

Weber, Max. 1978. *Economy and Society*. Edited by Guenther Roth and Claus Wittich. Berkeley, CA: University of California Press.

Wenger, Etienne. 1998. *Communities of Practice: Learning, Meaning and Identity*. Cambridge: Cambridge University Press.

Wenger, Etienne, Richard A. McDermott, and William M. Snyder. 2002. *A Guide to Making Knowledge: Cultivating Communities of Practice*. Boston, MA: Harvard Business School Press.

Wood, Stepan. 2008. "Will ISO 26000 corner the market for international social responsibility standards? Competition for transnational regulatory authority." Paper presented at the *SLSA Conference*, Montreal, Canada, May 1.

World Standards Services Network (WSSN). 2010. "About WSSN." www.wssn. net/

7 Climate re-public: practicing public space in conditions of extreme complexity

Matthew Paterson

In their Introduction to this volume, Best and Gheciu define "public practices as patterns of activity that involve an understanding in a given society at a particular moment in time that something is of common concern." That climate change governance entails public practices according to this definition is perhaps so obvious as to go unnoticed. It is more or less impossible to make any claim about climate change that does not refer to this quality. It is, for example, the foundational claim in the United Nations Framework Convention on Climate Change (UNFCCC). The first words of the Convention read "The Parties to this Convention, Acknowledging that change in the Earth's climate and its adverse effects are a common concern of humankind ... " (UN 1992: Preamble). The first principle enunciated in the Convention reads that "The Parties should protect the climate system for the benefit of present and future generations of humankind, on the basis of equity and in accordance with their common but differentiated responsibilities and respective capabilities" (UN 1992: Article 3.1). More or less any governance document focused on climate change makes some sort of claim about climate change as a "common concern."

But how might we say more about the qualities of public practices around climate change? Best and Gheciu's division of these into three types of argument – the public as eroded by the private, the reconstitution of the public sphere, and the notion of public goods – is a useful starting point. This chapter explores the reconstitution of the public in climate change governance. It suggests that while climate change is ubiquitously framed as a public-goods problem, thinking through how public is practiced in its politics is better understood by starting from its framing as a problem of complexity. The notion of public goods is ubiquitous in talk about climate change – but it arguably is not so useful in explaining what people *do* in relation to it.

I am grateful to Philippe Descheneau for research assistance in preparing this chapter, and to Jacqueline Best and Alexandra Gheciu for comments on an earlier draft.

The qualities of these practices are affected fundamentally by the character of climate change as a complex problem. The chapter suggests that in effect this character produces a reconstitution of rather classical accounts of the public as a specific sort of political space, a space characterized first and foremost in terms of deliberation. But the character of this deliberation, and thus the public spaces it serves to produce, are transformed by the character of climate change as a problem of complexity, which turns the practices that produce this particular sort of "public space" into open-ended collective learning rather than ones fixed on the production of authoritative texts. In the terms set out by Best and Gheciu (Chapter 2, this volume), this is thus a set of practices concerned first and foremost constituting the character of processes that are deemed public. As I will show, the question of "who" is part of the public, or what sort of issues are regarded as public, is a secondary question in the phenomenon the chapter explores. The public space of climate change operates both within many individual climate change governance initiatives, and in the overall space of what might be called a "global climate governance complex." It entails attempting to practice the qualities associated classically with the agora, but in radically changed circumstances.

The chapter starts by elaborating the most obvious way that climate change is framed in terms of a very conventional notion of the public – the concept of public goods in economics. It then contrasts this with an alternative framing of climate change as a "superwicked" problem, invoking theories of complex adaptive systems to understand the character of the problem. It then turns to the question of how we might adequately understand the practices that emerge as public practices, and argues that the combination of these framings of climate change (as public good and as complex system) suggests that the classical account of the public sphere in political theory cannot plausibly be regarded to exist in these conditions. Instead, some of the practices of climate governance can be interpreted as a form of reconstituted public space – a climate re-public, if you like – where politics is oriented strongly towards deliberative, inter-subjective learning processes in conditions of extreme uncertainty and complexity. These practices emerge for two principal reasons. One is that the innovations in climate governance are widely critiqued as privatizations of governance, and thus the actors involved engage in various sorts of public practice in order to secure their legitimacy. This in effect means that the claims about the erosion of the public by the private can themselves be understood as interventions that serve to reconstitute the public itself. The other is that the complexity itself of climate change generates a set of practices that are focused on learning and deliberation.

Climate change as a public-goods problem

To suggest that climate change is the quintessential global public good is to express a banality. It exhibits the qualities that economists and other theorists of collective action associate with such goods – indivisibility of benefits and jointness of supply – in paradigmatic fashion. The conventional literature on global climate governance routinely starts with this sort of conceptualization of the character of climate change as a problem. In Aldy and Stavins' terms, "Global climate change is the ultimate global-commons problem, with the relevant greenhouse gases mixing uniformly in the upper atmosphere, so that damages are independent of the location of emissions. Because of this, a multinational response is required" (Aldy and Stavins 2007: 1). Such framings of climate change as a problem are ubiquitous (e.g. Barrett 2003, 2007; IPCC 2001: ch. 10, 2007: ch. 13; Stern 2006: Part VI; Tickell 2008: ch. 3). From this framing, an enormous range of literature outlining the logic of climate change as a collective action problem has emerged, with the standard range of problems emerging (mostly understood in game-theoretic terms) – free riders and how to get around them, enforcement and compliance, and so on.

It is also now widespread to argue that the specific character of climate change as a public-goods problem means that traditional methods of pursuing public goods do not work. In other environmental areas (regimes to manage ozone depletion or acid rain are often taken as paradigmatic), such approaches tend to entail the pursuit of treaties that bind states to specific obligations. But it is now conventional to argue that climate change is simply too complex to manage in this way (e.g. Keohane and Victor 2010), given the way that it touches on a broader range of human activities, and across a more diverse set of scales, compared to any other issue – not just in the environmental "issue area," but in *any* domain of global politics.

Two sorts of conclusions can be drawn from this, however. For some it is an issue of making sure that the design of international agreements "fits" with the character of climate change as a problem; here there is a panoply of alternative proposals for different "architectures" for international climate treaties that are different – at times radically different – to existing models of cooperation (see for example Bodansky 2004; Haas 2008; Keohane and Raustiala 2008; Victor 2001; or various contributions to Aldy and Stavins 2007). Occasionally (e.g. Haas 2008), these analyses also contain pleas for a sort of complex multilevel governance involving a wider range of governance actors than simply states.

But a growing number of analysts argue that in response to the character of climate change as a problem of complexity (see below), the wider range of governance practices that Haas (2008) pleads for are in fact themselves already emerging (see in particular Bulkeley *et al.* 2012: Hoffmann 2011). Among those focusing solely on state-led governance, Keohane and Victor (2010) argue that climate governance is best understood as a "regime complex" involving a broad range of inter-state governance institutions that are involved in governing climate change. Variously termed transnational (Andonova *et al.* 2009; Bulkeley *et al.* 2012), private (Pattberg and Stripple 2008), or multilevel (Betsill and Bulkeley 2006) climate change governance, these terms attempt to capture an explosion of such initiatives since the late 1990s. The largest research project on this phenomenon, coordinated by Harriet Bulkeley, catalogued and analyzed sixty such governance initiatives (Bulkeley *et al.* 2012), recognizing that these were a long way from the entire universe of such projects.

So while climate change is routinely invoked as a public-goods problem, observers also routinely observe both the inability of multilateralism to address it effectively and the emergence of an enormous range of transnational, public–private, non-state, and other forms of governance that attempt variously to fill the gap. Another way of seeing this is to suggest that while a public goods framing of climate change is intuitively useful, the logic of climate change exceeds the capacity of this framing to generate adequate understandings of its dynamics. Instead, the public-goods account of climate change is performative – generating practices (the pursuit of collective action, the analysis of free-rider problems, and so on) that constitute climate change politics even while its frame is highly problematic.

Climate change as a "superwicked" problem

At the same time as it is widely conceptualized as a public-goods problem, climate change is also framed, if not so ubiquitously, in terms of being a problem of exceptional complexity, and thus to be understood in terms of complex systems theory (Hoffmann 2005, 2011; Homer-Dixon 2006; Levin *et al.* 2009; Urry 2010). Levin *et al.* (2009) refer to it as a "superwicked" problem, which they take to refer to four interlocking characteristics: "time is running out; the central authority needed to address it is weak or non-existent; those who cause the problem also seek to create a solution; and hyperbolic discounting occurs that pushes responses irrationally into the future" (Levin *et al.* 2009: 2).

In this way of understanding the problem, both the climate system itself and the social systems that mediate impacts of climate change and determine mitigation efforts are understood as intertwined complex, open systems. Empirically, this generates arguments about path dependency, "lock-in" (Unruh 2002), tipping points, and the like. Normatively it generates a set of arguments about the need to think through how we engineer or "steer" responses that might overcome the basic elements of its superwicked character – e.g. how to engineer quick changes, without central authority, which create changes in the practices of those who cause it, and which overcome the central time inconsistency problem in our behavior. Two foci here of the arguments are worth picking up on. One is to try to engineer technological transitions whereby the shift to new technologies becomes self-sustaining precisely through the systems-theoretic logic of rising returns to scale and path dependencies (e.g. Barrett 2007; Scrase and Smith 2010). Another is to focus on learning; in the absence of clear knowledge about the effect of our choices, the appropriate response is a sort of constantly reflective experimentation with novel practices.

In terms of governance and the argument I want to develop during this chapter, Matthew Hoffmann provides the best point of entry for framing climate change within this logic. Hoffmann (2011) argues that the proliferation of private, transnational, or multilevel governance initiatives around climate change should be understood as a series of "climate governance experiments." These in turn need to be understood in terms of the logic of complex adaptive systems that agents within those systems – finding the traditional tools (inter-state agreements, national regulatory policies) unable to deal with the problem, and recognizing the complexity of climate change – engage in as an attempt to find means of engineering shifts in the practices that generate climate change.

Classical accounts of public and the logic of climate change politics

The central question that animates this chapter is: What happens to the notion of "public" in climate change governance when we combine these two sorts of framings – of climate change as a public-goods problem, and climate change as a problem of complexity? The central argument I want to make in relation to this sort of a question is that the logic of these intertwining frames is a reconstitution of the meanings and practices of "public." There are two linked dynamics here.

First, the failure of traditional means of resolving public-goods problems spawns a range of governance experiments. But the legitimacy of these transnational, private, hybrid, partnership forms of governance is widely contested, precisely on the basis of normative claims that climate change should be addressed through public rather than private means.

These claims about privatized governance in turn create a range of interesting legitimation strategies adopted by the actors involved in such governance projects, specifically through making claims about the "public" character of their projects.

Second, the focus of many governance practices becomes about learning and deliberation rather than traditional rule-making. They are focused on the question of how to find levers to accelerate decarbonization in the absence of central authority or clear knowledge about what "works." Both of these elements raise questions about what is meant by "public" in the context of specific governance practices. How then is the practice of "public" transformed by these dynamics? In order to address this, we need first to go back to conceptual debates about what we mean by terms like public and private.

There are of course many versions of what is meant by the term "public." In existing debates on climate change governance (e.g. Andonova *et al.* 2009; Bulkeley *et al.* 2012; Pattberg and Stripple 2008), as well as more broadly in the debate about the emergence of "private authority" in global governance (Cutler, Haufler, and Porter 1999; Ruggie 2004; see also Best and Gheciu, Chapter 2, this volume), the prevailing account identifies public and private as different institutional locations within society. Thus "public" are those entities claiming some broad scope representing general interests in society, and whose legitimacy arises out of some sort of representational claim. So the state, or the "polis," is classically the site where the "public" *is*. In contrast, private refers to all those institutional sites where such claims about general social interests are not present but rather the interests of individuals or specific collectivities are what count. It is where individuals can *deprive* either other individuals, or the collectivity at large, from intervention. According to this sort of institutional view of public and private, it ought to be possible at any place and time to identify whether specific organizations, institutions, or people act in a public or a private capacity and context – the two being ontologically separate domains of social life.

What I want to draw on here are the classical accounts of the public, going back to the ancient Greeks, and in modern political thought perhaps most closely associated with Hannah Arendt (1958) as a space of deliberation and democratic decision-making (see also Ruggie 2004: 405, following Wolin 1960; and Best and Gheciu, Chapter 2, this volume). For Arendt, the public realm constitutes, on the one hand, the realm where a broad reality is produced, as individuals' personal experiences become validated through contact with others, and "the presence of others who see what we see and hear what we hear assures us of the reality of the world and ourselves" (Arendt 1958: 50). She connects this notion of public directly to the idea of "publicity" (Arendt 1958: 50). At the same time, "the term 'public' signifies the world itself, in so far as it is common to all of us and distinguished from our privately owned place in it" (Arendt 1958: 52). This aspect of the public implies a particular sort of social relation where individuals simultaneously recognize both their difference to and their connections to others, and it is in effect the recognition of this space that is the precondition of politics, properly so-called. Societies without a public realm do not have politics, but merely domination.

This classical conception of the public is perhaps a little thinner and open-ended than Habermas' account of the "public sphere" (see Best and Gheciu, Chapter 2, this volume), which entails assuming the transformation of the public/private distinction from a distinction between the individual and political as in Arendt's reading of classical political theory, towards one founded on the emergence of "civil society" as a sphere distinct from both state and individuals, specific to capitalist modernity, and underpinning Habermas' claims. Habermas' account of the "erosion" of this public sphere has much in common with more recent claims about the erosion of public authority by privatization, but what we need perhaps to be attentive to, unless we collapse into nostalgia, is that this may also be in part because of the erosion of the social conditions of the "bourgeois public sphere," namely clear distinctions between state, civil society, and individuals. If relations between these are changing, then we need to be attentive to how the public is being reconstituted, and not simply take for granted a narrative of decline and erosion.

The classical account of the public is highly pertinent in relation to climate change governance – as it entails in effect the processes by which collectivities deliberate and decide how to act. It is also more open-ended – in essence it is, like Habermas, focused on the public as "sphere," but arguably permits a range of possible ways in which this sort of space may be constituted. In this account, public refers perhaps most fundamentally to a notion of a specific sort of social space, which involves both deliberative and decisional processes, arising out of our recognition of our dwelling together in a "common world." It is a space where the individual agents are required in effect to attempt to transcend their own interests and consider the interests of the collectivity. But at the same time that collectivity is not held necessarily to have any particular interests a priori – those interests arrive out of the collective deliberation. The transcendence of their own interests arises in the course of the deliberation.

From this conception of the public, at least three things flow. First, the notion of public is already understood as a practice; it arises precisely out of the inter-subjective deliberations between agents. So even while the public is a sort of space, its quality is made precisely by the practices that constitute it – the ways that agents interact. The space does not logically exist prior to the practices themselves, and multiple types of public space might be created by different sorts of deliberative and/or agonistic practices. Second, it can be understood either as a process of consensus-formation, informing some standard accounts of democratic politics (e.g. Crick 1962), or as inevitably agonistic, as is perhaps more commonly emphasized in contemporary democratic theory (e.g. Mouffe 2000, 2005; in relation to environmental politics, see in particular Torgerson 1999). Third, whichever of these latter two accounts one privileges, it remains the case that this account of public as a sort of political space reinforces the deliberative turn in much recent democratic theorizing, including in attempts to think about democracy in global contexts (see especially Dryzek 2006, 2011).[1]

In relation to existing debates, what this account of the public as a certain sort of deliberative space suggests is that it is not possible or perhaps particularly useful, a priori, to decide on whether a particular actor is "private" or "public."[2] Rather, the notion of public applies to the character of their interaction, i.e. the practices by which their relations are sustained.

But the practice of the public in this classical account has various assumptions embedded in it about both the nature of the authority that the public operates through, and the nature of the decisions that are deliberated on and made in public spaces. The attempt to articulate a sense of a "green public sphere" (Torgerson 1999) within a state-centric framework presumes the existence of this central authority. Specifically, a central authority is presumed to exist, so that a single site of deliberation and decision-making exists that can both take and then enforce decisions. Simultaneously, the sorts of decisions that are presumed are single, one-shot decisions. Should we go to war or not? Should we raise

---

[1]   Mouffe in fact (e.g. Mouffe 2005: 5) contrasts the deliberative account of politics to the agonistic, or conflictual one. Dryzek however represents the approach I adopt here in emphasising that a deliberative account of politics can also emphasise the agonistic nature of that deliberative process (see in particular Dryzek 1999). For Arendt, whom Mouffe regards as in the "consensual" camp, "To be political, to live in a *polis*, meant that everything was decided through words and persuasion and not through force and violence" (Arendt 1958: 26). But the focus on "words and persuasion" does not necessarily imply a lack of conflict and agonism.

[2]   I cannot claim to have been able to totally avoid such categorizations in what follows. Where "public" and "private" are used as ways to categorize different actors, however, I try to restrict this to where others (academics or social movements) identify actors in relation to this dichotomy – this is most obvious in the debate about the privatization of governance, which I contend is itself a part of the reconstitution of the public around climate change. Ruggie (2004), notably, falls back into this characterization of actors as public or private, sitting uneasily with his conceptualization of the public as a domain.

a tax on *X* or not? Should we rebalance the powers of different elements of the polity? They may be *complicated* (given the dilemmas they involve, the competing values, and interests to be weighed), but they are not *complex* in the sense used within complexity theory.

In the context of complexity, without central authority, with ongoing, iterated decisions across a wide range of types of actors, with great changes implied in the daily practices of all people around the world, with decisions that generate non-linear and irreversible effects, and with great uncertainty about impacts of governance actions, this classical sort of public space exemplified by the agora cannot exist, and a "greened" version as elaborated by Torgerson (1999) fails to fully capture the dynamics of the situation. At this point we could get all nostalgic and bemoan the decline of democracy, as does a good deal of literature on "globalization" as a threat to democracy, or as Arendt (1958) herself did with regard to the "decline of the public realm." Or we could rethink the ways in which the qualities of the classic public space are being practiced in these sorts of conditions. The rest of this chapter explores what seem to me two of the central elements in which we can see such practices evolving. The analytic approach is illustrative rather than claiming to describe all the possible ways in which the public is being practiced in climate change governance.

Reconstituting publics I: legitimizing "privatized" governance

The first of these forms of reconstituted public practices in relation to climate change emerges in relation to the discursive contestation of the broad swath of private, transnational, multilevel governance projects. This has produced two types of public space: one set of deliberative spaces, as those involved in "privatized" governance set up stakeholder and other participative governance arrangements in response to legitimation problems they face; and another which is the agonistic space between proponents and opponents of such governance arrangements.

A commonplace argument is that these various forms of new governance practice should be interpreted principally as a "privatization" of (environmental) governance (e.g. Cashore 2002; Clapp 1998; Levy and Newell 2005; Mansfield 2008; Newell 2008; Saurin 2001; see also Best and Gheciu, Chapter 2, this volume). Both social movements and many academics have widely criticized environmental governance, and perhaps especially climate change governance, as operating through a privatized logic.

Arguments about the privatization of environmental governance highlight a number of distinct elements in this process. In some instances, it is that private sector actors are engaging directly in governance themselves, raising basic questions about accountability and democratic legitimacy (Bäckstrand 2008; Bernstein 2011). In others, it is that private sector actors start to make the rules serving their own interests, which then get rubber stamped by states (see Clapp 1998, on the International Organization for Standardization, for example). In others still, and notably in the climate change context, privatization entails the direct transformation of public goods into private ones. This is the logic of carbon markets – that it transforms the atmosphere from a common into a bundle of rights to emit carbon (cap and trade markets) or promises not to emit carbon (carbon offset markets) that are constructed as private property rights that can then be bought and sold in the marketplace. This initial privatization of the atmosphere has a colonial quality, in that it entrenches existing inequalities in use of the atmospheric commons by turning *de facto* emissions levels into *de jure* emissions rights (see variously Bachram 2004; Böhm and Dabhi 2009; Gilbertson and Reyes 2009; Lohmann 2005, 2006), and because the resulting carbon offset markets themselves produce a range of socio-ecological injustices.

In the context of these legitimacy challenges, those promoting such "privatized" governance seek to respond to shore up the legitimacy of themselves as actors and of the projects they promote. There are a variety of aspects to such re-legitimization processes (see also Paterson 2010, for other aspects); in this context, two are worth picking up on. Both can be understood in effect as public practices: reaffirmations of claims about climate change as a common concern, and engagements with what might be called a public space around climate change, as articulated above.

First is an attempt to deploy the notion of public goods as the *raison d'être* of the project itself – as outlined above, it is useful to see the notion of public goods as a performative discursive practice that helps to constitute issues as public, rather than a detached analytical account of climate change. In numerous legitimizing statements, those promoting such governance of the climate make such discursive moves. For example, James Cameron, chair of the Carbon Disclosure Project (on this, see in particular Harmes 2011; Kolk, Levy, and Pinkse 2008; or www.cdproject.net/en-US/Pages/HomePage.aspx) and of carbon finance company Climate Change Capital, stated to the UN General Assembly in 2008 at a meeting on climate change finance that "The scale of the problem and the time constraints require huge private capital investments today which can help deliver the public good associated with reducing emissions" (Climate Change Capital 2008). He went on to argue that states were unable to generate the amount of investment necessary, so the mobilization of financial markets was necessary to generate the flow of

Table 7.1 *Consultative arrangements in private climate governance projects*

Governance project	Main scope of consultation	Nature of consultation	Main organizations involved
Carbon Disclosure Project	Global/national	Web, meetings, letters	Private sector Government
Gold Standard	Global (for the program) Local (for projects)	Web, meetings, letters	Local communities NGOs
Voluntary Carbon Standard	Global	Meetings, letters	Private sector
VER+ program[a]	Global (for the program) National/local (for projects)	Not specified	Private sector Local communities

[a] *Note*: VER has become the standardized name for a credit issued in the Voluntary Carbon Market, referring to a "Verified Emissions Reduction." VER+ simply uses this acronym in its name.

funds to low carbon development. The CDP's own statements make similar claims about their public-goods provision rationale: "Climate change is a global problem which needs a global solution. It is only through collaboration and collective action that we will achieve a low carbon economy and that is why we work with partners and through alliances all over the world" (CDP 2011).

A second response to this legitimation problem is the deployment of a wide range of arrangements whereby the organizers of these governance projects assemble a diverse range of actors into the development of the project itself – in other words, to define who makes up the "public" for this initiative. So while a governance initiative may have specific sorts of actors behind them, they routinely enroll others into the initiative to at least portray the sense of it having the backing of a broad swath of global society. Table 7.1 gives a summary of such arrangements for some specific types of climate governance initiatives, the CDP as representative of investor-led governance projects, and three examples of certification projects in the Voluntary Carbon Market (VCM).[3]

[3] This refers to the part of the carbon market which is not created by regulatory measures, but rather through the desire of companies and to a lesser extent individuals to offset their carbon missions through investing in emissions reductions projects elsewhere, usually in the developing world. Beyond the general legitimacy problem of the marketization of climate, the specific legitimacy problem facing this market has been the credibility of claims about emissions reductions from projects. In response, many NGOs and business groups have stepped in with certification systems to validate the claims made by project developers. There are now around twenty such systems in place. On these certification systems, see Bumpus and Liverman (2008) or Newell and Paterson (2010: 7).

Many of these organizations also have boards that attempt to establish broad representation. The board of the Voluntary Carbon Standard (VCS), for example, contains members from various business sectors that are involved in the market (consultants such as Ecofys, financiers, and project brokers such as CantorCO2e, verifiers such as SGS, companies seeking to offset emissions such as BP or Taiheiyo Cement) and business lobbies (the International Emissions Trading Association, who in fact initiated the VCS process), but also a range of NGOs (the Climate Group, World Resources Institute), and one state-run quango (the California Climate Action Registry). The "public" here has a rather particular constitution: but while the representation is clearly business-dominated, it represents a broad variety of business interests, and the attempt to branch out to a broader range of interests is indicative of the desire to respond to the legitimacy crisis of "privatized" governance.

The Gold Standard is perhaps paradigmatic in relation to these consultative arrangements. It was a project developed by a group of environmental NGOs (ENGOs), led by the Worldwide Fund for Nature (WWF), and sought to gain wide acceptance among the ENGO community. It is backed by over sixty such NGOs (Gold Standard 2009a). The Gold Standard's certification scheme "was the result of an extensive 12-month workshop and web-based consultation process conducted by an independent Standards Advisory Board composed of NGOs, scientists, project developers and government representatives" (Gold Standard 2008: 4). The board comprises members from a broad range of social sectors, but "at least 50% of its members must be recruited from the Gold Standard NGO supporter community" (Gold Standard 2008: 4). For individual projects, the Gold Standard also requires extensive consultative arrangements with those affected by projects (Gold Standard 2009b).

One way to read these processes is as a dynamic of counter-hegemony and hegemonic co-optation. In this interpretation, the responses by the dominant social forces that promote various private governance practices are driven by a desire to forestall broader legitimacy crises, by bringing in relatively moderate elements from environmental movements, in order to weaken the force of more critical elements and split the environmental movement more generally. The logic of stakeholder processes, for example, in this interpretation, is to present what are effectively corporate-led processes as open deliberative ones, as Whitman (2008) argues in his detailed account of the emergence of "stakeholders" into policy discourse.

This interpretation certainly has a good deal going for it (Paterson 2010). It is perhaps best seen in the emergence of certification systems in the VCM. In the earlier days of this market, through to around 2006, the majority of project developers simply asserted the carbon reductions from a given project; there was little by way of third-party evaluation or a certification system against which the project was judged. By 2010, 93 percent of VCM projects use third-party verification and one of the certification systems such as VCS or the Gold Standard mentioned above (Hamilton *et al.* 2010: 57). Many of these certification systems can be thought of as alliances between business organizations and environmental NGOs, with varying degrees of initiating agency by each type of organization, in effect representing varying sorts of strategies to co-opt environmental NGOs into a market-led governance practice.

But to interpret this simply as a power struggle between "public" and "private," with private governance serving to shore up the power of transnational business, relies on the reading of public/private as two types of agent and institutional locations. From the point of view of the argument developed here, it is more important to think through the type of space that is created by the governance practice itself. In this light, the dynamic outlined above can be understood as creating public spaces in two sorts of ways. The first of these is that the consultative processes illustrated above can be understood as the construction of public spaces within the governance arrangements themselves. There are clearly power relations involved here; it would not be persuasive to suggest that they represent open spaces with equal participation by all types of actor. But the public sphere has never been free from power relations (from the formal exclusion of slaves, women, and foreigners in ancient Athens onwards), so this should not disqualify these practices from the category of "public."

But the second is that the overall process is itself a sort of agonistic deliberative space. This is the sort of conceptualization of transnational democracy developed by John Dryzek in particular. Dryzek argues in effect that global democratization should not be understood as an unfolding of a cosmopolitan logic associated most famously with David Held, but rather as the emergence of a space of discursive contestation, where competing discourses vie with each other for success in contexts where agents are engaged in both strategic and communicative action (Dryzek 2006). "Transnational democracy of this sort is not electoral democracy, and it is not institutionalized in formal organization. Instead it is to be sought in communicatively competent decentralized control over the content and relative weight of globally consequential discourses" (Dryzek 2006: 154). As suggested above, Dryzek's account refuses the idea that we must choose between visions of the public sphere and of politics as *either* deliberative *or* agonistic.

Seen this way, the public realm in climate governance is not only to be found in each individual governance initiative, but also in the contestation between competing discourses underpinning opposition to and promotion of this way of responding to climate change as a whole. Opposition to these "privatized" forms of climate governance is couched broadly in terms of what Dryzek elsewhere calls a discourse of "green radicalism" focused on the question of global social justice, while their promotion is framed variously in terms of economic rationalism, sustainable development, or ecological modernization (Dryzek 2005). Conceptually, what this implies is that the public as practice consists not so much in the claims any specific actor makes about the quality of climate change and their relation to it, but in the character of the interaction between these competing claims and the movements that articulate them. To the extent that climate change governance is practiced through these competing discourses, its governance has a public quality.

But as Dryzek emphasizes, the mere existence of "decentralised networked governance" (Dryzek 2005: 155) does not make it democratic. For this to be the case, it requires that there are processes that mean that attempts to forestall deliberation fail, so that a vibrant public sphere persists. In the case of climate governance, I argue that this occurs principally because the agents who might have the power to shut down debate (the targets of critiques of "privatized governance" – transnational corporations and their institutional allies in the World Bank, WTO, etc.) are themselves forced to engage in deliberation precisely because climate change confuses their capacity to engage in purely calculative and strategic practices – they are engaged in a series of learning processes about what their interests are.[4] I turn now to this point in more detail.

Re-constituting publics II: learning and deliberating

There is a second logic also at play, perhaps a bit deeper than the dynamic of de- and re-legitimation, arising out of the "superwicked problem" logic. Many practices of governance in climate, whether nominally "public" or "private," operate through a range of practices that in effect constitute an agora operating in the context of complex learning processes and in the absence of a single central authority. There are a variety of possible ways of illustrating and exploring these practices. I will focus here on two: the rhetoric and practice of "learning by doing," and the way that the space of "negotiations" is being organized to facilitate such learning and deliberation.

---

[4] I have long argued this is also the case in interstate climate change negotiations – in particular Paterson (1996: 6).

Learning by doing

The first, most obvious, way to illustrate this learning logic to climate governance is through the more or less ubiquitous invocation of "learning by doing" in relation to climate change.[5] Learning by doing is deployed in these contexts to illustrate precisely that we cannot know in advance of our actions their likely consequences. In many contexts it is intended to refer to a "phase" – that we start by "learning by doing" and what this should result in is better knowledge that would enable us to act more definitively. In other contexts, this conceit is lost and the recognition of an open-ended process of learning is present.

While this process could be illustrated in various contexts, the Clean Development Mechanism (CDM) of the Kyoto Protocol is exemplary here. It has its origins in the attempts by industrialized states to work out means of meeting commitments they were envisaging to undertake in the UNFCCC. The approach that emerged, promoted initially by the Norwegians and the USA, was for countries to be able to invest in other countries and get credited for this against their own emissions reductions obligations – termed in climate change debates "joint implementation." In response to a number of controversies, notably about whether developing countries would participate in such projects, a pilot phase of "activities implemented jointly" was developed in the run-up to the Kyoto Conference of the Parties in 1997, and termed explicitly a "learning by doing phase" (Newell and Paterson 2010). This phase aimed to deal both with the basic questions about such project-based mechanisms – how to measure emissions reductions from projects, how to allocate emissions reductions between participants, whether such projects are a good thing at all – but also with the more managerial or operational questions.

As projects started however, states were also negotiating what would become the Kyoto Protocol. The USA in particular made such "flexibility" mechanisms a condition of its signing such a treaty, and bargained hard for them to be included. As an outcome in particular of North–South conflicts on the issue, in the Kyoto Protocol there are two such mechanisms. The Joint Implementation provision deals with projects and investments between industrialized countries, while the CDM deals with projects between industrialized and developing countries. What is pertinent in this regard is that the early years of the CDM were themselves regarded as a "learning by doing" phase. Over time, however, the term "phase" fell by

---

[5] As a banal but instructive comparison, Google gives 359,000 hits for "learning by doing" and "climate change" combined, as opposed to 847,000 for what might seem the more obvious combination of "public goods" and "climate change."

the wayside and the CDM became a mechanism whose presumed mode of operation became "learning by doing." This is for the participants in the market – the project developers, investors, certifiers and verifiers, and so on – for whom a constant learning process about new types of projects, methodologies for measuring emissions reductions, or ways of working, has become the norm. But it is also for the governors of the CDM – the states and the institutional actors in the CDM Executive Board and Methodologies Panel – who are engaged in constant reflection on the governance principles and organizational format of the CDM. This "reflection" or learning process is also highly politicized, since within that context there are clearly identifiable actors pushing their interests. There are project developers and investors who wish to maximize the number and speed of project approvals. There are verifiers seeking to ensure their rents from their authority to verify projects are maintained. And there are environmental NGOs seeking to maintain or enhance the "environmental integrity" of the CDM process. As hinted earlier on, this could be analyzed as a process of hegemony, counter-hegemony, and co-optation between dominant and resistant social forces. Nevertheless, a key dynamic in the process has been the desire to act without anything like full knowledge of whether the actions undertaken will "work," and to reflect on those practices as they are developed, and a process whereby what is intended to be a discrete "phase" unravels into a more open-ended process.[6]

If climate governance involves practices that generate new sorts of public space, then the physical spaces it uses may give one hint to the quality of these public practices. Figure 7.1 shows the organization of the main space for the 14th Conference of the Parties to the UNFCCC, in Poznań in 2009. This involves two large formal meeting rooms (Halls 7A and 8), one hall transformed into offices for delegations, and another into a media center. But these formal spaces were integrated with four large concourses in which all of the booths for national delegations, NGOs, business organizations, think-tanks, and international organizations were mixed up, as well as a café and various spaces with comfortable chairs and coffee tables. The organization of space was designed to maximize the interaction between a wide variety of different types of actor.[7]

---

[6] This passage is based on direct observations undertaken while attending the 14th Conference of the Parties to the UNFCCC in Poznań, Poland, in December 2009.

[7] This is in part an arbitrary feature of the space in Poznań, which was in a large business convention centre. The contrast with the space at COP15 in Copenhagen a year later was striking. In Copenhagen, there was much more segregated space, with the NGO booths separated from the government booths, and both separated from the formal meeting rooms. The point here is that the organizers of climate negotiations sought to take advantage of the opportunities that such spaces enabled. In Copenhagen, the architecture impeded this desire, however.

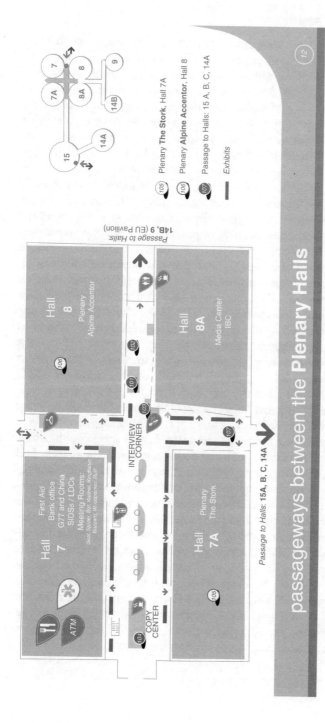

Figure 7.1 The space of climate governance: the climate change agora at Poznań. *Source:* United Nations (2008).

Anyone who has been to a more conventional UN space, such as the meeting rooms in the basement at the UN's headquarters in New York, would notice the striking difference. Those spaces can be understood as classic agoras, spaces for deliberation amongst citizens only (state representatives in this context), with other actors separated physically to relegate them to purely observer status. They also have the theatrical qualities associated with an agora; the space is organized to emphasize the grandeur of the setting and the decisions to be made in it (the UN Security Council room is iconic here) as well as to make the meetings a spectacle for onlookers. A number of spaces in global environmental governance have this theatrical or spectacular quality (Death 2010; Doran 1993), as does diplomacy more generally (Constantinou 1996: 95–124).

In Poznań, by contrast, space was organized to render the boundaries between formal negotiating spaces and informal spaces for conversations between a huge range of actors highly fluid, and maximize the possibilities for chance encounters with other actors or simply through noticing publications at booths. The possibility of agonism within the space was also envisaged; the environmental NGOs' daily "Fossil of the Day" awards,[8] awarded to the three countries judged to have blocked progress in the negotiations most during the day, were held at the Climate Action Network booth at the bottom of the map, in the corridor between Halls 7A and 8A, i.e. directly at the exit where delegates would have to pass in order to leave the convention centre.

Even the spaces for formal "negotiations" were very different to more traditional ones. While there was a stage for the chairs of meetings, the secretariat supporting the meeting, and any principal speakers, the space lacked the spectacular grandeur of more traditional diplomatic spaces. This change is mediated by other technologies. In the place of the fixed earpieces attached to desks, conventional in most UN meeting rooms, delegates picked up a mobile headset on entering a hall, and could thus walk through the room while listening to the current intervention in the UN language of their choice. Furthermore, the acoustic quality of the room is fundamentally different, enabling different kinds of public practice. Traditional UN negotiating rooms are designed to dampen sound, and participants listen to the debate via the headsets. These rooms have an eerie quietness to them, with someone's voice vaguely discernible but not their words. The engagement between speakers is correspondingly dry, technocratic. In contrast, in Poznań, the speakers were amplified through PA systems, enabling more theatrical, even impassioned interventions.

---

[8] See www.fossiloftheday.com.

Many of the meetings were also organized very differently to more traditional UN meetings. In the place of the basic negotiating text, around which a long series of interventions by delegations take place, many meetings were organized as workshops, around a specific theme or problem in the negotiations. Selected delegations, specifically representing broader groups of countries, as well as speakers from specific intergovernmental organizations, were invited to give short presentations, with the aid of PowerPoint, and then subjected to a question-and-answer period, more akin to an academic seminar than a negotiation. These workshops often had a specific question they would address, such as "What emissions reductions are feasible by 2020, 2030 and 2050?," or similar. The focus was thus clearly on a collective learning process rather than the more traditional line-by-line intervention around a specific negotiating text designed to set the scene for backroom bargaining.

This sort of architecture and the sort of public practice it enables can be seen in other sites of climate governance. At Carbon Expo, for example, the "global carbon market fair and conference," space is similarly organized where formal meeting spaces are closely integrated with booths for the organizations attending, multiple sites for coffee, lunches, and snacks, and ample open space for networking. Overall, if the emerging "global public domain" entails that the "system of states is becoming embedded in a broader, albeit still thin and partial, institutionalized arena concerned with the production of global public goods" (Ruggie 2004: 500), then these spaces are the physical organization of how this embedding is organized, especially when the precise nature of how these "global public goods" are to be produced is uncertain and thus needs to be constantly reflected upon.

Conclusions

These processes can be interpreted as part of the practice of public life – deliberation and decision-making, seeking consensus in agonistic situations (a paradoxical process, clearly) – in a radically different socio-ecological context than the classical accounts of public space were generated in. The practice of public life becomes pluralized, sites of decision-making become unclear, processes become much more highly focused on deliberation and inter-subjective learning than on decision-making per se, and thus become open-ended rather than closely circumscribed. Otherwise put, if we can identify, with Thomas Risse (2000; see also Best and Gheciu, Chapter 2, this volume), three logics of social action – bargaining, rule-guided behavior, and communicative action – then all three of these practices are transformed by the inability of agents to calculate the effects of their strategic action, decide what the appropriate norm or cause-and-effect relationship is, or identify the object around which a reasoned consensus might emerge. The public practices of climate change are precisely focused on establishing what each of these three logics might entail, without any sense that some sort of definitive account of any of the three might emerge. The process itself becomes the object.

Conflict is, however, far from removed from this process, and indeed one can argue that a good deal of the learning comes itself from the way that those involved in a variety of governance processes, whether inter-state or other, have to encounter those opposed to the governance initiatives being developed. I have tried to argue that they cannot shut down or ignore this contestation largely because they are themselves involved in a set of learning processes about how they want to respond to the radically novel set of challenges raised by climate change, a set of challenges that effectively involve the first ever globally organized socio-technical transformation of the global economy and everyday life (Newell and Paterson 2010), in conditions of great complexity which render the outcomes of any specific practice highly uncertain. In Chapter 2 (this volume), Best and Gheciu draw a distinction between transformative and reinforcing public practices. What strikes me about the dynamics explored here is that this question is undecidable. While we might see an inherent transformative logic in the argument just presented, and in the more general logic of climate change (as the pursuit of decarbonization of the global economy), many of the practices can themselves be understood as attempts to reinforce existing hierarchies of power, attempts to govern the emergent processes of responding to climate change in ways that forestall radical political realignments of power. But at the same time, the need to engage in learning processes and the uncertainties involved limits the ability of otherwise powerful actors such as transnational firms to impose their goals on society as a whole.

This sort of conceptualization of the evolving global sphere has much in common with Ruggie's (2004) account of the "reconstitution of the global public domain." But it extends Ruggie's logic by suggesting how the spaces of governance are significantly affected by the qualities of climate change as a "superwicked" problem. This means that the focus of the public practices of governance is more on learning processes than authoritative decision-making, since what actors are trying to achieve, and how they are to achieve it, are highly uncertain. It also means that these practices are plural – there is no one single "global public domain" but rather the emergence of a varied set of public domains and practices associated with them. The account here also draws more fully on Dryzek's account of global democratization as a process of discursive contestation. So, while for Ruggie, the public domain exists primarily in the way that those developing governance practices respond to criticism, for Dryzek, and in this chapter, the public domain exists as much in the agonistic space between opposing discursive forces.

REFERENCES

Aldy, Joseph, and Robert Stavins, eds. 2007. *Architectures for Agreement: Addressing Global Climate Change in the Post-Kyoto World.* Cambridge: Cambridge University Press.

Andonova, Liliana, Michele M. Betsill, and Harriet Bulkeley. 2009. "Transnational climate governance." *Global Environmental Politics* 9(2): 52–73.

Arendt, Hannah 1958. *On the Human Condition.* Chicago, IL: University of Chicago Press.

Bachram, Heidi. 2004. "Climate fraud and carbon colonialism: the new trade in greenhouse gases." *Capitalism, Nature, Socialism* 15(4): 5–20.

Bäckstrand, Karin. 2008. "Accountability of networked climate governance: the rise of transnational climate partnerships." *Global Environmental Politics* 8(3): 74–104.

Barrett, Scott. 2003. *Environment and Statecraft: The Strategy of Environmental Treaty-Making.* Oxford: Oxford University Press.

2007. *Why Cooperate? The Incentive to Supply Global Public Goods.* Oxford: Oxford University Press.

Betsill, Michele, and Harriet Bulkeley. 2006. "Cities and the multilevel governance of global climate change." *Global Governance* 12(2): 141–59.

Bernstein, Steven. 2011. "Legitimacy in intergovernmental and non-state global governance." *Review of International Political Economy* 18(1): 17–51.

Bodansky, Daniel, with contributions from Sophie Chou, Christier Jorge-Tresolini. 2004. *International Climate Efforts beyond 2012: A Survey of Approaches.* Washington, D.C.: Pew Center on Global Climate Change.

Böhm, Steffen, and Siddartha Dabhi, eds. 2009. *Upsetting the Offset: The Political Economy of Carbon Markets.* Colchester: Mayfly Books.

Bulkeley Harriet, Liliana Andonova, Karin Bäckstrand, Michele Betsill, Daniel Compagnon, Rosaleen Duffy, Ans Kolk, Matthew Hoffmann, David Levy, Peter Newell, Tori Milledge, Matthew Paterson, Philipp Pattberg, and Stacy VanDeveer. 2012. "Governing climate change transnationally: Assessing the evidence from a survey of sixty initiatives." *Environment and Planning C: Government and Policy* 30(4): 591–612.

Bumpus, Adam, and Diana Liverman. 2008. "Accumulation by decarbonization and the governance of carbon offsets." *Economic Geography* 84(2): 127–55.

Carbon Disclosure Project. 2011. "What we do – Alliances." www.cdproject.net/

Cashore, Benjamin. 2002. "Legitimacy and the privatization of environmental governance: how non-state-market-driven (NSMD) governance systems gain rule-making authority." *Governance* 15(4): 504–29.

Clapp, Jennifer. 1998. "The privatization of global environmental governance: ISO 14000 and the developing world." *Global Governance* 4(3): 295–316.

Climate Change Capital. 2008. "James Cameron speaks at UN General Assembly: urges UN to encourage entrepreneurship to help combat climate change." Press release, June 09. www.climatechangecapital.com/

Constantinou, Costas. 1996. *On the Way to Diplomacy*. Minneapolis, MN: University of Minnesota Press.

Crick, Bernard. 1962. *In Defence of Politics*. London: Penguin.

Cutler, Claire A., Virginia Haufler, and Tony Porter, eds. 1999. *Private Authority and International Affairs*. Albany, NY: State University of New York Press.

Death, Carl. 2010. *Governing Sustainable Development: Partnerships, Protests and Power at the World Summit*. New York: Routledge.

Doran, Peter. 1993. "The Earth Summit (UNCED): ecology as spectacle." *Paradigms* 7(1): 55–65.

Dryzek, John. 1999. "Transnational democracy." *Journal of Political Philosophy* 7(1): 30–51

Dryzek, John S. 2005. *The Politics of the Earth: Environmental Discourses*, 2nd edn. Oxford: Oxford University Press.

　　2006. *Deliberative Global Politics: Discourse and Democracy in a Divided World*. Cambridge: Polity Press.

　　2011. *Foundations and Frontiers of Deliberative Governance*. Oxford: Oxford University Press.

Gilbertson, Tamra and Oscar Reyes. 2009. *Carbon Trading: How It Works and Why It Fails*. Uppsala: Dag Hammarskjöld Foundation.

Gold Standard. 2008. *Gold Standard Toolkit 2.0*, July 2008. Geneva: Ecofys, TÜV-SÜD, and FIELD.

　　2009a. *Annual Report 2009*. Geneva: Gold Standard Foundation.

　　2009b. "The Gold Standard briefing for potential supporters." www. cdmgoldstandard.org/

Haas, Peter M. 2008. "Climate change governance after Bali." *Global Environmental Politics* 8(3): 1–7.

Hamilton, Katherine, Milo Sjardin, Molly Peters-Stanley, and Thomas Marcello. 2010. *Building Bridges: State of the Voluntary Carbon Markets 2010*. New York: Ecosystem Marketplace and Bloomberg New Energy Finance.

Harmes, Adam. 2011. "The limits of carbon disclosure: theorizing the business case for investor environmentalism." *Global Environmental Politics* 11(2): 98–119.

Hoffmann, Matthew J. 2005. *Ozone Depletion and Climate Change: Constructing a Global Response*. Albany, NY: State University of New York Press.

　　2011. *Climate Governance at the Crossroads: Experimenting with Climate Change after Kyoto*. Oxford: Oxford University Press.

Homer-Dixon, Thomas. 2006. *The Upside of Down: Catastrophe, Creativity, and the Renewal of Civilization*. Washington, D.C.: Island Press.

IPCC. 2001. *Climate Change 2001: Working Group III: Mitigation: Summary for Policymakers*. Geneva: World Meteorological Organization/United Nations Environment Programme.

2007. *IPCC Fourth Assessment Report, Working Group III: Summary for Policymakers.* Geneva: World Meteorological Organization/United Nations Environment Programme.

Keohane, Robert O., and Kal Raustiala. 2008. *Toward a Post-Kyoto Climate Change Architecture: A Political Analysis*, Discussion Paper No. 08–01. Cambridge, MA: Harvard Project on International Climate Agreements.

Keohane, Robert O., and David G. Victor. 2010. *The Regime Complex for Climate Change*, Discussion Paper No. 2010–33. Cambridge, MA: Harvard Project on International Climate Agreements.

Kolk, Ans, David Levy, and Jonatan Pinkse. 2008. "Corporate responses in an emerging climate regime: the institutionalization and commensuration of carbon disclosure." *European Accounting Review* 17(4): 719–45.

Levin, Kelly, Benjamin Cashore, Steven Bernstein, and Graeme Auld. 2009. "Playing it forward? Path dependency, increasing returns, progressive incrementalism, and the super wicked problem of climate change." Paper presented to the *Climate Change: Global Risks, Challenges and Decisions Congress*, March 10–12, 2009, Copenhagen, Denmark.

Levy, David, and Peter Newell, eds. 2005. *The Business of Global Environmental Governance.* Cambridge, MA: MIT Press.

Lohmann, Larry. 2005. "Marketing and making carbon dumps: commodification, calculation and counterfactuals in climate change mitigation." *Science as Culture* 14(3): 203–35.

2006. *Carbon Trading: A Critical Conversation on Climate Change, Privatization and Power.* Uppsala: Dag Hammarskjöld Foundation.

Mansfield, Becky, ed. 2008. *Privatization: Property and the Remaking of Nature–Society Relations.* Oxford: Blackwell.

Mouffe, Chantal. 2000. *The Democratic Paradox.* London: Verso.

2005. *On the Political.* New York: Routledge.

Newell, Peter. 2008. "The political economy of global environmental governance." *Review of International Studies* 34(3): 507–29.

Newell, Peter, and Matthew Paterson. 2010. *Climate Capitalism: Global Warming and the Transformation of the Global Economy.* Cambridge: Cambridge University Press.

Paterson, Matthew. 1996. *Global Warming and Global Politics.* New York: Routledge.

2010. "Legitimation and accumulation in climate change governance." *New Political Economy* 15(3): 345–68.

Pattberg, Philipp, and Johannes Stripple. 2008. "Beyond the public and private divide: remapping transnational climate governance in the twenty-first century." *International Environmental Agreements: Politics, Law and Economics* 8(4): 367–88.

Risse, Thomas. 2000. "'Let's argue!' Communicative action in world politics." *International Organization* 54(1): 1–40.

Rittel, Horst W. J., and Melvin M. Webber. 1973. "Dilemmas in a general theory of planning." *Policy Sciences* 4: 155–69.

Ruggie, John Gerard. 2004. "Reconstituting the global public domain: issues, actors, and practices." *European Journal of International Relations* 10(4): 499–531.

Saurin, Julian. 2001. "Global environmental crisis as the 'Disaster Triumphant': the private capturing of public goods." *Environmental Politics* 10(4): 63–84.

Scrase, Ivan, and Adrian Smith. 2010. "The (non-)politics of managing low-carbon technical transitions." In *Climate Change and Political Strategy*, edited by H. Compston, pp. 49–68. New York: Routledge.

Stern, Nicholas. 2006. *Stern Review: The Economics of Climate Change.* Cambridge: Cambridge University Press.

Tickell, Oliver. 2008. *Kyoto2: How to Manage the Global Greenhouse.* London: Zed Books.

Torgerson, Douglas. 1999. *The Promise of Green Politics: Environmentalism and the Public Sphere.* Durham, NC: Duke University Press.

United Nations. 1992. *United Nations Framework Convention on Climate Change.* New York: United Nations.

   2008. *United Nations Climate Change Conference, Poznań, Poland, December 1–12, 2008, COP 14 Plans.* Bonn: United Nations Framework Convention on Climate Change Secretariat. unfccc.int/files/meetings/cop_14/

Unruh, Gregory C. 2002. "Escaping carbon lock-in." *Energy Policy* 30(4): 317–25.

Urry, John. 2010. "Consuming the planet to excess." *Theory, Culture and Society* 27(2–3): 191–212.

Victor, David. 2001. *The Collapse of the Kyoto Protocol and the Struggle to Slow Global Warming.* Princeton, NJ: Princeton University Press.

Whitman, Darrell. 2008. "'Stakeholders' and the politics of environmental policymaking." In *The Crisis of Global Environmental Governance: Towards a New Political Economy of Sustainability*, edited by Jacob Park, Ken Conca, and Matthias Finger, pp. 163–92. New York: Routledge.

Wolin, Sheldon 1960. *Politics and Vision: Continuity and Innovation in Western Political Thought.* Boston, MA: Little Brown.

8 Transforming the logic of security provision in post-Communist Europe

Alexandra Gheciu

At first glance, scholars and practitioners seeking to understand the transformation of the field of security in post-Communist Europe might be tempted to interpret developments in those countries in terms of a straightforward evolution leading to the establishment of Western-style liberal-democratic arrangements.[1] From that perspective, processes of liberalization and European integration – involving the accession of most Central/East European countries to the EU and NATO – necessarily involved the creation of new types of public actors that are distinct from the (also newly created) private domain of activity. In contrast to the abusive behavior characteristic of the Communist era, we are told, the new public actors are engaged in the provision of domestic security in ways that conform to liberal-democratic norms and principles – above all, respect for human rights, transparency, and accountability.

Yet, a closer analysis of the dynamics of domestic security provision in former Communist states reveals a far more complicated – and normatively problematic – picture. As I suggest in this chapter, neither the nature of actors engaged in the provision of security as a key public good nor the practices performed by those actors can be understood unless we transcend conventional boundaries between public/private and domestic/international. In this chapter, I focus on developments in Bulgaria and Romania to illustrate my points. However, those developments are part of a broader set of transformations involved in the construction of liberalism in the former Communist bloc. Contemporary security providers in those countries are networks of actors that are not confined to a particular space or institutional domain; rather, they are both global and national, state and non-state, new and yet often with strong

This chapter draws on research sponsored by the Social Science Research Council of Canada (SSHRC). I would like to thank the fellows of the Bulgarian Centre for the Study of Democracy, in particular Philip Gounev, for their valuable research support.
[1] This is the prevailing discourse articulated by public officials in most Central/East European states.

connections to old (Communist-era) organizations. Those actors can be conceptualized as particular "communities of practice" that have emerged in a specific historical context – particularly post-Cold War processes of liberalization – and have been shaped by – but have also contributed to – a broader process of redefinition of what and where the "public" is.[2]

The analysis developed in this piece provides further evidence in support of the argument that if we are to understand the nature and role of contemporary security providers we need to question not only conventional, state-centered international relations (IR) approaches, but also much of the literature on private actors in global governance.[3] The problem with the literature on private actors and private authority is that, in general, it either fails to include private security in its analyses, or, when it does focus on the field of security, it portrays private actors as clearly distinct from if not opposed to the state. In essence, private security actors are largely depicted as being engaged in the exercise of an illicit form of authority (Hall and Bierstecker 2002: 1–21), or as marginal participants in practices of security provision (Börzel and Risse 2010). Yet, as we see below, security companies conventionally seen as belonging exclusively to the private domain are often constituted as agents of – rather than actors opposed to – public power.

Before going any further, let us clarify the various yet interrelated meanings of "public" in this chapter. To begin with – as noted in the framing chapter – the notion of "public" refers to public goods; for our purposes, the key public good is security and the provision of that particular public good has long been central to discourses of state legitimacy. As Max Weber (among others) reminded us, the existence of a public sphere of security that applies equally to all the citizens of a given state was a key dimension of the evolution of modern liberalism (Weber 1948; see also Loader and Walker 2007).

This idea of the security of the citizenry as a fundamental public good is linked to another idea of "public": the notion that certain actors (primarily state agents) can and should speak and act on its behalf, as opposed to pursuing their particular interests.[4] As a corollary to that, actors that protect the public good of security are recognized as having special duties but also special rights (e.g. the right to define norms of

---

[2] Following Adler, I define communities of practice as consisting of "people who are informally as well as contextually bound by a shared interest in learning and applying a common practice" (Adler 2005: 15).

[3] See also Abrahamsen and Williams 2011; Avant and Haufler (Chapter 3, this volume); Leander (Chapter 9, this volume).

[4] See Abrahamsen and Williams (Chapter 11, this volume).

appropriate behavior applicable to all citizens, and to resort to a multitude of measures, including coercion in support of those norms).[5] In the context of modern liberal thought and practice, the notion of special rights and special responsibilities is inextricably linked to norms of political legitimacy. These norms are concerned with the challenge of constituting and controlling the exercise of power within the social order "in a manner that simultaneously empowers institutions to perform valued collective functions, and prevents powerful institutions from degenerating into tyranny" (Macdonald 2010: 148). A key purpose served by liberal norms of political legitimacy is to set out the nature of the public goods/values and purposes that ought to be upheld by political institutions, and to prescribe institutional forms capable of upholding these public liberal values both by enabling a series of political actors to perform protective functions, and by constraining the abuse of their power. In essence, political legitimacy norms are concerned with public power: the power that needs to be institutionally enabled to promote public liberal values or goods, and at the same time institutionally restrained in order to protect those same values from a potential abuse of power (Macdonald 2010: 148).

There is another sense of the term "public" that is relevant to our study: the public as the community of citizens (or demos) that, as part of an imagined social contract, are the beneficiaries of the collective goods provided by the state and to whom the state is presumably accountable. As a host of scholars have noted, of key importance to modern liberal-democratic polities is the construction of a "responsible" public – in other words, the modern state needs to be, and has been, systematically involved in the socialization of citizens into liberal norms in an effort to ensure that those citizens exercise liberal freedoms in a rational, self-disciplined manner.[6] The analysis developed here shows that an effort to construct a responsible liberal public has also been part of the process of establishing liberal institutions – including in the field of security – in former Communist states. What is especially interesting in our case is that private entities have been able to take advantage of – and have also contributed to – practices through which the demos is being (re)constructed. The demos or general public being (re)constituted in former Communist polities has a specific set of duties to act as "responsible" participants in their own protection via a set of preventive measures of risk management. At the same time, however, this new public has a far

---

[5] See Walzer's argument about the "art of separation" that lies at the heart of liberalism (Walzer 1984: 315–30).
[6] See, for example, Dean 1999.

176   *Alexandra Gheciu*

more limited role than liberal theory would prescribe in debates about –
and in the process of holding accountable – domestic security providers.

The changing field of security in the era of globalization

At the risk of noting the obvious, let us start by recalling a point also made
by Avant and Haufler (Chapter 3, this volume): in the modern age, the
territorial state became synonymous with the provision of security. From
the point of view of citizens living in a modern state, the government's
commitment to provide equal protection to all of them was a defining
feature of the (imagined) social contract from which the rights and duties
of public authorities and private individuals derived. Indeed, it could be
argued that the very origins of the modern (and later liberal-democratic)
state were defined around the opposition between public and private
security (Abrahamsen and Williams 2011: 111). In principle – contrary
to the pre-modern age – security was not to be provided by private
individuals, nor was it to be offered only to some privileged groups or
classes. On the contrary, the modern state was based on the principle that
security was to be a public good, provided by the state and enjoyed by all
citizens regardless of their class or status.[7]

Yet, in parallel to almost ritualistic reaffirmations of the importance of
security as a public good provided by the state, in the past two decades
there has been a growing move to partly detach the provision of security
from the state and, contrary to the idea of a clear divide between public
and private actors in the sphere of security, to allow non-state entities,
especially private security companies, to play increasingly important roles
in the provision of that fundamental public good (Abrahamsen and
Williams 2008, 2011; Avant 2005, 2006; Haufler 1997, 2007; Johnston
1992; Leander 2005, 2011; Loader and Walker 2005, 2007; Percy 2007).

The proliferation of private security actors, both within the state and
across national boundaries, cannot be understood in abstraction from a
broad set of transformations of norms and practices of governance that
have occurred over the past two decades. To begin with, the late 1980s
and 1990s marked the rise to prominence of neoliberal norms and
policies. Neoliberal norms have served to legitimize the "outsourcing"
of functions that were previously seen as falling within the purview of the

---

[7] I am not denying the fact that, in practice, public force was sometimes used in support of
private interests under the pretext of promoting the public good (e.g. in dealing with labor
unrest in many countries). But, for our purposes, what matters is that the principle that
security should be a public good has continued to inform modern conceptions of politics,
and has also been systematically inscribed in modern legal and institutional arrangements
(e.g. recall the unique universal jurisdictional reach of the police).

state, and the partial commodification of security – leading to a situation in which, at least within certain limits, security becomes a service to be bought in the marketplace and a commodity capable of being exported as a set of technical capabilities, knowledge, and skills.[8]

The growing presence and importance of private security actors is also linked to the growing emphasis on prevention and risk management in the face of the uncertainties of the late modern world (Beck 1999, 2004; Coker 2002; Gheciu 2008; Ericson and Haggerty 1997). According to Beck, the current international concern with risk is largely a product of globalization, and a related sense of vulnerability in being part of a world system in which old protections (usually provided by nation–states) are increasingly becoming obsolete. In the context of neoliberal state retrenchment, the growing prominence of risk management has translated, among other things, into a shift towards "responsibilization" (Garland 2001; Abrahamsen and Williams 2011) as governments seek to convey to individuals and groups the message that they are, at least in part, responsible for their own safety and security. Not surprisingly, this focus on "responsible citizens" and communities has further facilitated the proliferation of private security companies who can presumably contribute to individual, corporate, and community security.

Taken together, all those transformations contributed to a complex process of diversification and fragmentation of the security field (Krahmann 2007). In today's world, security is not simply the responsibility of the state but also of individuals, local communities, corporations, and private security companies, all of whom participate – with various degrees of influence – in "hybrid security structures" (Abrahamsen and Williams 2011; Amoore 2007; Bigo 2006; Johnston 1992; Loader and Walker 2005).

The magnitude of neoliberal transformations that occurred in established liberal democracies pales in comparison to the massive changes that have occurred in former Communist states. Ironically, it is hard to imagine a type of polity that came closer to the Weberian ideal of state monopoly of violence than the pre-1989 Central/East European Communist polities. The contrast between the pre-1989 situation and the contemporary state of affairs, in which there are thousands of private security contractors providing services that range from the protection of business and private property to the protection of ports, airports, military sites, and nuclear facilities, could not be starker.

---

[8] It is revealing that the World Trade Organization includes private security in the General Agreement on Trade in Services and thus encourages Member States to allow free and fair competition in the security services.

With particular emphasis on Bulgaria and Romania, I suggest that the proliferation of private actors and their mobilization in practices of security provision has contributed to the reconstitution of the public in interesting, though sometimes problematic ways.[9] Why focus on these two countries? Romania and Bulgaria are extremely interesting because in the pre-1989 period they were governed by some of the most repressive Communist regimes – as such, they had very large and complex state agencies aimed at ensuring "domestic order," systematically monitoring the entire population and quickly silencing any actual or potential dissidents. These cases, therefore, can be seen as unique social laboratories, giving us insight into the ways in which particular types of practices can fundamentally alter the meaning of public security providers and the dynamics of security provision in just a few years.

To understand changes in the practices of security provision, it is useful to understand the broader context in which those changes were occurring. The 1990s were a time when most countries of the former Communist bloc in Europe embarked upon comprehensive and highly ambitious liberal reforms, aimed at turning their countries into Western-like democracies. Those reforms were strongly supported, monitored, and often systematically guided by international actors, including institutions ranging from the global financial organizations to regional bodies – particularly the EU and NATO (Epstein 2008; Kelley 2004; Vachudova 2005). In the context of post-Communist transition in Bulgaria and Romania, one of the key actors involved in the dissemination of liberal norms in the area of domestic security was the European Union. The EU has sought to promote free trade in security services across Europe as part of its Services Directive, and, as part of accession negotiations, has encouraged candidate states from the former Communist bloc to allow free and fair competition in the security services.[10]

International – coupled with some domestic – pressures for reform resulted in a series of legislative changes in the 1990s. Through those changes, it became possible for private companies to become involved in the provision of security in Bulgaria and in Romania (Gounev 2007; Prisicariu 2010). Legal transformations were accompanied by socio-political and economic developments that resulted in growing demand for private security services. Diminishing state involvement in the

---

[9] According to the Confederation of European Security Services (2011), both in Bulgaria and in Romania the number of private security guards is greater than the number of police officers.

[10] Interviews with EU officials and Romanian and Bulgarian political analysts, Brussels, Bucharest, and Sofia, May 2011 and May–June 2012.

security sector during the transition from Communism created a demand for protection of privatized goods and services in Romania and Bulgaria. In particular, an opaque and arguably abusive transfer of public goods into private hands during the transition period, coupled with a corrupt and poorly functioning judicial system (Gounev 2007; Prisicariu 2010) led to widespread distrust in the state as a security provider (Page *et al.* 2005).

Under those circumstances, many businesses came to rely on private security companies for protection (Gounev 2007; Tzvetkova 2008). Consequently, by the mid-2000s, the private security sector had already witnessed tremendous growth in Bulgaria and Romania, as well as in other ex-Communist states. Thus, by 2006 in Bulgaria about 9 percent of all employed males were engaged in a private-security-related activity; meanwhile, by the mid-2000s more than 1,000 private security companies (employing around 38,000 people) were operating in Romania (Gounev 2007; Page *et al.* 2005).

What is particularly interesting in ex-Communist countries is the way in which newly created private security companies were right from the start able to draw on their material sources of power as well as symbolic power to strengthen their position in the rapidly changing field of security. To understand this, it is useful to draw on Bourdieu's analysis of competition for power within a given field. As Abrahamsen and Williams (2006, 2011) have persuasively argued, Bourdieu's conceptualization of different forms of capital that shape (and can be mobilized in) a particular field can help us understand the dynamics of "assemblages" of actors that transcend the public/private divide in contemporary security. For Bourdieu, a field is analogous to a game in that it is a socially constructed, historically specific domain of activity that is governed by a specific set of rules (Bourdieu 1990; Haugaard 1997; Leander 2011; Williams 2007). The social space of a field is in important ways shaped by the distribution of capital among its players. Capital consists of the resources that actors can mobilize in order to act successfully in a given field, and in particular to exercise symbolic power. Thus, according to Bourdieu, fields are loci of symbolic power: "the power to constitute the given by stating it, to act upon the world by acting upon the representation of the world" (Bourdieu and Wacquant 1992: 116). Each field is characterized and shaped by particular forms of capital: a field, in short, is a structured space of positions, in which the positions and their interrelations are determined by the distribution of different kinds of resources or "capital." It might be tempting to think that the notion of capital refers exclusively to economic resources. But, in Bourdieu's view, the concept needs to be understood in a broader sense, involving different forms of capital endowed with various degrees of value. As Thompson has pointed out,

There are many different forms of capital: not only "economic capital" in the strict sense (i.e. material wealth in the form of money, stocks, and shares) but also cultural capital (i.e. knowledge, skill, and other cultural acquisitions, as exemplified by educational or technical qualifications), symbolic capital (i.e. accumulated prestige or honor), and so on. (Williams 2007: 32)

In Bulgaria as well as in Romania, private security companies were able to enhance their position within the security field by drawing on material capital – particularly money and technology acquired, in part, as a result of the lucrative contracts they were able to secure through their connections with former colleagues, especially the police and army officers. At the same time, private security companies were able to mobilize symbolic–cultural forms of capital – particularly the expertise in the provision of security that they had acquired while working for Communist state organs – to enhance their prestige and power in the rapidly evolving field of security.

In the first years of post-Communism in Bulgaria, there was a strong link between private security companies, which were often led by former members of the Communist security apparatus, and organized crime (Gounev 2007). As Bulgaria was embarking on market reforms in the early 1990s, it did not have the political, economic, and legal institutions in place to support market transactions and protect property rights. Unable to count on the public authorities to collect debts and enforce contracts, many Bulgarians turned to "muscle for hire" private firms that would use any method possible on behalf of their clients (Gounev 2006, 2007; Tzvetkova 2008; Vaglenov 2010). As a Bulgarian journalist who investigated their activities noted, private security companies were "so powerful because, after long years of activity for the Communist government, they knew exactly how to protect their clients and frighten potential enemies of those clients. At the same time, they also had a solid understanding of social attitudes towards crime and insecurity, and were able to exploit those attitudes to their advantage."[11] In that context, private firms resorted to protection rackets that were facilitated by a particular set of social attitudes well known to the private security companies. For instance, the street vendors systematically "taxed" by private security companies were constantly concerned about Roma thieves, and were – reportedly – pleased when they realized that, once

[11] Author's telephone interview with Bulgarian journalist, August 7, 2010.

they became "protected" by private security companies, they were carefully avoided by the Roma (Tzvetkova 2008). So powerful did some of those firms become that they soon came to be regarded as a potential threat to state authority. In the mid-1990s, then Chief Army Prosecutor General Yotsev referred to private security companies as a threat to the state because of their "military subordination, iron discipline, high-quality communication devices, ultramodern cars, and weapons that the police did not have" (Tzvetkova 2008: 333). In that context, the Bulgarian government sought to take firmer steps to limit the power of those firms. Following the promulgation of Regulation 14 in 1994, the government refused to license many security firms suspected of criminal activity (Gounev 2006, 2007; Tzvetkova 2008). Interestingly, however, while the Bulgarian government sought to push out of business certain private security companies, it continued to protect and promote the security companies owned by former policemen (Tzvetkova 2008). In short, the close connections between the state and the private security domain were maintained and even strengthened in the aftermath of the introduction of new rules in 1994.

Furthermore, while private security companies accused of criminal activity were pushed out of the official security business, they did not entirely disappear from the field of security. Thus, many of those companies re-emerged as insurance companies (Gounev 2006, 2007; Tzevtkova 2008; Vaglenov 2010). Those companies came to be known by the general public as "power insurers," as they engaged in "insurance" practices that were synonymous with protection rackets: the "insurer" would leave a sticker on a car or venue, and the price for having the sticker would have to be paid. Refusal to comply could result in car theft or damage of property (Stoytchev 2004, cited in Tzvetkova 2008). In other words, the violent side of the provision of security to individuals and businesses continued, and, in the mid-1990s at least, was tolerated by the state. As Stoytchev noted: "This went on from the local kiosks for newspapers and cigarettes to camping sites and beaches. Moreover, this was seemingly legal. There is a contract whereby the two sides have obligations ..." (cited in Tzvetkova 2008: 338).

Two aspects of this violent side of security provision practices are particularly relevant for our purposes: to begin with, "power insurers" were able to exploit the post-Communist government's new insistence on risk management and responsibilization of citizens. As part of the process of liberalization, Bulgaria (like other former Communist countries) followed established liberal democracies in transferring part of the responsibility for protection to citizens themselves, adopting legislation that allowed the establishment of private insurers and encouraged individuals to take out policies provided by those private insurers. In this case, the new emphasis on self-protection translated into a mafia-like approach, one which was nevertheless treated by the state as a private issue rather than a matter of common concern. In essence, in the mid-1990s, governmental authorities and "power insurers" were *de facto* (if not *de jure*) working together to (re)define the (public) realm of common concern, and to cast matters that had previously fallen under the purview of the state (protection of individuals from criminal activities) as private issues simply because those matters were assumed to be governed by an implicit contract between the "protector" and the "protected."

Second, those companies were able to use their material power (weapons and surveillance technology) as well as a particular type of symbolic capital (reputation for violence) to employ stickers as tools of extortion. Those who received the stickers knew the insurers' reputation for violence and thus – reports indicate – largely agreed to pay. By the same token, criminals who noticed the stickers on cars, kiosks, and shops were also aware of the insurers' reputation for violence and thus refrained from stealing "protected" goods (Tzvetkova 2008).

In a broader perspective, this form of security provision illustrates a point made in the framing chapter of this volume: practices through which the public is defined and enacted cannot be understood as long as we insist on retaining the divide between the material and ideational realms – a divide that has shaped so much of the conventional thinking about international politics. In our case, a type of practice that, on the surface, might be seen as having little to do with the ideational realm (the use of stickers) depends heavily on a set of inter-subjective ideas shared by participants in – and all those affected by – those practices. Thus, inter-subjective ideas about the power and modus operandi of the "power insurers" and about the inability or unwillingness of the state to control them enabled the use of a particular (on the surface, banal and unimportant) category of objects, i.e. stickers, as a relatively effective – albeit deeply problematic – instrument of protection.

Similar to Bulgaria, the process of liberalization in Romania did not result in the emergence of a private sector (including in the field of security) that is clearly distinct from the public domain. Rather, the move away from the rigid Communist monopoly over the provision of security translated into the emergence of a complicated community of practice, consisting of individuals who belong in both – or at least move effortlessly between – what we traditionally define as the public and private domains, and in the process mobilize material and symbolic power sources that are often closely connected to the state. Those power sources are drawn upon in the context of practices of security provision in which the boundary between public-good provision and private profit are often impossible to establish.

There is significant evidence that, particularly in the first years following the collapse of communism, there were close links between some senior state officials, private security companies, and organized crime. As reports issued by the Organized Crime and Corruption Reporting Project (OCCRP 2010) indicate, while Communism collapsed in 1989, many leaders of the Communist security apparatus (including the much-feared Securitate) went into business for themselves – and used the skills, know-how, and methods they had learned and used under Communism.[12]

As in the case of Bulgaria, several of the owners/employees of private security firms employed the symbolic and material capital they had acquired while working for the Communist government to advance their position in the field of security. Linked to this, they systematically portrayed themselves as knowledgeable and effective security providers in a situation widely seen as marked by the state's administrative and judicial weakness, corruption, and the police's inability or unwillingness to provide effective security to businesses. The capital mobilized in that context included not simply financial resources and specialized technology but also specialized skills (ranging from physical protection to monitoring of communications), and a general reputation as powerful actors, whose clients would enjoy preferential treatment in day-to-day activities and in interactions with government officials. The OCCRP investigation even discovered that some of the largest Romanian security firms had been used to "dig up dirt" on businesses and politicians, then use it against them. In some instances, those companies used wire-tapping skills and technology they had employed in their government jobs, in other instances they called in favors from old friends and former colleagues who had information against their political masters (Prisicariu 2010). As in the case of Bulgaria, some of those private security companies also operated as "power insurers" (though they did not necessarily register as insurance companies), and practiced protection racket with relative impunity (OCCRP 2009).

(Re)constituting public actors in Bulgaria and Romania

Given the growing power of private security companies in Romania and Bulgaria, the governments of both countries eventually came to regard

---

[12] In this section, I draw on Prisicariu 2010 and OCCRP 2009.

the regulation of those firms as a priority for ensuring domestic order and security. Interestingly, however, the measures taken in an effort to control private security companies did not involve an effort to outlaw them. Rather, the focus was on establishing legal and institutional arrangements through which such firms could operate – within certain limits – as agents of public power in the field of security. The Bulgarian and Romania laws adopted in an effort to better regulate the activities of private security companies are interesting illustrations of the way in which – as explained in this volume's framing chapter – discursive practices are potent tools for constituting the public in particular ways. In our case, through particular legal discourses, actors that, on the surface, could appear as entities that belong exclusively in the private domain are effectively constituted as legitimate participants in the provision of a key public good.

Consider, for example, the Bulgarian law governing the activities of private security companies, the Law for the Private Guarding Activity, which identifies these companies as active partners of the public authorities in everyday policing activities.[13] According to Article 3 of the Law, the private guarding activity shall be carried out by observing the following principles: "respect for the rights, freedoms, and dignity of the citizens; interaction with the Bodies of the Ministry of Interior in the fight against crime and the protection of the public peace; guaranteeing security and safety in the guarded sites; and carrying out preventive activity on the grounds of analysis of the causes of tort in the guarded sites." To enable them to perform their activities, the law gives private security companies the right and even the duty to detain persons in the region of the guarded site when those persons have committed a crime or even when they are deemed (by the companies themselves) to pose a danger to the life, health or property of others (Article 32). In addition, private security companies are granted the right to use force when they cannot fulfill their duties otherwise (Article 34).

It is particularly interesting to note the ways in which this law extends to private security companies the function of preventive policing – that is, a function which, following the rise to prominence of norms and practices of risk management, became a significant attribute of public authorities in the modern age. To understand this focus on prevention, we need to place it in the context of transformations that occurred in the area of policing liberal societies in the late twentieth century. Mariana Valverde and Michael Mopas, among others, have noted that in the nineteenth and the early to mid twentieth century, policing in liberal societies was

---

[13] The Law for the Private Guarding Activity was adopted in February 2004, and amended several times in 2005 and 2006.

aimed at normalizing if not each individual offender then at least the population of offenders (Valverde and Mopas 2006). Towards the end of the twentieth century, however, "neoliberal and managerial moves to displace therapy, to cut back state budgets, and to impose new knowledges more amenable to performance assessment, found the new logic of 'risk' more useful than the older, more ambitious and totalizing logic of 'discipline'" (Valverde and Mopas 2006: 238). In a world of risk management, the focus is on establishing "risk profiles," by using categories developed by experts and data gathered from a multitude of public and private sources, and then formulating strategies for managing those risk factors. And in the neoliberal world, which relies on local authorities and non-state actors, businesses as well as private individuals or groups are involved in providing information about – and thus helping to classify – "risky" subjects and objects.[14] As a corollary to this, non-state actors also came to participate in the exercise of public power through their involvement in measures aimed at excluding such (allegedly risky) subjects from the normal political and socio-economic life of the liberal community.

In our case, the Bulgarian Law for the Private Guarding Activity empowers private security companies to participate in the function of classifying people according to the degree of risk they allegedly pose, and on this basis apply different treatments to them. For example, Article 7 of the Law states that the activity of protection carried out by private security companies "may include the introduction of admission regimes on the sites [protected by those companies]." Individuals and groups deemed by the companies to be "risky" can be excluded from the particular events and/or sites that they are guarding (which can include not only private businesses and residences but also public sites, such as ports, just as they can include mass events). More broadly – consistent with the logic of preventive policing – private security companies are given the right to assess the security risks in the areas that they are protecting, and are also assigned the duty to detain individuals suspected of a crime or deemed as a risk to the health or property of others.

In a similar vein, the recent Romanian legislation in this area defines new norms of security provision that cast private actors in the role of (partial) agents of public power, endowed with special rights as well as responsibilities to contribute to the provision of public security. According to Article 2 of Law 333/2003 (the Law Regarding the Protection of Goods and Persons), it is the responsibility of individual

---

[14] See, for example, Ericson and Haggerty 1997.

companies and organizations to ensure the protection of goods/valuables on their premises, as well as of the goods they transport on Romanian soil. In other words, the duty of protection of property conventionally attributed to the police is devolved through Law 333 to private persons, companies, and organizations, which have the right – and indeed are encouraged – to resort to the services of specialized private security companies.

Furthermore, according to Law 333, private security companies can carry out the function of protecting the environment, and produce reports regarding the risks to private property, to particular individuals, or to society and the environment as a whole (Article 20). And – again, similar to the situation in Bulgaria – through the Law on the Protection of Goods and Persons, private security companies acquire the power to set up admissions regimes on the sites that they are protecting (involving the right to classify people and subject them to different treatment based on the degree of risk they allegedly pose). As a corollary to this, private security companies are also saddled with the legal duty to detain and surrender to the police all those individuals suspected of criminal activity in the sites that they are protecting (Article 48).

It should also be noted that this reconstitution of private security companies as public actors did not affect only national companies. In the early post-Communist years, most private companies were domestically owned, and in fact the early Bulgarian and Romanian legislation in this area discriminated against foreign individuals/companies. In the past decade, however, in part as a result of increased liberalization associated with accession to the European Union, global players have emerged both in Romania and in Bulgaria. Some leading global players (particularly UK-based G4S) have started to operate and have rapidly grown in prominence, coming to employ thousands of individuals and providing a multitude of functions ranging from individual/business protection to ensuring security and domestic order during public events.[15] This development is particularly interesting because it suggests that to understand the nature and practices of contemporary public actors, we need to transcend not only conventional thinking about the public/private divide but also mainstream IR ideas about the distinction between the domestic and the international arenas.[16]

---

[15] At the time of writing this chapter, G4S represents the second largest private security company in Bulgaria. Author's interview with Bulgarian two security experts, Sofia, June 15–17, 2012.

[16] There is an interesting similarity between this development in Eastern Europe and changes in security arrangements in Africa (see Abrahamsen and Williams 2011).

Policing society and the ethics of care in the age of globalization

Against the background of those initiatives, in recent years some leading private security companies have become deeply engaged in practices of policing by monitoring suspects, responding to burglary alerts, and apprehending alleged criminals. For example, between 2007 and 2010, one of the leading Romanian private security companies, BGS, has alone apprehended almost 2,000 alleged burglars, surrendering them to the police for questioning.[17] As noted above, these new partnerships concern global private security companies, as well as national companies. At present, both Romania and Bulgaria seem to be in the process of establishing systematic forms of cooperation between their key ministries (especially ministries of interior and justice) and global security firms such as G4S. Those practices are aimed at enhancing the capacity of the Bulgarian and Romanian states to carry out the surveillance and punishment of criminals. They include, *inter alia*, probation services and electronic surveillance as well as the transport of convicted criminals on Romanian and Bulgarian soil. The picture is likely to get even more complex in the near future, as G4S representatives seek to obtain permission from the Romanian government to build and run a private prison in Romania.[18]

In both cases, G4S seems to have effectively invoked its cultural–symbolic capital – specifically, its expertise and experience in working with government authorities in other countries, including liberal democracies, but also their knowledge of the Romanian and Bulgarian markets – to cast themselves as the kinds of security actors that can be trusted to participate in practices of policing that were, until very recently, strictly reserved for the state.[19] In short, we seem to be witnessing the consolidation of communities of practice that bring together actors which cannot be confined to a particular space or institutional domain. Those actors share specific knowledge of the nature of security needs, goals, and challenges in the age of risk management, and collectively enact practices of security provision that are grounded in that knowledge.

It is also worthwhile to note that the involvement of local and global private companies in the surveillance/control of the population in

---

[17] Interviews with two security analysts, Bucharest, June 15–16, 2011.
[18] Interviews with Romanian officials, Bucharest, June 1–3, 2011.
[19] Telephone interviews with a Romanian legal adviser and a Bulgarian journalist who followed these developments, May 12, 14, and 17, 2010.

Romania and Bulgaria is not limited to penal practices. What is involved here is a far larger and more complex process of growing participation of those companies in everyday practices of surveillance, often in situations in which state agencies are unable or unwilling to intervene. Take, for instance, the role of those firms in providing protection during major cultural and sporting events. Thus, exhibitions, musical and film festivals, rock concerts, and soccer games are increasingly protected by global security players such as G4S or Romanian/Bulgarian companies. In describing their involvement in the protection of those events, companies like G4S portray themselves as not simply expert security providers but also effective participants in a broader process of population management. Indeed, the G4S discourse casts the company as an actor that, through its management skills and commitment to the well-being of the public, effectively deals with problems such as accessibility to cultural/ sporting events for disabled individuals, and the well-being of children and other vulnerable individuals before, during, and after the event.[20]

That ostensible commitment to an ethic of care is not reduced to the provision of security during isolated events. As noted above, particularly since the mid-2000s, global as well as local security companies in Bulgaria and Romania have become involved in complex practices of surveillance of the population in areas/sites where they provide protection, be they government property or private venues. In those sites – ranging from government offices to shopping malls, banks, and ports – what seems to be involved is the emergence of "bubbles of governance" in which people are constantly monitored and classified into different categories of "risk," to be subject to very different kinds of treatment.[21] While state police agencies, facing limited resources and personnel, are unable to provide constant monitoring of (potentially) vulnerable sites, private security companies have stepped in to offer constant monitoring as well as a host of services designed to facilitate the management of crowds in busy offices or stores. Their involvement is generally characterized by a continuous presence, an infrequent recourse to physical coercion, and often a degree of involvement in the operation of the businesses they protect in ways that are uncharacteristic of contemporary police practices.

The growing involvement of private security companies in complex forms of surveillance/management can be seen as a partial revival of the types of links between policing and the governance of populations that were characteristic of liberal polities in the nineteenth and early to

[20] See, for instance, the activity reports provided by G4S Bulgaria (www.g4s.bg/bg-bg/) and G4S Romania (www.g4s.ro/).
[21] I borrow the term "bubbles of governance" from Wakefield 2005.

mid twentieth centuries. As Loader and Walker remind us, starting in the nineteenth century, in the name of looking after the well-being of citizens, the state became interlocked with other agencies – health, housing, social security – involved in the welfarist project (Loader and Walker 2007: 26). In becoming an instrument of social governance, Loader and Walker point out, the modern police retained traces of the pre-modern conception of *"polizei,"* concerned with producing a general condition of stability/prosperity. That complex form of policing, however, fell out of fashion in the context of the advent of neoliberal policies in late twentieth century, as the state retrenched and outsourced many of its tasks to the private sector. In the area of policing, that meant a growing emphasis on punishment/penal practices, and a move away from the more complex forms of policing as a form of "care."

Yet, the gap left by the retrenchment of the state seems to be in the process of being partially filled by private security companies which, as noted above, are becoming more and more involved in the close surveillance of the population and the provision of various services. A new type of partnership of care seems to be emerging, linking together private security companies and those individuals and businesses that are willing and (financially) able to act as responsible risk managers by resorting to the services of those companies. The problem, however, is that this trend only serves to reinforce the already significant gap between exclusive communities/segments of the population that enjoy superior protection and care, and those that are deprived of even a minimal level of security.

Security, accountability, and the new publics

If – as noted above – one of the key concerns in modern liberal thought and practice has been the empowerment of actors that can function as agents of public power, an equally important preoccupation has been the imposition of legal/institutional constraints upon those actors, in an effort to ensure that their power does not degenerate into abusive behavior. This preoccupation has certainly been evident in recent legal and institutional arrangements governing private security companies in ex-Communist Europe. While the early 1990s were a time where the newly created private security companies were operating in a very fluid and relaxed legal environment, in which they enjoyed extraordinary liberties, in subsequent years there was a growing consensus, both in Bulgaria and in Romania, that some of these companies had become too powerful and that new, more efficient rules and norms were imperative in order to keep private security actors from becoming a threat to the state.

In the aftermath of some high-profile incidents in which private security firms transgressed the law with impunity,[22] in the late 1990s and 2000s, the Bulgarian government took several steps to enact and implement legislation aimed at preventing private security companies and related companies from engaging in mafia-like activities. As Philip Gounev has pointed out, under pressure to meet NATO and EU membership criteria, Sofia took a series of measures to enhance the effectiveness of the criminal justice system, and in 2004 passed the Law on Private Guarding Activities, which was meant to bring Bulgaria to the level of European "best practice" – for instance, by strengthening the definition of private security activities, requiring all private security employees to undergo specialized training, and stipulating that private security companies can only operate in Bulgaria if they have a license issued by the Bulgarian authorities (Gounev 2006, 2007). These measures have indeed resulted in a situation in which violence or the threat of violence is much more rarely employed by private security companies (Gounev 2006, 2007; Tzvetkova 2008).

In Romania, too, the private security companies' freedom to maneuver started to diminish in the 2000s. At that time due to domestic concerns that some of those firms had become too powerful and were becoming a potential threat to the authority of the state, and also in response to EU demands that Bucharest accelerate its liberal democratic reforms and address the problem of corruption in preparation for membership, the Romanian government took some steps – as reflected in Law 333 adopted in 2003 and broadened in 2005 and 2006 – to constrain the activities of these companies and to revoke the licenses of those firms that had been involved in criminal activities.[23]

The official discourse in both Bulgaria and Romania depicts these legislative changes as clear indications of those countries' progress towards greater conformity with modern liberal democratic norms, in particular norms of respect for individual rights and freedoms, accountability, as well as commitment to the provision of a key liberal public good: security.[24] It is certainly true that some of the legal constraints imposed on Bulgaria and Romania represent a significant move away from the almost unlimited freedom of the early 1990s, and towards an acceptance of private security companies as actors that, by virtue of their ability to affect principal liberal freedoms (e.g. individual

---

[22] See Tzvetkova 2008.
[23] Interviews with two Romanian investigative journalists, Bucharest, June 2–3, 2011.
[24] Recall the language of the key laws on private security discussed above – those documents speak of the importance of ensuring that private security companies act in a manner consistent with the protection of fundamental liberties of citizens as well as in a way that advances public security.

freedoms) and collective goods (security), need to be constrained in order to ensure that their power does not become abusive.

Yet, this is not simply a story of unambiguous progress towards greater compliance with liberal-democratic norms. The key problem in this area is that recent legislative changes redefine the role of the general public (or demos) in a problematic way, by restricting the number of those that have the right and/or duty to monitor and regulate the activities of actors engaged in the provision of domestic security. As Abrahamsen and Williams (Chapter 11, this volume) explain, neoliberal practices of privatization and regulation have led to a redistribution of power inside states in favor of those elements of the state that are directly embedded in global structures (such as ministries of finance, elements of the judiciary that deal with international regulation, and the executive branch). Simultaneously, the rearrangement of power within the state tends to involve a relative decline in the influence exercised by legislatures, as global actors are now linked directly to globalized state institutions, and work together to overcome the opposition of other elements of the state.

This type of rearrangement of power within the state has also affected security governance in post-Communist states like Bulgaria and Romania. In essence, Sofia and Bucharest have promoted a type of legislation which reinforces norms that leave control over private security companies in the hands of a few organs of the state, and severely limit the involvement of legislatures and/or civil society groups in this area (Gounev 2007; Page et al. 2005). Through legislation governing the provision of security, ministries of the interior and the police are empowered to exert virtually unlimited power in regulating private security companies. There is no provision in that legislation requiring that such companies be subject to parliamentary or civil society scrutiny – in spite of their growing power in ex-Communist states. In essence, post-Communist polities like Bulgaria and Romania are witnessing a redefinition of the role of the demos in the field of security which is similar to transformations that have recently occurred in various other countries and in multiple-issue areas.[25] What is involved in all these areas is a normatively problematic process of narrowing the role of the general public, by limiting its access to information and processes of deliberation about the provision of key public goods.

There is yet another way in which contemporary security practices in Bulgaria and Romania construct the public in a manner that is problematic from the point of view of liberal-democratic principles of good

---

[25] As revealed in several contributions to this volume, e.g. Helliner (Chapter 4), Best (Chapter 5), and Bernstein (Chapter 6).

governance. This concerns the partial commercialization of certain public agencies responsible for security governance. In Romania, for instance, in the mid-2000s, agencies such as the national *gendarmerie* as well as guards under the authority of local councils came to provide not only public security but also commercial security services – and sometimes even competed with private actors for the provision of those services (Page *et al.* 2005). In a similar vein, the Bulgarian Ministry of Internal Affairs, which regulates the private security sector, also offers its own commercial security services to individuals and businesses, and has been systematically involved in competing with private firms over contracts to guard individuals and property (Vaglenov 2010).

In essence, post-Communist Romania and Bulgaria seem to have witnessed a peculiar redefinition of the role of the state: contrary to modern principles regarding the role of the state as provider of public goods, the state – or, rather, specific state agencies – seem to be playing the dual and arguably contradictory role of public protector and profit-seeking participant in market transactions, in competition with private security companies. This duality constitutes a significant departure from the assumption that, in a modern polity, state agencies involved in the provision of security have to be clearly differentiated from private actors and interests. Thus, the categories of citizen and paying customer seem to be combined in a normatively problematic way in contemporary Romania and Bulgaria. Anecdotal evidence from those countries suggests that at least in some cases police forces acting on behalf of private clients have privileged the profit of those (paying) customers over the security of the public at large (for instance, by spending more resources on missions paid for by their private "clients" than on regular policing duties).

Conclusion

This chapter has explored the emergence in post-Communist Bulgaria and Romania of new types of security practices enacted by actors that often belong in – or at least easily move between – what would be conventionally regarded as distinct ("public" and "private") domains. In post-Communist Bulgaria and Romania, the proliferation of private security companies – and their incorporation into a new community of practice – is part of broader processes of (re)defining the category of "public" in ways that do not conform to theoretical models developed around assumptions of political dynamics in established liberal democracies. These security providers are engaged in practices that have a profound impact on Bulgarian/Romanian societies by redrawing the boundary between acceptable/unacceptable behavior by public actors, by reshaping understandings of who has the right to provide key public goods (in this context, security), and by introducing a form of "care" of the general public that is not provided by the state.

Arguably, it is still too early to understand the impact that these practices will eventually have on norms and institutions governing the provision of security in Bulgaria and Romania. For instance, it is unclear if/to what extent these security practices will significantly erode the legitimacy of the state by undermining the citizens' belief in the ability of their government to perform its function of protection and to avoid a situation in which security comes to be seen as a luxury commodity granted primarily to paying customers. Nevertheless, it is not too early to conclude that the very existence of these practices is a clear indication that we need to question some established categories and divides through which we have long made sense of the world – above all, the distinction between public and private.

One might be tempted to think about the evolving role of private security in the two ex-Communist countries examined here as being highly unusual and thus of limited relevance. It is certainly true that certain aspects of the evolution of practices of security provision are particular to post-Communist societies. But those specific issues and developments are part of larger dynamics, which cannot be reduced to a particular geographical context. As we have seen, the very fact that private entities came to be regarded as legitimate security providers and sources of "care" in Bulgaria and Romania cannot be understood in abstraction from regional and global developments that compel us to question conventional assumptions about the nature, location, and reasonable functions of "public" subjects and objects.

REFERENCES

Abrahamsen, Rita, and Michael C. Williams. 2006. "Security sector reform: bringing the private in." *Conflict, Security and Development* 6(1): 1–23.
  2008. "Selling security: assessing the impact of military privatization." *Review of International Political Economy* 15(1): 131–46.
  2011. *Security beyond the State: Private Security in International Politics.* Cambridge: Cambridge University Press.
Adler, Emanuel. 1998. "Seeds of peaceful change: the OSCE's security community-building model." In *Security Communities,* edited by Emanuel Adler and Michael Barnett, pp. 119–60. Cambridge: Cambridge University Press.
Amoore, Louise. 2007. "Vigilant visualities: the watchful politics of the War on Terror." *Security Dialogue* 38(2): 215–32.

194   *Alexandra Gheciu*

Avant, Deborah. 2005. *The Market for Force: The Consequences of Privatizing Security*. Cambridge: Cambridge University Press.

2006. "The implications of marketized security for IR theory: the democratic peace, late state-building, and the nature and frequency of conflict." *Perspectives on Politics* 4(3): 507–28.

Beck, Ulrich. 1999. *World Risk Society*. Cambridge: Polity Press.

2004. "The silence of words: on terror and war." *Security Dialogue* 34(2): 255–67.

Bigo, Didier. 2000. "When two become one: internal and external securitisations in Europe." In *International Relations Theory and the Politics of Europe Integration*, edited by Morten Kelstrup and Michael C. Williams, pp. 171–204. New York: Routledge.

2006. "Security, exception, ban and surveillance." In *Theorizing Surveillance: The Panopticon and Beyond*, edited by David Lyon, pp. 46–68. New York: Willan Publishing.

Börzel, Tanja A., and Thomas Risse, 2010. "Governance without a state: can it work?" *Regulation and Governance* 4(2): 1–22.

Bourdieu, Pierre. 1990. *The Logic of Practice*. Translated by Richard Nice. Stanford, CA: Stanford University Press.

2002. "Social space and symbolic power." In *Power: A Reader*, edited by Mark Haugaard, pp. 225–44. Manchester: Manchester University Press.

Bourdieu, Pierre, and Loïc Wacquant. 1992. "The purpose of reflexive sociology (The Chicago Workshop)." In *An Invitation to Reflexive Sociology*, edited by Pierre Bourdieu and Loïc J.D. Wacquant. Chicago, IL: University of Chicago Press.

Coker, Christopher. 2002. *Risk Management Goes Global*. www.spiked-online.com/

Confederation of European Security Services. 2011. *Private Security Services in Europe: Facts and Figures*. http://coess.eu/

Cutler, Claire A., Virginia Haufler, and Tony Porter, eds. 1999. *Private Authority and International Affairs*. Albany, NY: State University of New York Press.

De Goede, Marieke, and Louise Amoore. 2005. "Governance, risk and dataveillance in the war on terror." *Crime, Law and Social Change* 43(2–3): 149–73.

Dean, Mitchell. 1999. *Governmentality: Power and Rule in Modern Society*. London: Sage.

Epstein, Rachel. 2008. *In Pursuit of Liberalism: International Institutions in Postcommunist Europe*. Baltimore, MD: Johns Hopkins University Press.

Ericson, Richard V., and Kevin D. Haggerty. 1997. *Policing the Risk Society*. Oxford: Oxford University Press.

Garland, David. 2001. *The Culture of Control: Crime and Social Order in Contemporary Society*. Chicago, IL: University of Chicago Press.

Gheciu, Alexandra. 2008. *Securing Civilization? The EU, NATO and the OSCE in the Post-9/11 World*. Oxford: Oxford University Press.

Gounev, Philip. 2006. *Police Ethnic Profiling in Bulgaria*. Sofia: Centre for the Study of Democracy.

2007. "Bulgaria's private security industry." In *Private Actors and Security Governance*, edited by Alan Bryden and Marina Caparini, pp. 109–28. Geneva: Centre for Democratic Control of the Armed Forces.

Hall, Rodney Bruce and Thomas J. Biersteker, eds. 2002. *The Emergence of Private Authority in Global Governance*. Cambridge: Cambridge University Press.

Haufler, Virginia. 1997. *Dangerous Commerce: State and Market in the International Risks Insurance regime*. Ithaca, NY: Cornell University Press.

2007. "The private sector and governance in post-conflict countries." In *Governance in Post-Conflict Societies: Rebuilding Fragile States*, edited by Derick Brinkerhoff, pp. 143–60. New York: Routledge.

Haugaard, Mark, 1997, *The Constitution of Power: A Theoretical Analysis of Power, Knowledge and Starcture*. Manchester: Manchester University Press.

Johnston, Les. 1992. *The Rebirth of Private Policing*. New York: Routledge.

Kelley, Judith. 2004, "International actors on the domestic scene: membership conditionality and socialization by international institutions." *International Organization* 58(3): 425–57.

Krahmann, Elke. 2003. "Conceptualizing security governance." *Cooperation and Conflict* 38(1): 5–26.

2007. "Regulating military and security services in the European Union." In *Private Actors and Security Governance*, edited by Alan Bryden and Marina Caparini, pp. 189–212. Geneva: Centre for Democratic Control of the Armed Forces.

Leander, Anna. 2005. "The market for force and public security: the destabilizing consequences of private military companies." *Journal of Peace Research* 42(5): 605–22.

2011. "The promises, problems and potentials of a Bourdieu-inspired approach to international relations." *International Political Sociology* 5(3): 294–313.

Leander, Anna, and Rens Van Munster. 2007. "Private security contractors in the debate about Darfur: reflecting and reinforcing neoliberal governmentality." *International Relations* 21(2): 201–16.

Loader, Ian, and Neil Walker. 2005. "Necessary virtues: the legitimate place of the state in the production of security." In *Democracy, Society and the Governance of Security*, edited by Jennifer Wood and Benoit Dupont pp. 165–95. Cambridge: Cambridge University Press.

Loader, Ian, and Neil Walker. 2007. *Civilizing Security*. Cambridge: Cambridge University Press.

Lyon, David. 2003. *Surveillance after September 11th*. London: Polity Press.

Macdonald, Terry. 2010. "Corporations and global justice: rethinking 'public' and 'private' responsibilities." In *Fair Trade, Corporate Accountability and Beyond*, edited by Kate Macdonald and Shelley Marshall, pp. 137–48. Farnham: Ashgate.

Mandel, Robert. 2001. "The privatization of security." *Armed Forces and Society* 28(1): 129–51.

OCCRP. 2009. *Prosecuting Organized Crime in Romania*; Organized Crime and Corruption Reporting Project. www.reportingproject.net/security/

2010. *Security Chaos.*, Organized Crime and Corruption Reporting Project. www.reportingproject.net/security/

Page, Michael, Simon Rynn, Zack Taylor, and David Wood. 2005. *SALW and Private Security Companies in South Eastern Europe: A Cause or Effect of Insecurity?* Belgrade: SEESAC.

Percy, Sarah. 2007. *Mercenaries: The History of a Norm in International Relations.* Oxford: Oxford University Press.

Prisicariu, Catalin. 2010. *Romania: New System, Same Players,* Organized Crime and Corruption Reporting Project. www.reportingproject.net/security/index.php/stories/7-romania

Rasmussen, Mikkel Vedby. 2002. "A parallel globalization of terror: 9–11, security and globalization." *Cooperation and Conflict* 37(3): 323–49.

Ronit, K. 2001. "Institutions of private authority in global governance: linking territorial forms of self-regulation." *Administration and Society* 33(5): 555–78.

Slansky, David. 2006. "Private police and democracy." *American Criminal Law Review* 43(89): 89–105.

Thirkell-White, B. 2006. "Private authority and legitimacy in the international system." *International Relations* 20(3): 335–42.

Tzvetkova, Marina. 2008. "Aspects of the evolution of extra-legal protection in Bulgaria 1989–1999." *Trends in Organized Crime* 11(4): 326–51.

Vachudova, Milada, 2005. *Europe Undivided: Democracy, Leverage and Integration after Communism.* Oxford: Oxford University Press.

Vaglenov, Stanimir. 2010. *Bulgaria: The Public, Violent Side of Private Security,* Organized Crime and Corruption Reporting Project. http://www.reportingproject.net/security/

Valverde, Marina, and Michael Mopas. 2006. "Insecurity and the dream of targeted governance." In *Global Governmentality: Govening International Spaces,* edited by Wendy Larner and William Walters pp. 233–50. New York: Routledge.

Volkov, Vadim. 2002. *Violent Entrepreneurs: The Use of Force in the Making of Russian Capitalism.* Ithaca, NY: Cornell University Press.

Wakefield, Alison. 2005. "The public surveillance functions of private security." *Surveillance and Society* 2(4): 529–45.

Walters, William. 2006. "Border/Control." *European Journal of Social Theory* 9(2): 187–204.

Walzer, Michael. 1984. "Liberalism and the art of separation." *Political Theory* 12(3): 315–30.

Weber, Max, 1948. *From Max Webers Essays in Sociology,* edited by H.H. Gerth and C.W. Mills. London: Routledge.

Williams, Michael C. 2007. *Culture and Security: Symbolic Power and the Politics of International Security.* New York: Routledge.

9 Understanding US National Intelligence: analyzing practices to capture the chimera

Anna Leander

In July 2010, the *Washington Post* (WP) published the results of a project on "Top Secret America" on which twenty investigative journalists had been working for two years. The project drew attention to the change and growth in National Intelligence following 9/11 (Washington Post 2010a). The initial idea had been to work on intelligence generally, but given that this proved overwhelming, the team narrowed down to focus only on intelligence qualified as "top secret." Even so, the growth in this intelligence activity is remarkable. This public is returning, or in this case expanding at an impressive speed confirming the general contention of this volume. Between 2001 and 2010 the budget had increased by 250 percent, reaching $75 billion (the GDP of the Czech Republic). Thirty-three building complexes for top secret work had been or were under construction in the Washington area; 1,271 government organizations and 1,931 private companies were working on programs, while over 850,000 Americans had top secret clearances. The project built up a searchable database on the basis of "hundreds of interviews" combined with the scrutiny of "innumerable publicly available documents" (Washington Post 2010c). This has proved to be a gold mine of information available from the project website (Washington Post 2010a).[1]

Yet, the exact nature of this public transformation is surprisingly difficult to pin down. At the end of their two-year project, the journalists still refer to their findings as "estimates" and underscore the "opaque" and "elusive" nature of the top secret programs they studied (Washington Post 2010d). Even more surprising, their interviews and documents

Thanks to Ester Baringa, Christian Borch, Mikkel Flyverbom, Beatrice Hibou, Paul Highgate, Åshild Kohlås, Ronnie Lipschutz, Iver Neumann, Ronen Palan, Maria Stern, Linda Weiss, the members of the Security Program at PRIO, and the participants in the graduate colloquium at PUC Rio de Janeiro for their inspiring comments on the earlier versions, as well as to the editors for comments inspiring this version and to Stefano Guzzini for discussing all of it.
[1] The quotes in the text that are not explicitly attributed to someone else are statements made by the WP team journalists.

show that the leaders inside Top Secret America share their uncertainties. They do not know its dimensions or purpose, nor do they feel capable of controlling it. This paradoxical combination has begun to define US intelligence. It has turned into a fleeting omnipresence, there for any observer to see (which justifies and creates the ambition for a team of twenty journalists to investigate it) *and* a mirage fading away when attempts are made to understand it, hold it accountable, or just simply quantify or describe it. This tension is not only analytically intriguing; it is unsettling. Considering the resources spent on US National Intelligence as well as the implications of US intelligence activities for people across the planet – including misinformation leading to war, torture, extrajudicial assassinations, and extraordinary rendition programs, as well as transformations of the handling of migrants, borders, and personal information – "capturing" National Intelligence in the dual sense of "understanding" and "detaining" is urgent (e.g. Bigo and Tsoukala 2008; Kessler and Werner 2008; Leander 2011b, 2010b; Salter and Mutlu 2010).

This paradox is the point of departure for this chapter. The argument is first that the reason this expansion of the public is so difficult to capture (understand, arrest, and control) is its hybridity – and more specifically the "chimerical" side of this hybridity – and second that analyzing "the public as practice" is a way of dealing with this difficulty.[2] This is a hybridity of the public and the private, in the strong sense of the two categories being *joined* into a new kind of "public" practice. It is not possible to understand this hybridity from the starting point of the traditional distinction between the public and the private – a distinction that is integral to the liberal "art of separation" (as emphasized in the Introduction) and that also acts as a "practical category" structuring the world of intelligence and most observations of it. This kind of tidy public/private distinction splits up the hybrid obscuring its enmeshment, elusiveness, and power. Efforts to study this phenomenon that start from the public/private divide can therefore do little more than (re-)produce an opaque and powerful elusiveness; that is the chimerical side of this hybrid. Inversely, conceptualizing the "public as practice" makes it possible to endogenize the public/private divide and analyze how its capacity to obscure hybridity is integral to reconstituting the public as an enmeshed, elusive, and powerful hybrid. This chapter shows how.

---

[2] I use public as defined in Chapter 2 of this volume: the "public" is that "recognized to be of common concern." I restrict the use of practice to cover the theoretical approach and analytical strategy informing this volume and also introduced in Chapter 2.

To make this argument, the first three sections demonstrate the enmeshed, elusive, and powerful character of US National Intelligence at the level of the actors/activities, purpose(s), and the regulation governing US National Intelligence. These sections paint a rather discomforting picture of a public transformation in which (in the terms of the actors) a national security enterprise is expanding according to its own zombie-like logic falling largely outside anyone's regulatory reach. The last section directs attention to the conceptualization of the public as practice which underlies this account, a conceptualization that paves the way for engaging and contesting this reconstitution of the public as a hybrid.

The *hybrid* Top Secret National Security Enterprise

The hybrid nature of US National Intelligence is captured by Marcus Brauchli, executive editor of the WP, who introduces "Top Secret America" by referring to it as "this country's *Top Secret National-Security Enterprise*" (Washington Post 2010f, emphasis added). As the formulation underscores, the WP project demonstrates the overlapping of logics that are conventionally regarded as operating in distinct public and private domains. Hence, even if the WP team and intelligence professionals constantly separate the public and the private, particularly when they make general or principled statements, as soon as they begin to describe and discuss them, the two become *enmeshed*: the actors, their activities, their purposes, and the applicable rules and regulations *turn out to be public and private simultaneously*.

Enmeshed actors/activities

The WP estimates that out of 854,000 people with top secret clearances, 265,000 are contractors, and close to 30 percent of the workforce in the intelligence agencies are contractors (Washington Post 2010d). Presented in these terms, one is left with the impression that there are two sets of distinguishable individuals interacting. In the details of the descriptions, however, this neatness disappears.

Companies are often set up by former service staff who have the necessary knowledge, training, and contacts; they are part of the "intelligence community" and often live inside the "intelligence clusters" such as that in Fort Meade which the WP describes in detail (Washington Post 2010e). Hence, contractors very often have their top secret clearances before they become contractors. The move to the private sector has indeed been extensive: "Companies raid federal agencies of talent [so that] the government has been left with the youngest intelligence staff ever while more experienced employees move into the private sector" (Washington Post 2010d). But moving to the private sector in this case means continuing to work for the state, in some cases even doing exactly the same things – sometimes even in the same physical location. The move is thus, in many ways, fictional. Moreover, a contractor may not only be a contractor or a state employee, but may actually be both at the same time, holding state and private positions simultaneously – taking a leave from one, working part-time for both, or combining the two full-time. This being public and private at the same time is what I refer to as enmeshment. It is for this reason that Mark M. Lowenthal, former senior CIA official, terms public–private contracting a "false economy" (Washington Post 2010d).

Enmeshment is even more apparent in intelligence activities. The WP introduces contracting by stating that "federal rules say contractors may not perform what are called "inherently government functions." Yet they do: "all the time and in every intelligence and counterterrorism agency" as former Defense Secretary Robert Gates and former CIA Director and current Defense Secretary Leon Panetta confirm in interviews (Washington Post 2010d). At the Department of Homeland Security, the number of contractors equals the number of federal employees. In the office handling intelligence, six out of ten employees are from the private industry. The captain in charge of information technology at the Office of Naval Research explains that he works with "the employees of 70 information technology companies who keep the place operating" (Washington Post 2010d). The activities of contractors and insiders are not only jointly undertaken (and often in the same place), they actually resemble each other to the point of being identical. As the WP comments, "it is hard to distinguish its [a private IT company's] work from the government's because they [are] doing so many of the same things" (Washington Post 2010d).

Enmeshed purposes

In view of this overlap in activities, it should come as no surprise that the purposes and reference points of state and private actions are also enmeshed. Despite constant referencing of the idea that there is a "market/private" and a "security/public" rationale at work, in the more precise accounts, security and market logics overlap all the time.

The contractors make it very explicit that they are *also* following a security rationale. The website of SGIS (a small IT company) features "navy sailors lined up on a battleship over the words 'Proud to serve' and another image of a Navy helicopter flying near the Statue of Liberty over the words 'Preserving freedom'" (Washington Post 2010d). This is the same language and images used on the websites of the state agencies. Moreover, their actions demonstrate that they *also* have a security purpose. They have "invented a technology that made finding the makers of roadside bombs easier and helped reduce the number of casualties from improvised explosives," "produced blueprints and equipment for the unmanned aerial war fought by drones, which have killed the largest number of senior al-Qaeda leaders and produced a flood of surveillance videos," and "created the transnational digital highway that carries the drones' real-time data on terrorist hide-outs from overseas to command posts throughout the United States." Contractors are simultaneously part of a commercial market order and a security order (Washington Post 2010d).

Inversely, the state agencies are *also* referring to a market purpose. The increase in contracting was itself motivated partly by the wish to cut costs. It would make it "easier for the CIA and other agencies involved in counterterrorism to hire more contractors than civil servants" and "to limit the size of the permanent workforce ... because they [the Bush administration] thought – wrongly, it turned out – that contractors would be less expensive" (Washington Post 2010d). Similarly, economic motivations are perfectly legitimate for intelligence professionals. This comes out clearly in the communication to and about state employees. If the market logic was absent, SGIS would hardly try to recruit public intelligence professionals with a video showing an SGIS employee "walk [ing] into the parking lot one day and be[ing] surprised by co-workers clapping at his latest bonus: a leased, dark-blue Mercedes convertible [and then show] him sliding into the soft leather driver's seat saying, 'Ahhhh ... this is spectacular'" (Washington Post 2010d). Nor would it appear self-evident that people leave the state because the private pays "often twice as much [and offers] perks such as BMWs and $15,000 signing bonuses" (Washington Post 2010d). The presence of the market order is also visible in the emergence of a secondary industry: 300 headhunting "bodyshops" charging fees that often "approach $50,000 a person" (Washington Post 2010d).

Enmeshed regulation

The contracting of intelligence services is covered by extensive regulations that have been expanding in recent years (Chesterman 2011; Kierpaul 2008). This regulation can be neatly compartmentalized into legal subfields such as administrative law, contractual arrangements, regulations of the Use of Force such as the uniform code of military justice, etc. (e.g. Martin 2007; Waits 2008; Zamparelli 1999). These compartmentalized subfields are, however, continuously enmeshed.

One expression of this enmeshment is the recurrent concern of intelligence actors with the many contradictory rules. As one would expect, intelligence professionals complain about being limited by overly extensive rules and the micro-management of their activities. A whole consultancy industry has emerged, geared to support them when they try to navigate the maze of regulations (Shorrok 2008), but they complain especially about the tensions and contradictions which the extensive rules generate. For example, a senior defense official recalls his frustration when dealing with a subordinate responsible for a top secret program who refused to brief him about it. "What do you mean you can't tell me? I pay for the program," he told the subordinate who answered that the contract was secret. The senior official was obviously referring to the regulations governing his own unit, whereas the employee considered himself in another regulatory context.

A second example of actors' concern with enmeshment is their difficulty in locating regulatory authority and the resulting ineffectiveness of regulatory initiatives. The fate of the Office of the Director of National Intelligence (ODNI), which was established "to bring the colossal effort [in National Intelligence] under control," is illustrative in this regard (Washington Post 2010b). The many contradictory regulatory systems were a source of weakness from the outset. "The law on ODNI passed by Congress did not give the director clear legal or budgetary authority over intelligence matters" (Washington Post 2010b). Subsequently, the work of ODNI has been severely hampered by the possibility of shifting between regulatory systems. Examples include times when "the Defense Department shifted billions of dollars out of one budget and into another so that the ODNI could not touch it," as well as when "[t]he CIA reclassified some of its most sensitive information at a higher level so the National Counterterrorism Center staff, part of the ODNI, would not be allowed to see it" (Washington Post 2010b).

Enmeshment is at the core of the Top Secret National Security Enterprise. It not only shapes regulations, but also defines who does what and with reference to what kind of purpose. The activities, purposes, and regulations enmeshed in this way cannot simply be separated back out again. The contractors can be separated from the CIA officials, the market purpose from national security purpose, and regulation of contracts from regulations administrations. Such separation is, however, a formalistic exercise that hides more than it reveals and blinds itself to the hybrid and its implications.

The *elusive* Top Secret National Security Enterprise

As Army Lt.-Gen. John R. Vines suggests, the arrangements that have come to characterize National Intelligence maintain a "complexity that defies description" (Washington Post 2010b). Indeed, even those who stand squarely in the middle of it (and who thus have more information and a deeper understanding of it than anyone else) claim that they do not have a precise grasp of it. For example Robert Gates makes "a terrible confession: I can't get a number on how many contractors work for the Office of the Secretary of Defense; not even as a whole" (Washington Post 2010d). Where secrecy is a virtue, this may not seem strange. Cheney sums it up when he explains that contracting has grown because it facilitates "work in the shadows" (quoted in Chesterman 2011: 96). The public/private divide, however, compounds the challenge: it makes enmeshed actors and activities, purposes, and regulations slide out of sight. This elusive character of the secret intelligence hybrid is one of its sources of power.

Elusive/expansive actors and activities

The WP Project's attempt to pin down the actors is a case in point. According to the WP, Top Secret America consists of forty-five governmental organizations that can be broken down into 1,271 subunits and 1,931 companies (not divided into subunits) (Washington Post 2010c). This estimate, however, misrepresents the things it purports to capture. One reason is that enmeshed activities can be classified as either public *or* private *or* both, or they can simply slide out of the picture entirely because the activity in question moved to the private when the public was measured or vice versa. An additional reason for this elusiveness is that the estimate excludes things located outside the divide (namely the formally private or the foreign). Yet, these are often integral to National Intelligence. In the formally private sector (private companies hiring private intelligence agencies), operatives with a background in the state intelligence services make up the bulk of the staffing of the "private" agencies, which do assignments for the state agencies and share their results with the state agencies (Donovan 2011, former employee of Shell Corporate Affairs Security). The same is often the case with foreign agencies. The combination of misrepresentation and exclusion generated by a reliance on the public/private distinction explains why observers and insiders share the impression that the beast they are trying to capture eludes them. Observing these practices through the public/private divide makes it impossible to capture who and what is part of US National Intelligence.

The elusiveness produced by the public/private divide facilitates an expansionary dynamic. By obscuring existing activities and actors, it makes it easier to argue that more projects and activities are needed.

As Elena Mastors, leader of a team studying the al-Qaeda leadership for the Defense Department, puts it, the overall logic is: "'Let's do another study' and because no one shares information, everyone does their own study" (Washington Post 2010d). This insulates actors and activities from attempts to curb their expansion. The complexity (and informality) of the arrangements combined with the intertwining of professional interests makes even those in charge feel powerless. As Vice-Adm. Dorsett (who claimed he could save millions by cutting contractors) stated, I "converted one contractor job and eliminated another out of 589 . . . It's costing me an arm and a leg" (Washington Post 2010d). This expansion goes so far that, according to some, the intelligence world is becoming entirely self-sustaining; "like a zombie, it keeps on living" as an official said after discovering sixty classified analytic websites still in operation despite orders to have them closed (Washington Post 2010b).

Elusive/expansive purposes

As the WP journalists highlight, "the amorphous mission" of defeating transnational violent extremists can, in principle, be interpreted in innumerable ways (Washington Post 2010b). In a context where actors/ activities take on zombie-like qualities, the purpose of intelligence missions becomes elusive. Part and parcel of becoming an intelligence operative and engaging in intelligence activities is to have an intelligence purpose; preferably a unique and central one. "You have to differentiate yourself" as the executive of a small IT company, InTTENSITY, explains (Washington Post 2010d). Along similar lines Kevin P. Meiners, deputy undersecretary for intelligence, gave contractors the recipe of the "the secret sauce" that will make their contracting thrive: "You should describe what you do as a weapons system, not overhead . . . You have to foot-stomp hard that this is a war-fighting system that's helping save people's lives every day" (Washington Post 2010d). The elusive status of hybrid actors makes it possible for them to engage in this kind of "stomping" in many contexts, and to do so simultaneously. Such competing efforts to define the purpose of intelligence activities therefore end up sounding more like a stampede, making their ultimate goal elusive.

Even if it becomes increasingly difficult to pin down intelligence purposes, it is not so difficult to recognize that this kind of stampede generates an expansion of intelligence purposes. This is most clearly expressed in the increasingly loud controversy over these purposes. Academics and practitioners alike criticize intelligence for not serving "national security." Maj.-Gen. John M. Custer, director of intelligence at US Central Command at the time, recounts a visit to the director of the National Counterterrorism Center (NCTC) during which "I told him that after 4.5 years, this organization had never produced one shred of information that helped me prosecute three wars!" (Washington Post 2010b). At times, developments in National Intelligence are presented as merely self-serving. These complaints about a disjuncture or even total delinking of security and intelligence activities from national security presuppose that there is a national security to which intelligence ought to be linked. Yet defining what this would be is precisely what the competitive foot-stomping is all about. The critics of the expanding intelligence purposes can identify the stampede. Unless they also prevent the public/private divide from obscuring the stampers, however, they are bound to do more to reinforce than to stem it.

Elusive/expansive rules

A common reaction to the expansion and multiplication of the purposes of top secret intelligence is to call for clearer leadership and rules. Maj.-Gen. Custer suggests that there is a need for someone "who orchestrates what is produced so that everybody doesn't produce the same thing" (Washington Post 2010b). Army Lt.-Gen. Vines, for his part, calls for a "synchronizing process" to ensure continuity of purpose. Nonetheless, such calls have gone unheeded (Washington Post 2010b). Instead there remains a lack of clear rules and regulations, and a subsequent overlapping of multiple and contradictory regulatory frameworks enmeshed in the Top Secret National Security Enterprise.

In the abstract, it may be possible to deal with this lack of clear rules by re-establishing a hierarchy and priority of norms, that is by reinstating the public/private divide and enforcing it more consistently (but see Fischer-Lescano and Teubner 2004). In US National Intelligence, however, as in most contemporary contexts, this is an unlikely scenario. Instead, the preferred strategy has been to create "coordination" and communication mechanisms. Hence, the ODNI does not exercise leadership by imposing rules of a unifying character. Rather, the DNI and his managers hold "interagency meetings" every day to promote collaboration between the different agencies (Washington Post 2010b). Similar approaches are echoed elsewhere. Coordination is also a core role of the handful of senior officials (so-called "Super Users") in the Department of Defense who have insight into, and overview of, all the programs located in the department (Washington Post 2010b). This coordination-based approach to rules and regulation cannot resolve the tensions and contradictions between regulatory systems. Instead it perpetuates them, reinforcing the ambiguity concerning which rules apply and when.

These contradictions and tensions between multiple rules and regulations are all the more likely to be perpetuated and multiplied as professionals and observers reinforce them through their own strategies. Even when they suggest that upholding multiple forms of regulation may be the most effective route to regulation (e.g. Dickinson 2008), they draw on and reinstate the public/private divide. Regulatory thinking, practical and academic, is constructed on past thought in which the inside/outside and the public/private are constitutive divisions (Cutler 2003). The resulting contradictions generate new forms of elusiveness, enabling certain professional to escape accountability (Michaels 2004). For instance, Michael Leiter, Director of the NCTC, complains that he cannot even govern his own work routines: "There is a long explanation for why . . ., and it amounts to this: some agency heads don't really want to give up the systems they have" (Washington Post 2010b). Other agency heads have mobilized contradictory regulations and their rules prevail over Leiter's.

Elusiveness is pervasive in National Intelligence. The deeply anchored categorical divides (most importantly in this case the public/private divide) allow actors – as well as their purpose and the rules governing them – to expand in ways that evade capture. While they are seen and sensed, they slide out of view. Creating an overview of the Top Secret National Security Enterprise is therefore a fool's errand. Even to gain a firm grip on specific groupings of activities is a daunting task. According to James Clapper, Undersecretary of Defense for intelligence, "there's only one entity in the entire universe that has visibility on all Special Access Programs [an ultra-secret group of programs in the Pentagon], that's God" (Washington Post 2010b).

The *powerful* Top Secret National Security Enterprise

Last but not least, the transformed National Security Enterprise is powerful. Not because specific actors or institutions are (or even can be) identified as masterminding it as a whole. Rather, its power is diffuse and capillary in form. It resides in the presence and spread of intelligence priorities across contexts and in its grip over understandings of national security. This section shows this by looking at how actors/activities, purposes, and regulations have become increasingly geared towards intelligence. It does so by showing that there has been a reshuffling of options, purposes, and forms of regulation which places intelligence on the agenda, rendering certain actions more self-evident, and bolstering/generating certain subject positions within the security field. In other words, the security field is shaped by a bias for intelligence, which is (re-)produced in actor strategies and understandings across the public/private divide.

Powerful intelligence actors/activities

The transformation of US National Intelligence has involved an expansion of the number of intelligence staff and activities. The recruitment has been constantly increasing and still grows. "Just last week, typing 'top secret' into the search engine of a major jobs Web site showed 1,951 unfilled positions in the Washington area, and 19,759 nationwide," the WP team writes (Washington Post 2010d). These figures partly reflect the constant reshuffling and shifts in already existing positions inside "Top Secret America." They are also indicative, however, of its capacity to absorb outsiders. "Contract analysts are often straight out of college and trained at corporate headquarters," an ODNI analyst explains (Washington Post 2010b). Similarly, many of the companies and government institutions that now work with intelligence have been created since 9/11, including a third of the 1,814 small to midsize companies that do top secret work (Washington Post 2010d). According to a member of the Senate Armed Services Committee, "we've built such a vast instrument. What are you going to do with this thing? It's turned into a jobs program" (Washington Post 2010d).

This "jobs program" is changing the value attached to different types of competence. The value of working on top secret matters – and hence of having a top secret clearance – has increased. It becomes important for getting jobs and contracts. It gives access to the networks and meetings in which these are distributed, many of which are informal. The WP team gives the example of the Defense Intelligence Agency's (DIA) annual information technology conference in Phoenix where General Dynamics hosted a Margaritaville-themed social event and Carahsoft Technology hosted a casino night. "These gatherings happen every week. Many of them are closed to anyone without a top secret clearance" (Washington Post 2010d). The companies' willingness to pay for these events underlines the significance of participating. The DIA event was entirely company sponsored. General Dynamics spent $30,000 on it (Washington Post 2010d). Also, drawing on intelligence competencies has become an important way of influencing hierarchies and jumping the career ladder. It can be used to short-circuit the hierarchy, or to "undermine the normal chain of command [as] when senior officials use it to cut out rivals or when subordinates are ordered to keep secrets from their commanders" (Washington Post 2010b).

The move into National Intelligence is not necessarily a move away from other activities. The activities may overlap. Nor is the related revaluation of competencies necessarily matched by a zero-sum devaluation of other competencies. "Dual use" (civil–military) technologies are matched by dual-use competencies. They do reveal, however the grip National Intelligence has gained over actors, the way they think of their options and hence the "strategies" they pursue.[3]

Powerful intelligence purposes

The Top Secret National Security Enterprise is not only redefining the purposes of intelligence, but also of politics more generally. Intelligence concerns are present across a wide (and growing) range of areas and activities. The "stampede" mode of defining intelligence purpose is also an expression of a clear, explicit effort to promote the dissemination of intelligence concerns across various areas. Erik Saar (whose evocative job title is "knowledge engineer") explains that his "job is to change the perception of leaders who might drive change" (Washington Post 2010d). Similarly, the founder of a small company that has rapidly grown explains that the company defined its activities as falling within the realm of "intelligence" because "we knew that's where we wanted to play. There's always going to be a need to protect the homeland" (Washington Post 2010a).

These efforts do not stop at the US border. Rather, "within the Defense Department alone, 18 commands and agencies conduct information operations, which aspire to manage foreign audiences' perceptions of U.S. policy and military activities overseas" (Washington Post 2010b) and "in September 2009, General Dynamics won a $10 million contract from the U.S. Special Operations Command's psychological operations unit to create Web sites to influence foreigners' views of U.S. policy" (Washington Post 2010d). These knowledge engineering and perception shaping efforts are likely to be influential, not necessarily because they are blindly accepted and hence capable of displacing civilian orders and understandings in a zero-sum fashion, but rather because they place intelligence/security concerns on the agenda. They focus attention, debate, and discussion on them. In the process, they make intelligence/security concerns integral to an increasing number of areas. Consequently, and even if they fail on their own terms, the opinion making efforts skew thinking about purpose in these areas towards intelligence and security.

One way of conveying this grip of intelligence concerns is by observing the transformation of Washington's "social morphology"[4] which both the WP team and intelligence professionals resort to when they want

---

[3] Strategy is obviously used in a Bourdieuian sense as reflecting the *habitus* generated by and reproducing the agents positions and dispositions in a field.
[4] The material landscape expressing the self-understanding of societies (Mauss 1950: 389)

to highlight the power of National Intelligence. The architectural landscape of Washington has been transformed by building complexes for top secret work that according to a senior military intelligence officer, "occupy the equivalent of almost three Pentagons or 22 U.S. Capitol buildings" and are "edifices on the order of the pyramids" (Washington Post 2010b). But as the WP team notes "it's not only the number of buildings...it's also what is inside: banks of television monitors. 'Escort-required' badges. X-ray machines and lockers to store cell phones and pagers. Keypad door locks that open special rooms encased in metal or permanent dry wall, impenetrable to eavesdropping tools and protected by alarms and a security force capable of responding within 15 minutes" (Washington Post 2010b). A constructor insists on the transformation of public buildings more broadly: "in D.C., everyone talks SCIF, SCIF, SCIF."[5] Finally, the transformation is visible in how people position and project themselves in the landscape. For example, according to a three star general: "you can't find a four-star general without a security detail...Fear has caused everyone to have that stuff. Then comes: 'If he has one, then I have to have one.' It's become a status symbol" (Washington Post 2010b).

Powerful intelligence regulations

Last but not least, the Top Secret National Security Enterprise has a strong grip on regulatory ideas and horizons, and hence on the regulatory debates and strategies pursued. In spite of the despair about the absence of synchronization and orchestration, when confronted with the problems created by the amorphous maze of intelligence activities, academics and professionals alike are prone to request more of the same. For example, after explaining a major oversight failure by suggesting "there are so many people involved here...Everyone had the dots to connect... but it was not clear who had the responsibility," the NCTC Director proceeds to plead for "more analysts; 300 or so" (Washington Post 2010b). Similarly, when faced with a mistake, the DNI suggested the creation of a "team to run down every important lead" as well as the need for "more money and more analysts to prevent another mistake" (Washington Post 2010b). There is a "bootstrapping" (i.e. self-sustaining) logic at work here (Sabel 2007). The consequence is not that regulatory alternatives are eliminated. Rather, the effect is that the web of loosely coordinated regulations expands further to cover ever increasing

---

[5] SCIF is a "Sensitive Compartmented Information Facility," i.e. an enclosed area (room or building) used to process information classified as "sensitive compartmented."

areas. In the process other forms of regulation, and particularly those following a different logic, become relatively less significant. An expression of this is the resistance this process generates in the form of the recurring call for more outside or independent – of intelligence professionals – oversight and control in the discussion surrounding the transformation of US National Intelligence (e.g. Verkuil 2007).[6]

The bootstrapping logic is reinforced by the devaluation of alternative regulatory forms. Indeed, the web of overlapping and contradictory regulations is inherent to a hybrid organizational form that is adopted because it grants flexibility and promotes synergies. As Grant M. Schneider, DIA's chief information officer, suggests, "Our goal is to be open and learn stuff...We get more synergy...It's an interchange with industry" (Washington Post 2010d). Synergies of this kind demand a high degree of regulatory flexibility. The approach to regulation is one which self-consciously resists the temptation to either create more centralized regulations or to strengthen the specific local regulations. As in other areas the "implicit message for legal policies...is: 'strengthen the networks' polycontextuality!" (Teubner 2002: 321).[7] Reverting to (and positively valuing) regulatory polyphony and the associated "sense of dissonance" (Stark *et al.* 2009) pushes aside regulatory alternatives – in particular, it devalues hierarchically organized regulatory structures.

The intertwining of enmeshment, elusiveness, and power just described (and summarized in Table 9.1) is at the core of US National Intelligence. As shown in the account, the public/private divide is not only a passive representation, but an active force in (re-)producing these characteristics of US National Intelligence. The public/private splits up enmeshed actors/activities, purposes/values, and rules/regulations and therefore engenders a dual misrecognition of the expansionary dynamics and the power implications at the core of hybridity. Observers and practitioners fall back on the divide and mobilize it for their own ends, hence perpetuating and reinforcing the difficulty of pinning down enmeshment, halting its expansion, and understanding its power. The public/private divide in other words reproduces the intelligence world as chimerical, as the lion–goat–snake (and sometimes dragon) monster of Greek mythology. The question is what can be done to break this (re)production and hence to capture this hybrid being.

---

[6] www.janschakowsky.org/
[7] By "polycontextuality" Teubner refers to the plurality of contexts that the networks he is studying span. Here it expresses the refusal to establish a hierarchy of contexts in favor of flat regulatory structures.

Table 9.1 *The Top Secret National Security Enterprise*

	Level			
		Actors	Purposes	Regulations
Characteristic	Enmeshment	Dual identities: The public Contractor	Dual purposes: Security The market	Dual origins: The clashing logics
	Elusiveness	Expanding presence: The zombies	Expanding purpose: The stampede	Expanding regulations: The divine regulator
	Power	Reshaping of options: The top secret clearance	Reshaping of purposes: The SCIF landscape	Reshaping regulatory imaginaries: Bootstrapping reforms

Capturing the Top Secret National Security Enterprise by analyzing the public as practice

Hybrids and hybridity figure prominently in many areas of the social sciences – including postcolonial theory, gender studies, anthropology, and sociology – precisely because they focus attention on situations where multiple logics co-exist, overlap, and are intertwined (e.g. Canclini 1995; Harvey 1996; Patel 2004). Although scholars in IR and IPE have engaged these notions, they have tended to ignore the chimerical side of hybridity, as an enmeshed, elusive, and powerful phenomenon (an exception is Graz 2006, 2008). Without attending to this, the awareness of the specific analytical challenges involved in capturing hybrids is lost, including the awareness of the pivotal importance of divides such as that between the public and the private. Adopting a practice approach is a way to deal with this. It paves the way for an analysis of the role of hybridity in public transformations. It makes the divides (and their productivity or performativity) endogenous to the analysis instead of placing them as exogenous points of departure – as will be briefly illustrated with reference to the three core characteristics of US National Intelligence: its hybridity, its elusiveness, and its power.

Looking "from below" to capture the enmeshment at the core of hybridity

In biology *chimera* is a technical word used to designate a being that combines two incompatible genetic codes. This usage suggests that hybridity is not just about the co-existence of different logics; rather, it is about their enmeshment. The chimera is a single being. As Teubner, who has worked extensively on hybrids in law, insists, "hybrids are not simply mixtures, but social arrangements in their own right" where contradictory systems co-exist and overlap (Teubner 2002: 331). Hybridity in this sense is difficult to understand. The overlapping and contradictory logics create paradoxes that are difficult to fit into the linear and hierarchical understanding usually deployed in social analysis (Teubner 2011). But on a more basic level, chimeras are difficult to capture mainly because observers fall back on well-established categories – in the above analysis the public/private – splitting the hybrid into its constituent parts. They will look at how the public and the private interact (as "revolving doors": e.g. Seabrook and Tsingou 2009) rather than at the hybrid as a whole. More broadly, these deeply anchored categories are also reproduced as actors and institutions use them to define their identities, conceptualize the world, and formulate strategies in pursuit of their interests. "Reality" is therefore likely to confirm the divide that obscures enmeshment.

As explained in Chapter 2, practice-based approaches enable us to transcend this problem; they do so by refusing to take the public/private divide as pre-given and fixed, and insisting that categories of "public" and "private" need to be understood as constituted in a particular historical context. Indeed, as Elias explains, practice theorists assume that the variability of social life is one of its permanent features (Elias 1970: 47). Under these circumstances, the analyst has to provide context-sensitive interpretations of the meaning of – and relationships between – categories such as "public" and "private." Seen from this perspective, the public/private divide is a construct that may conceal an enmeshment that tends to be reinforced by the continued usage of the divide by actors engaged in, as well as by observers to, particular types of social practices. There is a "stickiness" of the terminology, as Neumann (2001) puts it. The most straightforward way to come to terms with this is to "look from below." This explains the proximity of practice analysis to anthropology/ethnography and the insistence on "empirical work" in all practice traditions (Leander 2010a, 2011a), including the notion of "field analysis" (Bourdieu 1980), the tracing of "networks" (Latour 2005), and the analyses of the everyday (De Certeau 1984).[8]

---

[8] As also flagged in Chapter 2 (this volume), these approaches are usually considered diverse and even incompatible. As I have argued elsewhere (Leander 2011a), although they are of course different, they have more in common than usually acknowledged.

The above analysis has captured the centrality of enmeshment to the US Top Secret National Security Enterprise. By focusing on how the actors and observers described who was inside the enterprise, what they were doing, why, and how this was formally regulated, this chapter has demonstrated that the public/private divide continues to structure most thinking and statements about US National Intelligence. When intelligence actors are pushed to provide more detailed accounts of the US Top Secret National Security Enterprise, however, it becomes clear that the divide effectively masks and reinforces a de facto public/private enmeshment. Hence, although the analysis developed in this chapter was clearly no fully fledged ethnography, field analysis, or network tracing, by drawing on the WP database it was able to capture the ways in which the public/private logics constantly overlap in the field of intelligence, giving actors, purposes, and regulations their dual character.

Acknowledging the productivity of conceptual divides to capture elusiveness

Practice analysis is also central for tackling a second analytical challenge linked to the study of hybrids, namely the elusiveness produced by conceptual divides. As illustrated above, the public/private divide is productive. It hides US National Intelligence. Hybrid intelligence is located in what modern system theory adequately terms a "blind spot," i.e. the distinction that establishes the system and hence makes it possible to think about it, or in this case the public/private distinction (Teubner 2006). Something located in that blind spot cannot be fixed. It slides out of sight. This is mirrored in status of the Greek chimera as the example par excellence of something that cannot *be* (Ashworth 1977: 63). Preventing hybrids from sliding out of view therefore requires an analytical strategy that displaces the blind spot while drawing explicit attention to the productivity of the conceptual divides for the observed. Yet, even those rare analyses that *do* focus on the productivity of conceptual divides often end up eliminating rather than analyzing the hybrid. This is done, for example, in analyses that show how distinct logics are integrated to form a new system (e.g. Frankel 2004), or that denaturalize the distinction on which the hybrid rests (e.g. Bevir 2008). Since hybrids and the blind spots in which they are located are likely to persist, the failure to analyze them hampers serious engagement with their productivity, and hence helps to reproduce the elusiveness of the hybrid.

Practice approaches can usefully be drawn upon to navigate away from this Scylla and Charybdis of ignoring the productivity of conceptual divides and of analyzing them out of existence. Practice approaches keep the productivity of conceptual divides inside their analyses and focus on how they produce elusiveness and misrecognition. Hence, a core point for Latour is to show how the modern misrecognition of the "seamless fabric" formed by nature-culture (Latour 1993: 7) has been produced, making science and social life more broadly elusive to observers and practitioners alike who nonetheless reproduce this misrecognition. Similarly, processes of misrecognition including those produced by the naturalization of conceptual divides are at the heart of Bourdieu's intellectual project. In analyzing the state, he urges against "seeing like a state" and proceeds to show how doing so (and accepting the public/private divide inherent in this vision) makes it impossible to recognize the imprint of the state on our innermost thoughts, including in matters of life and death. His conclusion is that the state monopoly on symbolic violence is more significant than its control over physical violence (e.g. Bourdieu 1994: 102). From the perspective of these practice approaches, a core task of sociological analysis is therefore to pinpoint misrecognition and its role in reproducing common understandings, including for example of the state or "the public."

This attentiveness to the productivity of conceptual divides and specifically their central and continuing role in producing misunderstanding, informed the above analysis of the US Top Secret National Security Enterprise. The analysis traced the recurring reference by practitioners and observers to the elusiveness expansion of the National Security Enterprise to the performative effects of the public/private divide. It suggested that the public/private divide is core to the elusive expansion of the range of actors, the stampede making intelligence purposes elusive/expanding, and the elusiveness of a regulation that has become so complex that "only God" can grasp it.

Analyzing reflexive processes to capture power

The difficulty of controlling the Top Secret National Security Enterprise evokes a last analytical challenge related to the analysis of hybridity, namely the question of how to capture its power. As discussed above this power resides mainly in the grip and spread of intelligence thinking over the understandings of what options, purposes, and regulations are available and appropriate across contexts. As such it is a power linked to the misrecognition at the origin of the expansionary dynamics tied to hybridity. This is underscored by the etymological link between hybrid and hubris: the ease with which hybrids impose themselves makes them overconfident (Godin 1996: 37). It is in other words a power that works by reorganizing understandings at the inter-subjective level, or a form of what Bourdieu would term "symbolic power" (e.g. Bourdieu 1990;

Guzzini 1993; Leander 2005). This kind of power tends not only to be difficult to capture in analysis, but to be reproduced in observation. The reason is that observers and observed alike usually remain trapped by their own situatedness and the categories inherent in it, and hence reproduce the symbolic power inherent in them; they remain trapped by limits of their own reflexivity. This holds also for this volume (including this chapter) which is constantly reproducing established connotations of "the public" simply by naming it as such, although its main ambition is to show how it has been reconstituted.

To break these "reflexive traps" requires focusing squarely on them in the analysis, and hence the practical import and reproduction of categorizations and understandings which Bourdieu would refer to as categorization effects. Doing precisely this is at the heart of practice analysis. Reflexivity traps ("self-fulfilling prophesies") and how to "resist" or "destabilize" them stand as core research objectives on the practice approach research agenda (Ashley 1989; Scott 1998). Practice scholars explicitly repeat and insist that they span, overcome, or simply work beyond (Latour) the divide between observers and observed (and they are also charged with failing, see e.g. Turner 1994). They also insist on broadening the range of observer–observed relationships they analyze to include observers such as movie-makers, designers, computerized technologies, or clowns (Shapiro 2011; Lacy 2008; Knorr-Cetina 2005; Amoore and Hall 2013 respectively). Reflexivity is a hallmark of the practice approach. This is epitomized by Bourdieu's insistence that his approach is "reflexive" (Leander 2002; Rask-Madsen 2011), but it is so widely shared that practice approaches have turned it into their most frequent foundation for their claim to authoritative knowledge to the considerable irritation of those who think no such claim is warranted (Lynch 2000). Consequently, practice approaches are particularly attuned to capturing the reflexive processes/ traps pivotal to the power of hybrids.

This is also how the practice approach plays into the analysis of the power of the US Top Secret National Security Enterprise above. The analysis shows that the power of intelligence (in the sense of its grip over understandings) is reproduced as it becomes integral to how actors reflect on themselves and the world around them. The way they organize their activities including their professional strategies, the way they see purpose, extending to that of the buildings that make up their physical surroundings, and the way they deal with regulation is increasingly marked by intelligence concerns. Even as there are persistent, explicit, and loud complaints about precisely this, both actors and observers (such as the WP journalists) seem to find it difficult to break out of this way of thinking.

Table 9.2 *Capturing US National Intelligence by analyzing practices*

Chimera characteristic	Difficult to capture because	Practice approaches can capture because they
It is Hybrid	The hybridity is split up in constitutive parts	"Look from below" (at "fields, "networks", the everyday . . .)
It is Elusive	The productivity of conceptual divides is ignored or dissolved	Analyze the implications of "conceptual divides" (as *illusio*, assumptions, performativities . . .)
It is Powerful	The link between observers and "strategies" is severed	Focus on reflexivity (on the observer–observed relation in practice)

In short, analyzing "the public as practice" makes it possible to capture hybrids such as the US Top Secret National Security Enterprise (see Table 9.2). The reason is that a practice approach problematizes the nature of conceptual divides and hence opens the road for an analysis of their "productivity" and their power. A practice approach can consequently avoid simply (re-)producing the blind spots in which hybrids such as US National Intelligence are located. Instead, it can identify these blind spots and engage the analysis of the mechanisms through which they produce elusiveness and power.

Conclusion

"A living, breathing organism impossible to control or curtail" is how a conservative member of the Senate Armed Service Committee describes US National Intelligence since 9/11 (Washington Post 2010b). This chapter has demonstrated that this imagery of a living, breathing organism is widely shared. It has also relied on a practice approach to locate its origins in the performative effects of the public/private divide. The salience of the public/private divide is no novelty. It has no doubt often obscured the work of national intelligence agencies across the world and in history. The encouragement of market-based governance forms has, however, placed "privatization logics" at the heart of the state. They have transformed the state from within, reconstituting it as hybrid. In the process, the performativity of the public/private divide has also become more salient. This chapter has insisted that this reconstituted (no longer public?) hybrid is chimerical: enmeshed, elusive, and powerful. It has also insisted that *pace* the many statements to the contrary, this hybridity does *not* make secret intelligence "impossible to control or curtail." Although this chapter has shown that "capturing" the logic of secret intelligence is exceedingly difficult as its elusiveness is constantly (re-) produced both by observers and observed, it has shown that analyzing the public as practice makes it possible. A focus on practice makes it possible to avoid the blind spots generated by splitting the hybrid into its constituent parts and by ignoring the productivity of conceptual divides and the power anchored in reflexive processes.

This argument is important for debates about the transformation of the public beyond US National Intelligence. Not because replicas of the US Top Secret National Security Enterprise are burgeoning everywhere but because its chimerical hybridity is likely to be found (with variations) in many other contexts of intelligence operatives, their values and the rules governing them are no doubt more internationally connected than is commonly acknowledged. Similarly, the transformation of intelligence is no doubt closely related to transformations of other areas of the state, such as health care, education, and local government (see e.g. Åkerstrøm-Andersen and Sand 2012). This suggests that the mechanisms through which chimerical hybridity is (re-)produced in the domain of intelligence – including the pivotal, performative, role of the public/private divide – may also play important roles in various other fields or domains of social life.

REFERENCES

Åkerstrøm Andersen, Niels and Inger-Johanne Sand, eds. 2012. *Hybrid Forms of Governance: Self-Suspension of Power*. London: Palgrave.

Amoore, Louise, and Alexandra Hall. 2013. "The clown at the gates of the camp: Sovereignty, resistance and the figure of the fool." *Security Dialogue* 44(2): 93–110.

Ashley, Richard K. 1989. "Imposing international purpose: notes on a problematique of governance." In *Global Changes and Theoretical Challenges: Approaches to World Politics for the 1990s*, edited by Ernst-Otto Czempiel and James Rosenau, pp. 251–90. Lanham, MD: Lexington Books.

Ashworth, E. J. 1977. "Chimeras and imaginary objects: a study in the post-medieval theory of signification." *Vivarium* 15(1): 57–77.

Bevir, Mark. 2008. "What is genealogy?" *Journal of the Philosophy of History* 2(3): 263–75.

Bigo, Didier and Anastassia Tsoukala. 2008. *Terror, Insecurity and Liberty: Illiberal Practices of Liberal Regimes*. New York: Routledge.

Bourdieu, Pierre. 1980. *Le sense pratique*. Paris: Minuit.

1990. "Social space and social power." In *In Other Words: Essays towards a Reflexive Sociology*, edited by Pierre Bourdieu, pp. 123–40. Oxford: Polity Press.

1994. *Raisons pratiques: sur la théorie de l'action*. Paris: Seuil.

Canclini, Nestor Garcia. 1995. *Hybrid Cultures: Strategies for Entering and Leaving Modernity*. Minneapolis, MN: University of Minnesota Press.

Chesterman, Simon. 2011. *One Nation under Surveillance: A New Social Contract to Defend Freedom without Sacrificing Liberty*. Oxford: Oxford University Press.

Cutler, Claire A. 2003. *Private Power and Global Authority: Transnational Merchant Law in the Global Political Economy*. Cambridge: Cambridge University Press.

De Certeau, Michel. 1984. *The Practice of Everyday Life*. Berkeley, CA: University of California Press.

Dickinson, Laura. 2008. "Accountability of state and non-state actors for human rights abuses in the 'War on Terror'." *Tulsa Journal of Comparative and International Law* 12: 53.

Donovan, John. 2011. *Inside the Shadowy World of Shell Corporate Security*. http://royaldutchshellplc.com/

Elias, Norbert. 1970. *What is Sociology?* Cambridge: Cambridge University Press.

Fischer-Lescano, Andreas and Gunther Teubner. 2004. "Regime collisions: the vain search for legal unity in the fragmentation of global law." *Michigan Journal of International Law* 25(4): 999–1045.

Frankel, Christian. 2004. *Virksomhedens Politisering [The Politicization of the Firm]*. Copenhagen: Samfundsliteratur.

Godin, Christian. 1996. "L'hybride entre la puissance et l'effroi." *Uranie* 6: 37–47.

Graz, Jean-Christophe. 2006. "Hybrids and regulation in the global political economy." *Competition and Change* 20(2): 230–45.

2008. "Gare aux hybrides: mythes et realités de la gouvernance de la mondialisation." *Etudes internationales* 39(3): 361–85.

Guzzini, Stefano. 1993. "Structural power: the limits of neorealist power analysis." *International Organization* 47(3): 443–78.

Habermas, Jürgen 1989. *The Structural Transformation of the Public Sphere: An Inquiry into a Category of Bourgeois Society*, Cambridge, MA: MIT Press.

Harvey, Penelope. 1996. *Hybrids of Modernity: Anthropology, the Nation State and the Universal Exhibition*. New York: Routledge.

Kessler, Oliver and Wouter Werner. 2008. "Extrajudicial killing as risk management." *Security Dialogue* 39(2–3): 289–308.

Kierpaul, Ian. 2008. "The rush to bring private military contractors to justice: the mad scramble of congress, lawyers, and law students after Abu Ghraib." *University of Toledo Law Review* 39(2): 407–35.

Knorr-Cetina, Karin. 2005. "How are global markets global? The architecture of a flow world." In *The Sociology of Financial Markets*, edited by Karin Knorr-Cetina and Alex Preda, pp. 17–37. Oxford: Oxford University Press.

Lacy, Mark. 2008. "Designer security: control society and MoMA's SAFE – design takes on risk." *Security Dialogue* 39(2–3): 333–57.

Latour, Bruno. 1993. *We Have Never Been Modern*. Cambridge, MA: Harvard University Press.

2005. *Re-Assembling the Social: An Introduction to Actor Network Theory*. Oxford: Oxford University Press.

Leander, Anna. 2002. "Do we really need reflexivity in IPE? Bourdieu's two reasons for answering affirmatively." *Review of International Political Economy* 9(4): 601–09.

2005. "The power to construct international security: on the significance of private military companies." *Millennium* 33(3): 803–26.

2010a. "Practices (re)-producing orders: understanding the role of business in global security governance." In *Business and Global Governance*, edited by Morten Ougaard and Anna Leander, pp. 57–78. New York: Routledge.

2010b. "The paradoxical impunity of private military companies: authority and the limits to legal accountability." *Security Dialogue* 41(5): 467–90.

2011a. "The promises, problems and potentials of a Bourdieu-inspired approach to International Relations." *International Political Sociolgy* 5(3): 294–313.

2011b. "Risk and the fabrication of apolitical, unaccountable military markets: the case of the CIA 'Killing Program'." *Review of International Studies* 37(5): 1–16.

Lynch, Michael. 2000. "Against reflexivity as an academic virtue and source of privileged knowledge." *Theory, Culture and Society* 17(3): 26–54.

Madsen, Mikael Rask. 2006. "Transnational fields: elements of a reflexive sociology of the internationalisation of law." *Retfærd* 3(114): 23–41.

2011. "Reflexivity and the construction of the international object: the case of human rights." *International Political Sociology* 5(3): 259–75.

Martin, Jennifer S. 2007. "Contracting for wartime actors: the limits of the contract paradigm." *New England Journal of International and Comparative Law* 14(Fall): 11–33.

Mauss, Marcel. 1950. "Etude de morphologie sociale: essai sur les variations saisonnières des sociétés Eskimos." In *Marcel Mauss: sociologie et anthropologie*, edited by Peter Gurvitch, pp. 389–478. Paris: Presses Universitaires de France.

Michaels, Jon D. 2004. "Beyond accountability: the constitutional, democratic and strategic problems with privatizing war." *Washington Univeristy Law Quarterly* 82(3): 1003–48.

Neumann, Iver B. 2001. *Mening, materialitet, makt: en innføring i diskursanalyse.* Bergen: Fagbokforlaget.

Patel, Geeta. 2004. "Home, homo, hybrid: translating gender." In *A Companion to Postcolonial Studies*, edited by Henry Schwarz and Sangeeta Ray, pp. 410–27. Malden, MA: Blackwell.

Sabel, Charles. 2007. "Bootstrapping development: rethinking the role of public intervention in promoting growth." In *On Capitalism*, edited by Victor Lee and Richard Swedberg, pp. 305–41. Stanford, CA: Stanford University Press.

Salter, Mark and Can Mutlu. 2010."The other transatlantic: practices, policies, fields." In *Mapping Transatlantic Security Relations: The EU, Canada and the War on Terror*, edited by Mark Salter, pp. 259–65. New York: Routledge.

Scott, James C. 1998. *Seeing Like a State: How Certain Schemes to Improve the Human Condition Have Failed.* New Haven, CT: Yale University Press.

Seabrook, Leonard and Eleni Tsingou. 2009."Power elites and everyday politics in international financial reform." *International Political Sociolgy* 3(4): 457–61.

Shapiro, Michael J. 2011. "The presence of war: here and elsewhere." *International Political Sociology* 5(2): 109–25.

Shorrok, Tim 2008. *Spies for Hire: The Secret World of Intelligence Outsourcing.* New York: Simon & Schuster.

Stark, David, David Beunza, Monique Girard, and Janos Lukacs. 2009. *The Sense of Dissonance: Accounts of Worth in Economic Life.* Princeton, NJ: Princeton University Press.

Teubner, Gunther. 2002. "Hybrid laws: constitutionalizing private governance networks." In *Legality and Community,* edited by Robert Kagan and Kenneth Winston, pp. 311–31. Berkeley, CA: Berkeley Public Policy Press.

2006. "In the blind spot: the hybridization of contracting." *Theoretical Inquiries in Law* **8**(1): 51–72.

2011. "Self-constitutionalizing TNCs? On the linkage of 'private' and 'public' corporate codes of conduct." *Indiana Journal of Global Legal Studies* **17**: 17–38.

Turner, Stephen. 1994. *The Social Theory of Practices.* Chicago, IL: Chicago University Press.

Verkuil, Paul. 2007. *Outsourcing Sovereignty: Why Privatization of Government Functions Threatens Democracy and What We Can Do about It.* Cambridge: Cambridge University Press.

Waits, Elizabeth K. 2008. "Avoiding the 'legal Bermuda Triangle': the military extraterritorial jurisdication act's unprecedented expansion of U.S. criminal jurisdiction over foreign nationals." *Arizona Journal of International and Comparative Law* **23**: 493–540.

Washington Post. 2010a. *Top Secret America.* http://projects.washingtonpost.com/top-secret-america/

2010b. *Top Secret America: A Hidden World Growing beyond Control.* http://projects.washingtonpost.com/top-secret-america/

2010c. *Top Secret America: Methodology and Credits.* http://projects.washingtonpost.com/top-secret-america/

2010d. *Top Secret America: National Security Inc.* http://projects.washingtonpost.com/top-secret-america/

2010e. *Top Secret America: The Secrets Next Door.* http://projects.washingtonpost.com/top-secret-america/

2010f. *The Washington Post's Press Release.* http://projects.washingtonpost.com/top-secret-america/

Zamparelli, Steven J. 1999. "Competitive sourcing and privatization: Contractors on the battlefield." *Air Force Journal of Logistics* **23**(3): 1–17.

IV

Conceptualizing the public as practices:
theoretical implications

10 Constitutive public practices in a world of changing boundaries

Tony Porter

Once upon a time – indeed not that long ago – it was quite easy to say what was public and what was private. *Public* was associated with the state and its citizenry as a whole, the general public. These were counterposed to the *private*, which referred to individuals, on their own, or organized in some particular or intimate way, in firms or families. As Best and Gheciu argue (Chapter 2, this volume), we are emerging from a period in which the private was greatly expanded at the expense of the public, to one in which the public is re-emerging, but in different forms than previously. These new forms involve public *practices*. We can no longer simply assume that activities associated with the state or its citizenry as a whole are public. Instead we need to pay close attention to the "knowledge-constituted, meaningful patterns of socially recognized activity that structure experience and that enable agents to reproduce or transform their world," to use Best and Gheciu's definition of practices. As they argue, *public* practices are ones that involve matters of common concern.

Already in these definitions the greater difficulty of identifying what is public is evident. The definitions involve a complex interplay between their social aspects (knowledge, social recognition, common concerns), which are closer to the collective character of older conceptions of the public, and the role of agents, which could be individuals or collectivities, but operating in a more particular manner that is closer to the older conceptions of the private. As Best and Gheciu note, this public is a more ad hoc construction involving certain actors or processes at certain moments.

In this chapter I examine the interaction between this complexity, and another aspect of the complexity of this new approach: the interaction between ideas and materiality. In the above definition, knowledge and social recognition primarily belong to the realm of ideas, while the process of reproducing or transforming the world brings in a material dimension.[1] I argue, however, that the ideal and the material are even

---

[1] As Best and Gheciu (Chapter 2, this volume) note "As this definition demonstrates, practices always bring together the *ideal* and the *material*." The material dimension is

more closely entangled than a casual reading of this definition might suggest. The definition could be taken to imply that agents are motivated by collective ideas, and then they act on the material world. I will argue that the agents themselves are also constituted materially, however. This is consistent with Bourdieu's concept of *habitus*, where the understandings that inform agents can be materially embodied or embedded in objects. It also includes, however, physical barriers or open architectures that prevent or enable people, ideas, or processes to assemble in a collective manner. These physical barriers and architectures themselves were constructed at a previous time, highlighting the continual recursive looping through the individual and the social, and through the ideal and the material, that is characteristic of a practice conception of the public.

A third type of complexity in this new approach should also be noted. This is the fading of the national/international distinction as an implicit starting point for identifying the public. Older definitions of the public simply assumed that it was constituted nationally. This assumption shaped Habermas' (1989) seminal work on the public sphere, which subsequent work on transnational public spheres has criticized (Fraser 2007). In contrast, today it is increasingly difficult to claim that public boundaries should correspond to national boundaries. Many problems and communities are inherently transnational (Djelic and Quack 2010), and to assume they cannot have a public character would be arbitrary and difficult to defend. The current volume, which treats the public as transnational, is consistent with this new aspect of contemporary public practices.

I will develop and explore these conceptual points by examining two cases: border security and internet governance. These two cases are crucial locations at which the reconstitution of the public can be found. Territorial borders are a key defining characteristic of the state, helping constitute publics organized around older logics. The internet has been widely associated with contemporary publics that previously would have been associated with citizens gathering in public squares or coffee houses, or communicating through newspapers. We shall see that it is impossible to make meaningful assessments of the degree to which state borders and the internet are public without taking the above complexity into account. The chapter starts by further developing the above points about complexity conceptually, and then turns to a more empirical examination of the two cases.

---

more explicit in the definition from Adler and Pouliot which they cite, which refers to practices acting in and on the "material world" (Adler and Pouliot 2011).

Complexity in contemporary transnational public practices

In this section I further develop the points introduced above, looking in turn at the relationship between the individual/collective, the ideal/ material, and the national/transnational distinctions that make contemporary public practices more complex than older and simpler associations of the public with the state and the national citizenry as a whole.

Individual/collective complexity

As noted above, it used to be that *public* was unproblematically associated with a national collectivity, whether this took the form of the state, or the national citizenry. In contrast *private* was closely associated with the individual. This was most evident in the association of the private with privacy or intimacy, but even meanings of private associated with business, such as private enterprise or the private sector, have been associated with individual entrepreneurship, or individual property rights. Prevailing legal approaches to corporate governance treat the firm as owned and exclusively responsible to its individual shareholders (Hansmann and Kraakman 2000).

There are multiple indications that this older association of the public with national collectivities has broken down, and is no longer useful. These can be grouped into three themes. The first is the evident presence of multiple publics in national spaces. The second is the increasingly obvious private individual elements in institutions such as the state which were previously seen as public and collective. The third is the increasingly apparent public elements in activities and spaces previously seen as private. I discuss each of these briefly. In general older public/private distinctions are rapidly losing their relevance.

With regard to multiple publics, Weintraub (1997), who provides a useful survey, points out that, even before our current period, the public could refer to not just collective political action but also to the disinterested sociability of a city street; or to aspects of the market when counterposed to the intimate sphere or family. This more casual recognition of multiple publics has been more forcefully developed by critics of Habermas' (1989) emphasis on a single national public in his hugely influential analysis of the emergence of a public sphere. Much of this criticism highlighted the role of counter-publics reflecting social categories such as class, gender, or race that were obscured by Habermas' focus on a more liberal bourgeois public sphere (Fraser 2002; Hill and Montag 2000).

There are two main ways that private elements of institutions such as the state that previously had been seen as public and collective are becoming more obvious. The first is reforms that have privatized various aspects of the state or that have introduced competition or other measures designed to make it more like private industry. The second is the problem of capture, where industry actors are able to manipulate regulators or other state agencies to promote their own private interests at the expense of the public interest (Pagliari 2012). Mattli and Woods (2009) address the difficulty of identifying the public interest in international regulation due to such problems, and they develop a useful set of criteria: whether the process is inclusive, open, transparent, fair, and accessible, along with robust societal demand, which is dependent on allies with resources, power, and expertise. These approaches begin to move away from the assumption that the state necessarily expresses the public interest to take more seriously the role of practices.

There are many ways in which locations or actors that previously would have been easily categorized as private are displaying public qualities. One is the carrying out of functions previously associated with the state by private actors, including private regulatory arrangements, or the private military companies discussed by Avant and Haufler (Chapter 3, this volume) and by Best and Gheciu (Chapter 2, this volume) in their discussion of the private authority literature. Another is the intervention of the state and its laws in personal matters. Cohen has illustrated this in her analysis of sexual harassment laws. As Cohen has noted, "The naturalness of the old public/private dichotomy, along with the gender assumptions that informed previous strategies of juridification, have more or less collapsed" (Cohen 1999: 443). Fahey argues that the public sphere "emerges not as a single, vast, open social space, but as a complex, multi-layered warren of zones and sub-spaces with different degrees and forms of privacy attached to them and different forms of interconnections between them" (Fahey 1995: 690) He further notes that "the term 'private' is thus a symbolic flag which draws on shared cultural meanings to give day-to-day effect to myriad zones of exclusion and inclusion in day-today life" (Fahey 1995: 699).

These types of complexity, which challenge an older association of the collective with the public and the individual with the private, confirm the value of the practice approach that informs this book. As noted above, the public cannot be identified automatically through its association with the state or citizenry as a whole, and instead we need to rely on the degree to which practices express common concerns. The practice approach, with its mix of collective knowledge, ideas, and concerns, and individual action, also blends elements previously associated with public and private in a new way. It maintains the crucial ideational collective element while avoiding prematurely and simplistically labeling large complex institutions as public because they have been seen as public in the past. Together these are helpful in addressing the types of complexity identified above.

Ideal/material complexity

In the past the relationship between ideas and materiality was not seen as particularly relevant to understanding the public. Sometimes this relationship would be casually referenced, such as when world public opinion was seen as too weak to constrain the more material power of states with their militaries. Altruism, which has often been associated with the collective other-regarding aspects of the public, also has often been associated with idealism, while markets and private enterprise have been associated with materialism. However there are many contrary inconsistent associations between the public and the ideal/material distinction, and it is safe to say that their relation was not well defined.

Today it is important to examine this relationship more carefully. If we wish to move beyond simply labeling institutions such as states as public and if we accept that the public can be constituted through decentralized practices, then the question of how the public can have an enduring enough presence to matter becomes important. Traditionally a key function or effect of the state was to preserve the common or collective aspects of societies through time, using such devices as constitutions, monuments, museums, and national archives (Adam 2004; Stockdale 2013). The ponderous weight of the state facilitated this. If the public depends, however, on shared ideas implemented by more individual agents in decentralized locations, it is less clear how the public can be sustained.

An important insight from the practice approaches associated with actor–network theory (ANT) is the role of materiality in making the effects of actions more durable (Latour 1991). If an idea is written down on paper or expressed in concrete architectures it is more likely to last. If it is encoded in computer systems which then continually implement it, its enduring effects may be even greater. Bringing the role of materiality into practices helps ensure that they are not conceived as being just about endless flows of ephemeral clashing ideas with no enduring effects.

In addition to the issue of the public's endurance, materiality is also important in the constitution of the public. This has been much more prominently recognized in analysis of public spaces in urban architectures (Low and Smith 2006) than in the literature on public spheres, which tends to focus instead on ideas, even if the role of particular architectures, such as coffee houses or the media, have been acknowledged to some degree. The displacement of public squares by privately owned shopping malls is an example of the relevance of urban architectures. Open architectures can facilitate the emergence of publics, while the erection of fences can convert public spaces to private ones. Common concerns are unlikely to emerge if they depend on people speaking to one another, one person at a time. Publics need to be built and not just be listened to.

One of the reasons that practice conceptions of the public are displacing more traditional ones is that contemporary technologies facilitate decentralized interactions (Sheller and Urry 2003). Where previously it may only have been possible to constitute the public by having representatives travel to a legislature in a capital city to deliberate and govern, today much more complex publics can be sustained by new media. Even within relatively recent forms of media, the shift from broadcast or print media which distributed pre-set packages of ideas to real-time interactive electronic media has greatly increased the variety of publics that can be sustained (Hansen 2009). Since interactions are increasingly mediated in various ways, the architectures of these media become crucial for the degree to which the public can be produced and sustained.

In analyzing public practices, then, we must pay careful attention to the interplay between the ideal and the material. We should be interested not only in the content of ideas, and whether they reflect common concerns, but also whether these ideas are carried through open architectures that help build publics, or are instead discussed in closed spaces that limit their public character. It is important to analyze both the constraining and enabling effects of materiality. We should be alert to the temporal dimension of practices, where architectures that are constructed at one point in time can then shape subsequent practices, which may or may not be able to change those architectures. Materiality therefore plays a key part in the question of whether practices are reinforcing or transformative in their social dynamics.

The national/transnational distinction

As noted above, traditionally the public was seen as based in nation–states. The state provided the security and stability that could sustain a public, in contrast to the violent anarchy beyond its borders. Today, however, there are many public actors, concerns, and processes that cross state boundaries. The idea of a transnational public sphere, developed especially by Fraser, has provoked debate (Conway and Singh 2009; Fraser 2007; Preston 2009). Some problems, like climate change, have material effects that cross borders. The governance processes and common concerns that interact with these effects are likely to cross borders as well. The question of who should be included in the public increasingly is shaped by factors other than nationality. In a globalized world, national borders can operate in an exclusionary manner that more closely resembles a private practice in its particularity, rather than a public practice.

In today's more complex public practices, the national/transnational distinction is displaced by more general questions related to communities, scale, and boundaries. Nationality is one possible basis for a public, and its selection as such may be influenced by emotional or practical considerations. Nationality, though, is only one type of community among many, some of which are transnational (Djelic and Quack 2010). It is hard to see why nationality should always trump other communities in defining the boundaries of publics. For example, communities concerned about climate change, poverty, or human rights could constitute alternative publics, and the ethical valence of these publics could be stronger than those based on nationality. In general, the larger and more open the community and the public associated with it, the easier it is likely to be to meet the criterion of common concern that this book has identified.

This discussion of scale and boundaries does not imply that there are universal criteria for publicness that are independent of public practices. The public or private quality of actors, ideas, and processes are constituted by these practices, and this process may be independent of scale. For instance a small group of actors may identify a concern associated with a relatively small scale, such as the rights of a local indigenous community, and succeed in defining this as a public issue. As Best and Gheciu argue (Chapter 2, this volume), publics are also constituted by logics, and these are not necessarily tied to ethical superiority of larger-scale publics. For instance the public-goods logic promotes a smaller public as an ethical value. Moreover, as Best and Gheciu suggest, the constitution of publics can exclude, and can involve an arbitrary pre-emption by powerful actors of alternative agendas, as happens with securitization. This means that publics can be constituted without reference to the ethical idea that the larger open publics have stronger claims than smaller exclusive ones. This section instead simply argues that nationality is no longer the obvious community upon which to base publics, and this should be taken into account in analyzing any particular public claim.

Case studies: border security and internet regulation

In this section I examine two cases, border security and internet regulation. The first case involves efforts to secure the boundaries of states, one of the most traditional aspects of the international, while the second case is a newer development that seems often to challenge those boundaries. As noted above, the first exemplifies an older public logic (as secured within the nation–state) and the practices associated with it are likely to be reinforcing, in the sense specified by Best and Gheciu (Chapter 2, this volume). The second exemplifies a more contemporary logic of a global public sphere (as produced transnationally by new media) and is typically seen as involving transformative practices.

The goal in analyzing these two cases is to show the inadequacy of older conceptions of the public, and to illustrate the relevance of public practices involving the three types of complexity discussed above, not to provide an exhaustive account of the cases.

Border security

The territorial borders of states are one of the most important fundamental defining properties of the sovereign state. The national interest and national security have been closely entwined with the public interest historically, and nationality and security can be treated as important public logics (on the concept of public logics see Best and Gheciu, Chapter 2, this volume). Borders often seem to be remarkably fixed, as the lines that represent them on maps have changed very little in the past half century. This stability contributed to the ease with which the public could be associated with the nation–state. On closer examination, however it becomes apparent that borders are experiencing dramatic changes that are consistent with new public practices set out in this book – they involve transformative practices. These changes do not mean that borders are becoming more permeable – on the contrary, they reinforce more effective forms of control and exclusion, often linked to older rhetorical anxieties about foreigners, and thereby also involve reinforcing practices with regard to the public. These changes are occurring throughout the world, but since full consideration of these is not feasible this section will focus especially on the borders of the United States, where they are particularly visible.

The increasing complexity of borders is evident in the ways that they are no longer fixed territorially at the line demarcated on maps, but are instead constructed in various locations connected to one another in complex ways. Already for many decades air travel has relocated borders to airports that are often far away from the more traditional border that those traveling on land or sea encounter. There is also a lengthy history of having some of the functions associated with borders, such as the approval of visas, shifted out to foreign embassies (Koslowski 2005). This type of complexity and reflexivity has accelerated dramatically since 9/11.

Borders are being pushed out in numerous ways. One is the delegation of travel document inspection and data collection to the foreign check-in counters of airlines, which are subject to stiff penalties if they allow passengers deemed to be inadmissible onto incoming flights (Fungsang 2006: 526). Airlines, like other modes of public transport, are required to send electronic data on their passengers or freight to border officials before they arrive at the border (Cate 2008: 447). A second is the further shifting of border functions to foreign embassies. A third is the delegation of inspection and securing of cargo outside US borders to firms in exchange for faster entry of that cargo into the USA, as with the Fast and Secure Trade (FAST) program used at the USA–Canada border, one of the most active borders in the world. This shifting out of the border is partly motivated by the desire to intercept travelers on foreign soil before they can make use of legal instruments, such as refugee claims, that they would have a right to should they be on a state's territory, or, in the case of terrorists, before they can launch an attack. It is also motivated by the practical difficulty of centralizing inspection at the original territorial border, evident for instance in the lengthy waits at many land borders.

Borders are also being shifted inward. This is evident in the shifting of border control functions originally restricted to territorial border posts to be applicable in multiple ways and places within the state's borders. For instance, the US Immigration and Nationality Act of 1996 separated a traveler who "has effected an entry" from those who have been "admitted." Those who have effected entry without being admitted, even if they are located far from the territorial border, can be subject to the relatively unconstrained authority of immigration officials that previously was restricted to territorial border crossings (Shachar 2009: 816). Similarly the USA aggressively uses civil and criminal law to force employers to step up monitoring of job applicants and employees to ensure that illegal immigrants are not hired (Green and Ciobanu 2006). Border controls increasingly rely on electronic access to databases that are in multiple locations away from the territorial border. Authorities have carved out certain spaces that are geographically inside the border and have deemed them legally to be outside the border. For instance, US Department of Homeland Security regulations first introduced in 2002 allow immigration officials to use "expedited removal" procedures previously restricted to the territorial border in spaces up to 100 miles from the border and for 14 days after crossing, and the Australian Migration Amendment Act "excised" certain parts of its coast that were vulnerable to unauthorized access (Shachar 2009: 818, 832).

A second change in borders is the degree to which their management has been delegated to private sector actors. One mentioned above is the reliance on private sector actors such as airlines or potential employers of undocumented worker to enforce border controls. The procedures followed by airlines are developed in part by their private association: the International Air Transport Association (Shachar 2009: 831). The data used by border authorities are often produced or managed by private sector actors, in some cases involving firms that otherwise have little to do with borders, such as when data on financial activities or phone calls are used. There is a large-scale awarding by states of contracts to private sector actors to develop or administer various aspects of the border. A Bermuda-based technology consulting company, Accenture, in coordination with a private sector consortium called the Smart Border Alliance, was awarded a US government contract, valued at $10 billion, to keep track of US border crossings electronically through the use of digital photos and fingerprints (Koulish 2008: 486). Other initiatives to include private firms in border controls include the use of sensors, unmanned drone aircraft, surveillance towers, and more integrated flows of information among these. Delegation of border security functions like the detention of unauthorized immigrants by companies like Blackwater (Koulish 2008) have raised concerns about the lack of public accountability for their treatment of detainees. At times these arrangements have involved ties with policy-makers that some might see as examples of excessive private influence within the public sector. For instance, during the Bush administration, Department of Homeland Security contracts were awarded to Sybase, which was controlled financially by the President's brother Marvin (Koulish 2008: 475).

These changes in the border also display complexity with regard to the interaction of the public and personal privacy. A key legal and political issue is the degree to which privacy rights constrain the policing of borders (Rishikof 2008). In the USA there are long-standing legal exemptions of border enforcement activities from the privacy protections of the Fourth Amendment to the US Constitution. Courts have generally been hesitant to restrict the access of border officials to new data that developments in electronic technologies have facilitated. For instance, searches at the border of the contents of laptops have been treated as similar to searches of luggage despite the very different implications they have for privacy (Bector 2009). Similarly, data such as bank or phone records have been treated as having a sufficiently public character to be released to authorities with minimal restrictions, even though they were provided by customers to private firms and could reveal personal information. New matching capacities of databases, such as the ability to use mathematical data associated with "eigenfaces" – summaries of the unique relationship of an individual's facial features – to link identifiable photographs of individuals with multiple other sources of personal data, create new threats to privacy (Adkins 2007).

In these conflicts privacy rights can still restrict border controls in important ways. For instance, the US Defense Advanced Research Projects Agency (DARPA) project entitled "Total Information Awareness" which aimed to vastly expand the government's ability to connect personal records across different public and private electronic data sources created a political backlash and the termination of its funding by Congress. A similar proposal of the US Transport Security Administration to expand data mining, the Computer Assisted Passenger Pre-Screening System II, was halted after public concern about privacy rights. The USA's attempt to subpoena financial data from the US operations of the EU-based Society for Worldwide International Financial Telecommunications was restricted after the EU protested on privacy grounds (Cate 2008: 446, 451, 447–48).

These changes also involve crucial interactions between the ideational and material worlds. The border itself, which previously was seen as fixed by the physical properties of the terrain across which it ran, is increasingly constructed in complex ways by new legal and technical ideas. Biometrics and data mining construct, modify, and transport identities that previously were seen as natural expressions inseparable from the human body. For instance, the US incorporation of RFID chips into passports involved multiple modifications of the materiality of border control (Lorenc 2007). The chips store digitized and coded versions of the information that was previously printed on the pages of the passport. A reader can send a signal that activates the ability of the chip to broadcast the data back to the reader, which then checks it against a remote database. The old markers that constituted membership in the national community, and thereby in the public, which were based on simpler verifications of residence and birth, are replaced by more complex mediated ones. Concerns about privacy and identity theft provoked by the ability of readers to access and track this information at a distance led to a decision to encrypt the transmissions and put protective covers on the passports (Bamberger and Mulligan 2008: 94). The passport, which used to be a relatively inert object, has become an active transmitter of information, part of a far-flung electronic surveillance network that helps constitute and manage membership in the nation and its public.

The case of border security illustrates the diminishing relevance of older public and private logics, and the relevance of the complexity discussed in the first part of this chapter. Changes in the location of borders illustrate the degree to which one important boundary of the public is constructed through practices. Traditionally territory was an important material dimension of the state and the public associated with it. The idea of national territory was reinforced by the physical character- istics of the land, such as its shorelines. This contributed to the percep- tion that the community on which the public was based was fixed and natural. However today these boundaries are being continually con- structed, and their link to the physical properties of national territories is attenuated.

The extensive private sector involvement with border security further illustrates the difficulty of treating activities conducted by the state as necessarily public. The public character of border maintenance is not automatically established by its association with the state. Indeed if we were simply to rely on the question of who manages border maintenance, it is more easily characterized as private. Of course, these private activ- ities are given a public quality by the claim that they are ultimately controlled by the state, and by the idea that the work they carry out, namely protecting the homeland, is a public concern for citizens. This involves rhetorical assertions that can be undermined by examples of activities that more closely fit the criteria for private actions.

The examples of the interplay between the public and individual privacy rights show how the public and its boundary are creatively reconstructed through time. More traditional approaches would focus on the state's public interest in governing the border, with private rights having little relevance. This older more simplistic view was not able to sustain itself. Instead transformative practices, including court cases, new identification technological developments, and sharp conflicts over privacy rights, worked to update the meaning and reach of the public. Throughout, however, these practices also reinforced traditional notions of the nation and the public.

The border security case also confirms this chapter's emphasis on the interaction between ideas and materiality. It shows that the practices that constitute the boundaries of the state and associate these with the public are carried out through technical artefacts that have material properties, even if these are distant from the physical properties of the territory which used to constitute the boundaries of the state and the public in the past.

These architectures play a key role in determining who gets in and who does not, and how the balance between public interest and private rights is settled. The more border security is automated, the more resistant it becomes to challenges over what should be public and what should be private. This process of automation however can itself provoke contestations, as was evident with privacy rights. Throughout, the emphasis on exclusion is a reminder of the arbitrariness in a globalized world of the nation as a basis for the public.

Internet governance

Superficially, the internet seems to be the contemporary equivalent of the emerging liberal public sphere of the eighteenth century sustained by coffee houses and literary salons that Habermas (1989) analyzed in his work on the history of the public sphere. As such, it is emblematic of the public logic associated with the idea of a public sphere, while departing from that logic in its transnational character. Like that earlier public sphere, the internet is a space between states and the personal that fosters open deliberation, where the content of the ideas matters more than the wealth or power of those who express them. The internet is not a free floating cyberspace that operates independently of humans or objects, though, but instead consists of humans and objects that are coordinated and governed through a complex set of practices and institutions (Eriksson and Giacomello 2009: 206). The practices and institutions that coordinate and govern the internet involve intense conflicts over the degree to which they are public or private.

This is evident, for instance, with the Internet Corporation for Assigned Names and Numbers (ICANN), which organizes high-level domain names that are essential for the computers to link to one another through the web. ICANN is a private non-profit corporation, incorporated under US law. The private and US character of this important institution has been sharply criticized by many governments which would prefer to see its functions carried out by an intergovernmental organization such as the International Telecommunications Union (ITU) in which all governments would have greater input. Similarly, most internet service providers (ISP) are private, but even private providers can be subject to government pressures or control. This was evident in the 2010 termination of Paypal services to Wikileaks in response to US government anger at the latter's release of confidential cables, or the ability of the Egyptian government to cut Egypt off from the internet in 2011 with a few calls to the private firms that carried Egypt's internet traffic, a governmental initiative which would be less possible in countries like the USA with a much larger number of ISPs. The complexity of these public/private relationships is evident in the way that some see the private character of both ICANN and ISPs as very important in enabling their public functions with regard to the free flow of information, while others call for a greater role for government in promoting the public interest, especially in equitable access (Arthur 2012).

Control of activity on the internet involves similar contestations over the meaning and boundaries of the public, further complicated by difficulty of relying on old nationally based public rules. For instance Yahoo. fr was sued by two French NGOs after Nazi paraphernalia was displayed on Yahoo.fr in France, where the display of Nazi paraphernalia is against the law (Meehan 2008).[2] After a French court supported the suit, Yahoo then sued the French NGOs in California courts asking that the foreign order be declared unenforceable because of the US First Amendment. This type of complexity, and the disruption it can produce on the internet, has led courts and scholars to consider many alternative governance arrangements. Meehan notes that one proposal has been to declare the internet a Common Heritage of Mankind in international law, like the High Seas, Antarctica, or Outer Space, but this seems impractical considering both state sovereignty and the complexity of the internet. At the opposite extreme, some have proposed relying on competition between dispute settlement provisions in internet service contracts, so for instance customers could choose their preferred forum governing their interactions on each website that they enter. A more feasible solution is for courts to apply certain criteria to determine jurisdiction, such as whether there is evidence that a website targets a jurisdiction (for instance by accepting its currency). Much more conduct is controlled by private rules rather than formal law. For instance, Paypal claimed that they terminated services to Wikileaks because of violations of the rules specified in their service contract.

The complexity of the public in internet governance is especially evident in conflicts over digital rights management (DRM). This involves the coding of restrictions on the use of digital products into computer hardware or software (Cesarini 2004; Lessig 2006). It has developed in response to widespread alarm on the part of owners of content, such as the music industry, that internet file-sharing and other new digital technologies were violating their property rights and destroying the revenues that give them the incentive to create the content. One industry response to this was to successfully lobby governments to create provisions in

---

[2] The discussion throughout this paragraph draws heavily on Meehan 2008.

public international law at the World Intellectual Property Organization and the World Trade Organization to require Member States to create new intellectual property rights and enforce them legally. The industry tried to enlist the full weight of these states, especially the USA, for instance by making access to US capital or markets conditional on a vigorous enforcement of intellectual property rights. Another industry initiative was to use private litigation, suing college students and others suspected of illegal file-sharing. By 2006 the industry had launched 18,000 lawsuits in the USA against music file-swappers and 5,500 outside the USA, especially in Europe (BBC 2006). The industry also very actively sought to delegitimize file-sharing by associating it with labels like piracy, theft, and stealing. Over time, however, it has put greater emphasis on DRM.

Digital rights management involves contestations over the character and boundaries of the public, but also the interplay between ideas and materiality. It involves the encoding of ideas of private and public into material objects such as CDs or computer hardware, which then circulate internationally. For instance, a Rights Expression Language (REL) like XrML aims to specify a wide variety of rights to content that will govern users, such as the length of time a file can be possessed, and whether it can be sampled, copied, printed, or modified. Unlike copyright laws RELs provide complete discretion to their coders in specifying public access and private rights (Bechtold 2003; Coyle 2003). Because most current DRMs can eventually be hacked, however, DRM supporters have successfully lobbied governments to back up the process by which private actors create private rights by criminalizing unauthorized modification of DRM systems, for instance through the US Digital Millennium Copy Right Act or the European Copyright Directive. This criminalization is being globalized through international law initiatives such as the Anti-Counterfeiting Trade Agreement.

In theory, the DRM technology can be used to safeguard the public character of knowledge, such as the coding that the Creative Commons License and Linux use to prevent commercialization (Bechtold 2003), but in practice most DRM is oriented towards the private interests of content owners. Further, DRM is not only implemented privately in its coding, but its long-range development is guided by consortia of private companies. Critics fear that public interest exceptions to copyright restrictions, such as for criticism or education or to facilitate market competition will be overridden by DRM. Companies may use DRM strategically against competitors, as Apple was accused of doing with its iTunes DRM, which is incompatible with competitors' devices (Willoughby et al. 2008). Privacy rights are an issue, especially with emerging DRM technologies that require a user's computer to constantly communicate with a central site to determine whether the user's conduct is authorized. At the same time critics of DRM have drawn very effectively on arguments that mix emotional attachments to personal freedom and expression with themes of openness associated with the public, provoking major firms in the music industry to forgo the use of DRM (Dobusch and Quack 2011).

The case of internet governance illustrates the complexity of contemporary public practices, and the inadequacy of older conceptions of the public. There is no clear link between the internet and older conceptions of public and private. The influence of states and national citizenries is no more decisive than many other influences. Although individuals and firms are active in internet governance, much of their activity has the characteristics associated with the logic of the public sphere with regard to openness and common concerns. This mix of collective ideas and individual action fits well with a more contemporary approach to public practices. It is clear that the determination of which elements of the internet are public and which are private cannot be made by simply drawing pre-set associations with old definitions. Instead these questions are answered through ongoing practices and contestations over what should be public and what should be private.

The interaction of ideas and materiality is especially evident with DRM. This is a decentralized encoding and enforcement of public access and private rights that takes material form in CDs, DVDs, and other digital media. Once it is established it limits and enables the public character of future practices. Its implementation is not entirely controllable by individuals, however. Rather it must also draw on and consider public law and public opinion to work.

Conclusion

This chapter has explored three types of complexity associated with contemporary public practices. Each of these differs from earlier simpler ways of identifying the public by associating it with the state or a national citizenry. The first type of complexity was the interplay between collective ideas and more individual actions which is expressed by this book's definition of practices, formulated by Best and Gheciu (Chapter 2). The second type of complexity was the interplay between the ideal and the material. The chapter argued that we need to examine this more carefully since we can no longer rely on the stability of the state to preserve the public and need to consider how the expression of elements of the public in material form contributes to its endurance. As well, the materiality of open architectures or private fences can facilitate or limit the ability of agents to identify or express common concerns, and thus the development of publics. The third type of complexity was the relationship between nationality and publics. Instead of nationality being the primary community upon which publics are built, it has become one of multiple communities, some of which are transnational. In its more exclusionary forms, nationality can operate in a manner more reminiscent of the meanings associated with "private" relative to larger and more open transnational publics.

The two case studies confirmed the importance of considering these types of complexity when trying to determine the public or private character of important institutions such as states or the internet. States with their national borders have been associated with the more traditional public logics, while the internet has been associated with new transnational public spheres. In both cases, however, there are complex mixes of public and private logics in these institutions. These mixes are not simple expressions of unchanging links of public logics to states and private logics to markets or individuals. Instead these logics are being continually produced and reproduced through often conflictual practices. At times practices attempt to reinforce more traditional logics, as with border security or the efforts of some governments to assert their right to control the internet. More often practices are transformative, reworking older logics in new ways.

These practices involve complex interactions between collective ideas and the actions of agents, as evident for instance with privacy rights at the borders, or the use of DRM to control information on the internet. They involve complex interactions between the ideal and the material, as evident in the encoding of border control practices in biometric and other technical systems, or the encoding of public access and private exclusions with DRM. They challenge simpler models of the public based on nationality, as the constructed and arbitrary character of national borders becomes more obvious, and as debates sharpen over whether nation–states or non-state governance is the best way to protect the public character of the internet.

By recognizing this type of complexity we can better understand the construction and meaning of publics today. By ignoring it and relying on older simpler public logics, we would underestimate the ongoing importance of the public, and the ways in which it is re-emerging after a period in which the private and the individual had started to eclipse the public. Ongoing political conflicts related to the construction and meaning of publics testify to the importance of publics and their boundaries to those involved, and to the importance of recognizing the complex changes these are displaying today.

240   *Tony Porter*

REFERENCES

Adams, Barbara. 2004. *Time*. Cambridge: Polity Press.

Adkins, Lauren D. 2007. "Biometrics: weighing convenience and national security against your privacy." *Michigan Telecommunications and Technology Law Review* 13 (Spring): 541–55.

Adler, Emanuel, and Vincent Pouliot. 2011. "International practices." *International Theory* 3(1): 1–36.

Arthur, Charles. 2012. "Internet remains unregulated after UN treaty blocked." *Guardian*, December 14. www.guardian.co.uk/technology/

Bamberger, Kenneth A., and Deirdre K. Mulligan. 2008. "Privacy decisionmaking in administrative agencies." *University of Chicago Law Review* Winter: 75–107.

BBC. 2006. "File-sharers face legal onslaught." *BBC News*, April 4. http://news.bbc.co.uk/

Bechtold, Stefan. 2003. "The present and future of digital rights management: Musings on emerging legal problems." In *Digital Rights Management: Technological, Economic, Legal and Political Aspects*, edited by Eberhard Becker, W. Buhse, D. Günnewig, and N. Rump, pp. 597–654. Berlin: Springer.

Bector, Sunil. 2009. "'Your laptop, please': The search and seizure of electronic devices at the United States border." *Berkeley Technology Law Journal* 24: 695–718.

Cate, Fred H. 2008. "Government data mining: the need for a legal framework." *Harvard Civil Rights – Civil Liberties Law Review* 43: 435–89.

Cesarini, Paul. 2004. "Contextualizing digital rights management: past, present and future." *Journal of Industrial Technology* 20: 1–8.

Cohen, Jean L. 1999. "Personal autonomy and the law: sexual harassment and the dilemma of regulating 'intimacy'." *Constellations* 6: 443–72.

Conway, Janet, and Jakeet Singh. 2009. "Is the World Social Forum a transnational public sphere? Nancy Fraser, Critical Theory and the containment of radical possibility." *Theory, Culture and Society* 26(5): 61–84.

Coyle, Karen. 2003. "The technology of rights: digital rights management." Based on a talk given at the Library of Congress. www.kcoyle.net/

Djelic, Marie-Laure, and Sigrid Quack, eds. 2010. *Transnational Communities: Shaping Global Economic Governance*. Cambridge: Cambridge University Press.

Dobusch, Leonhard, and Sigrid Quack. 2011. "Mobilizing competing standards: transnational private regulation in the field of copyright." Paper for the Florence Workshop on Transnational Business Governance Interactions, May 23–24, European University Institute, Florence.

Electronic Frontier Foundation. 2005. *Digital Rights Management: A Failure in the Developed World, a Danger to the Developing World*, Report to the International Telecommunications Union. www.eff.org/

Eriksson, Johan, and Giampiero Giacomello, eds. 2009. "Who controls the internet? Beyond the obstinacy or obsolescence of the state." *International Studies Review* 11: 205–30.

Fahey, Tony. 1995. "Privacy and the family: conceptual and empirical reflections." *Sociology* **29**: 687–702.

Fraser, Nancy. 2002. "Rethinking the public sphere: a contribution to the critique of actually existing democracy." In *Habermas and the Public Sphere*, edited by C. Calhoun, pp. 109–42. Cambridge, MA: MIT Press.

2007. "Transnationalizing the public sphere: on the legitimacy and efficacy of public opinion in a post-Westphalian world." *Theory, Culture and Society* **24**(4): 7–30.

2009. *Scales of Justice: Reimagining Political Space in a Globalizing World*. New York: Columbia University Press.

Fungsang, Francis. 2006. "Government information collection: U.S. E-Passports – ETA August 2006: recent changes provide additional protection for biometric information contained in U.S. electronic passports." *I/S: A Journal of Law and Policy for the Information Society* **2**: 521–46.

Green, Thomas C., and Ileana M. Ciobanu. 2006. "The state of federal prosecution: Article: Deputizing – and then prosecuting – America's businesses in the fight against illegal immigration." *American Criminal Law Review* **43**: 1203–23.

Habermas, Jürgen. 1989. *Structural Transformation of the Public Sphere*. Cambridge, MA: MIT Press.

Hansen, Mark B. N. 2009. "Living (with) technical time: from media surrogacy to distributed cognition." *Theory, Culture and Society* **26**(2–3): 294–315.

Hansmann, Henry, and Reinier Kraakman. 2000. *The End of History for Corporate Law*, Discussion Paper No. 280, Harvard Law School. www.law.harvard.edu/

Hill, Mike, and Warren Montag. 2000. *Masses, Classes, and the Public Sphere*. London: Verso Books.

Kemp, Randy, and Adam D. Moore. 2007. "Privacy." *Library Hi Tech* **25**: 58–78.

Koslowski, Rey. 2005. "Smart borders, virtual borders or no borders: homeland security choices for the United States and Canada." *Law and Business Review of the Americas* **11**: 527–45.

Koulish, Robert. 2008. "Blackwater and the privatization of immigration control." *St. Thomas Law Review* **20**: 462–89.

Latour, Bruno. 1991. "Technology is power made durable." In *A Sociology of Monsters: Essays on Power, Technology and Domination*, edited by John Law, pp. 103–31. New York: Routledge.

Lessig, Lawrence. 2006. *Code: Version 2.0*. New York: Basic Books.

Lorenc, Margaret L. 2007. "The mark of the beast: U.S. government use of RFID in government-issued documents." *Albany Law Journal of Science and Technology* **17**: 583–614.

Low, Setha, and Neil Smith, eds. 2006. *The Politics of Public Space*. New York: Routledge.

Mattli, Walter, and Ngaire Woods. 2009. "In whose benefit? Explaining regulatory change in world politics." In *The Politics of Global Regulation*, edited by Walter Mattli and Ngaire Woods, pp. 1–43. Princeton, NJ: Princeton University Press.

Meehan, Kevin A. 2008. "The continuing conundrum of international internet jurisdiction." *Boston College International and Comparative Law Review* **31**: 345–69.

Pagliari, Stefano, ed. 2012. '*The Making of Good Financial Regulation: Towards a Policy Response to Regulatory Capture.*' London: International Centre for Financial Regulation. www.icffr.org/

Preston, Paschal. 2009. "An elusive trans-national public sphere?" *Journalism Studies* **10**(1): 114–29.

Rishikof, Harvey. 2008. "Combating terrorism in the digital age: a clash of doctrines: the frontier of sovereignty – national security and citizenship – the fourth amendment – technology and shifting legal borders." *Mississippi Law Journal* **78**: 381–431.

Shachar, Ayelet. 2009. "Territory without boundaries: immigration beyond territory – the shifting border of immigration regulation." *Michigan Journal of International Law* **30**: 809–39.

Sheller, Mimi, and John Urry. 2003. "Mobile transformations of 'public' and 'private' life." *Theory, Culture and Society* **20**(3): 107–25.

Stockdale, Liam. 2013. "Temporality, sovereignty, and risk: the critical potentialities of taking time seriously in international relations." Ph.D. dissertation, McMaster University, Hamilton, Ontario.

Weintraub, Jeff. 1997. "The theory and the politics of the public/private distinction." In *Public and Private in Thought and Practice: Perspectives on a Grand Dichotomy*, edited by Jeff Weintraub and Kirshan Kumar, pp. 1–42. Chicago, IL:University of Chicago Press.

Willoughby, Kelvin W., Alejandra Castañeda Andrade, Stéphane Dassonville, Tim Heitmann, and Marc Mimler. 2008. *Should Apple Open up its 'FairPlay' Digital Rights Management System? Untangling the Knot of Copyright and Competition Law for Online Businesses*, Working paper prepared for the 2007–08 Congress of EIPIN (the European Intellectual Property Institutes Network). www.drkelvinwilloughby.com/

11 Publics, practices, and power

Rita Abrahamsen and Michael C. Williams

Like the divide between domestic and international politics, the public/ private distinction has long served as a foundational assumption of international theory; and as with the categorical division between politics inside the state and politics between states, the public/private dichotomy has also become subject to extensive critical interrogation. As the editors of this volume outline in their Introduction, this critique has recently been intensified by three concerns. First, a sense that after a long period of the ascendance of the "private," we may now be witnessing a reassertion of the "public," particularly in the wake of the 2009 financial crisis. Second, a suspicion that prior assessments of the increasing role of the private in international politics may well have underestimated the role of the public in these processes, and thus provided incomplete or potentially misleading foundations from which to assess the "return" of the public. And finally, the possibility that the entire idea that the rise of the private necessarily marked a retreat or diminishment of the public may be misguided, and that what has been occurring is instead the development of new hybrid institutions and forms of governance. In turn, these new forms of governance may demand a reconsideration of the deeply embedded visions of the public and the private that structure scholarly analysis and public discourse about domestic and international politics.

These are tremendously complicated questions, and it would be folly to try to address them, or the rich studies collected here, with the aim of comprehensiveness. In this concluding chapter, we have two more modest ambitions: one historical and philosophical, and the other sociological and political. In the first, we argue that while explicit concern with the public–private relationship is relatively recent in the field of IR, the question of the public and the private is in fact at the heart of IR theory as a whole. A concern with these issues should not be seen as standing outside IR in even its most traditional and narrowly state-centric forms.

This chapter draws on research supported by the Social Science Research Council of Canada (SSHRC), grant number 410–2010–2121.

On the contrary, the dominance of state-centrism is often an unspoken (and sometimes unrecognized) consequence of complex historical attempts to determine what or where the public is, as well as its relationship to the private. The public–private question is inextricably a question of representation – a very old question of who or what is capable of representing the people, and which people. As we seek to show, the question of representation was central to the emergence of the tradition of "reason of state," and we misunderstand its importance if (as is often the case in IR) we identify it only with the external relations between states.

Our second ambition is to locate these foundational theoretical challenges within wider sociological transformations in contemporary global governance, and to illustrate some of the challenges that arise when the relationship between the public good and private goods moves beyond the confines of the national good to which it was restricted until perhaps the 1980s. Although the question of the public and the private is a very old one, it is clearly taking on new forms and salience in the context of the changing nature of the state and its relationship with other institutions and actors, both private and public. Placing the question within this framework reveals that although we may be currently witnessing, or perhaps just seeing more clearly, an increased role for the public in the form of the state, this does not necessarily entail the reassertion of the public in the wider sense of the constituent power of the people, not to mention an answer to the vexing question of how to determine issues of common concern.

Opening up the question of the public–private thus reveals issues that engage both explanatory theory and cross-cutting philosophical lineages and political valuations that continue to play central roles in political perceptions and practices. By addressing the question simultaneously through its expression in the historical tradition of reason of state and in contemporary sociologies of the global system, we suggest that it is possible to examine how the entwinement of these two dimensions lies beneath some of the most striking and puzzling aspects of contemporary global politics. Locating the studies in this volume against this wider backdrop helps bring out how even specific sectoral transformations in public–private relations today raise questions that go to the heart of foundational visions of modern politics and with them, key issues and debates in IR.

Situating the public

The innovative conceptualization at the heart of this volume, that the public is a "practice" (rather than a place or person) that is defined by an engagement with issues of "common concern" demonstrates clearly that thinking seriously about transformations in the relationship between public and private requires an engagement with the former as much as the latter. Yet if the public is "back," this raises a disarmingly simple question: what or where is it? This is, of course, by no means a new question. The simple answer (and the one that underpins many theories of international politics) is this: the state. But as many of the chapters in this collection demonstrate, and as Marxists have long claimed, an institution's formally "public" status scarcely means that it acts for purely public purposes in the sense of any unmediated or collective relation to issues of "common concern." As the authors of the previous chapters show in impressive depth and detail, the fact that putatively private agents now routinely participate in processes or carry out tasks previously dominated or monopolized by formally public actors only complicates further an already intricate set of issues over how we define public and private interests, concerns, agents, and even institutions.

At one level, then, a focus on the state as the locus of the public looks remarkably naïve, and the commitment to state-centrism that continues to captivate large parts of the field of IR, patently anachronistic. This certainly can be true, and it is a charge that has been leveled at "state-centrism" for at least a century, and perhaps even longer. But the very resilience of the commitment to the state as the definition of the public in the face of such critiques merits further investigation, because historically the idea of the state as the locus of the public was not a simple empirical observation, nor is the identification of the public with the state, as well as the centrality of "reason of state" in IR, just an unreflective commitment to state-centrism. On the contrary, it is a direct if often unacknowledged legacy of historical attempts to address the relationship between the public and the private, to determine precisely what and where the public is, and to resolve crucial issues surrounding the source and location of legitimate authority in modern politics. While reason of state has often become an unreflective assumption of theories of IR and thus a barrier to thinking critically and creatively about the public–private, in its genesis, reason of state was precisely an attempt to develop a viable conception both of the public and of the relationship between the public and the private. The adequacy and implications of this problematic has been at the heart of political debate ever since, and if the location of the public is today shifting, it is useful to recall some of the ways in which it came to be located within the state in the first place.

As is so often the case, one of the most revealing figures to turn to is Thomas Hobbes. For Hobbes, the public could not be identified simply with "the people." Without a common form of representation, the people were not in fact a public at all, but remained what Hobbes called a "multitude": a shifting, indeterminate set of individuals or groups with diverse interests and desires, but lacking the form of a public in any unified sense of the word. As he memorably phrased it: "the *people* is not in being before the constitution of government as not being any person, but a multitude of single persons" (Hobbes 1991: 196). Indeed as Murray Forsyth (1981: 193) insightfully pointed out, in his early writings Hobbes went so far as to assert the common identity of the people and its representative. In *Man and Citizen*, he strikingly argued:

The people is somewhat that is one, having one will, and to whom one action may be attributed; none of these can properly be said of a multitude. The people rules in all governments. For even in monarchies the people commands; for the people will by the will of one man; but the multitude are citizens, that is to say, subjects. In a democracy and aristocracy, the citizens are the multitude, but the court is the people. And in a monarchy, the subjects are the multitude and (however much it seems a paradox) the king is the people. (Hobbes 1991: 250)

For Hobbes, it was only through this process of representation that the people could come to form a public in any unified sense, as opposed to a public understood as simply a multitude of individual wills. Only through such sovereign representation could a public interest be distinguished from a shifting and unstable collation of private interests and their domination over (or conflict with) the interests of others. Here, the public only becomes a public through its representation, although the representative is not the public in any simple sense. In his later writings, most particularly *Leviathan*, Hobbes softened the stark division between a multitude and a people, developing instead a two-part understanding. While a representative is still required to bring the people into existence, the people authorize a unifying sovereign power in order to carry out what they all will (or should rationally will) – in Hobbes's case, their mutual safety and security – rather than just what a majority or a powerful minority might desire. In short, the idea of the public is separated from a conception of the people's interests as the actual desires or interests of groups (or even a majority) of citizens, and indeed the latter could clash with pursuit of the public interest which the state was authorized to represent and which was the basis of its authority.

In the two moments of Hobbes's conception of sovereign representation, therefore, the genesis of the people as a public required a corresponding recognition by the public authority – the sovereign state – that its end must be to represent the public as the constituent power of the people. Failure to do so would destroy the possibility of a commonwealth and the construction of sovereign public along these lines. As Forsyth nicely phrases it, if the sovereign power merely said with Louis XIV, "*L'Etat c'est moi!*" – the whole body politic is encompassed in one – there was no future for the commonwealth. If however he said with Frederick the Great that "the Prince is the first servant of the state" then there was a future for it. Princedom plus service: that was the essence of Hobbes' conception of political representation. Its weakness was precisely that it rested on the insight or enlightenment of particular sovereigns for its fulfilment, their ability to perceive, like Hobbes, where the true source and legitimacy of their power lay. (Forsyth 1981: 203)

In other words, the representative had to stand apart from the actual public and its interests and desires (or the dominant expressions of them), as well as from its own interests, to somehow represent the interests of the public as a whole.[1]

In this way, Hobbes, along with Sieyès,[2] founded a vision of the public based on what is generally called the "constituent power" of the people (Sieyès 2003).[3] This creation of a public becomes complexly entwined with the logic of reason of state. The latter is an expression of the former: an attempt to conceive and create a public, and a sovereign agent capable of representing it and acting in its name, which is separate from a vision of the public interest as the simple collation of individual desires and their expression, even via a majority. This conception of representation was central to the emergence of the tradition of reason of state, and we misunderstand its importance if we identify it only with the external relations between states, or with the domination of the state over its members.[4]

Difficult as these issues are within a classically "Hobbesian" vision of sovereignty they were multiplied, as Istvan Hont has brilliantly illustrated, once the dynamics and concerns of the public and the private moved substantively beyond a territorially bounded polity.[5] This is, of course, the classic question of the relationship between capitalism, commercial society, and the state. From amongst a vast cast of characters, David Hume provides a telling exposition of how reason of state and private commercial interests could come together to act against the public interest as constructed by someone like Hobbes. For Hume, the new capitalists of modern "commercial society" were different from

[1] Working through the implications of this conception was the goal of Meinecke's (1988) classic study.
[2] Sieyès' term for the people in this sense was, of course, "the nation" and the genealogy of some of the substantial understandings of the national interest can be traced to it.
[3] For a superb tracing of the complex relations between the state, the nation, and nationalism, see Hont 2005: 447–527.
[4] For diverse treatments of this complex trajectory, see Runciman 2005; Skinner 1989; Viroli 2005.
[5] Indeed, Hont argues that properly modern politics only really began when commerce became central to it.

individuals who engaged in trade: "The capitalist was not simply a rich person, but an individual who invested in interest-bearing government bonds issued to finance war. On its own accord, trade could never produce such a creature. The capitalist was the commercial child of political Machiavellianism, of competition for power and hegemony among nations" (Hont 2005: 84). Hume's capitalists were a new interest group, neither landowners nor merchants, nor traders or laborers, and their interest in government borrowing "could easily diverge from those of the nation" as they pushed for imprudent expansion or refused to fund necessary projects, even as an increasing state debt caused rising taxes. In the eyes of Hume and many like him, the result was that "the financial revolution had created a monster that would eventually destroy Europe's liberty" (Hont 2005: 85), a prospect that led both Hume and Kant to advocate voluntary state bankruptcy under the justification of public necessity (Hont 2005: 86–88) – and a stance that contrasts (but also resonates) intriguingly with the actions of most contemporary states in the face of the recent financial crisis.

Our point in rehearsing some of these relatively familiar elements of political thought is to stress that the question of the public/private should not be treated simply as one of arbitrary definitions or settled assumptions, or of grasping the inevitably historically and socially constructed nature of the divide and its shifting inclusions and exclusions, or as a recent set of concerns. They also need to be placed alongside the wider problematic of legitimate sovereignty, and the dominance of state-centrism which so often seems to stand as a barrier to thinking about them is actually and paradoxically a largely unrecognized inheritance of attempts to address these issues and to determine what or where the public is, and what therefore qualifies as legitimate, or properly public, power.

Placing the issue in this context can help us see how coming to terms with contemporary transformations demands an appreciation of historical legacies as well as current innovations and transformations. However distant in history and sociology they may be – and remaining mindful of anachronism – it is hard not to see fascinating affinities between the concerns of Hobbes, Sieyès, and others with the creation of the "people" and a representative sovereign as the public and the contemporary international attempts to build national "publics" capable of holding their governments accountable, as discussed by Jacqueline Best (Chapter 5, this volume). Similarly, Deborah Avant and Virginia Haufler's history (Chapter 3, this volume) of how public and private force were entwined historically is also the story of how sovereign power became disconnected from its identification with the person of the monarch and gradually recast as a public representing the people. Their account, as well as Alexandra Gheciu's revealing analysis (Chapter 8, this volume) of the role of private force and the dilemmas generated by the "rebirth" of private security in "transitional" societies, also show the difficulties that these developments pose for both political analysis and judgment – difficulties which find their source in the problem of locating the public, in the past and in the present.

Situating the public in the global

Today, situating the public requires not only an awareness of these historical lineages and legacies, but also an empirical analysis of the global and the reshaping of the state. In the early days of the globalization debate, the conventional fear was that the public would be undermined as the power of the state was eroded. More recently, a series of analyses have demonstrated that the relationship is much more complicated than this allowed. In her analysis of globalization and the shifting relationship between territory, authority, and rights, for instance, Saskia Sassen (2008) argues that globalization involves more than the mere existence or increase of global flows of products, capital, or people, and that it cannot be equated with the simple erosion of the position and power of the state. As she puts it:

We generally use terms such as deregulation, financial and trade liberalization, and privatization to describe the changed authority of the state when it comes to the economy. The problem with such terms is that they only capture the withdrawal of the state from regulating its economy. They do not register all the ways in which the state participates in setting up the new frameworks through which globalization is furthered, nor do they capture the associated transformations inside the state... (Sassen 2008: 234)

In line with a number of analyses in this volume, Sassen argues that it is precisely the national state that has made today's global era possible. Echoing the arguments of scholars such as Linda Weiss (2003), she holds that many of the activities, institutions, and structures now identified with globalization came into existence at the direct instigation of national governments, and continue to operate through transformed national institutions that enable and facilitate their operation. More specifically, Sassen suggests that the development of contemporary global structures involves three key elements: a process of "disassembly" in which previously public functions are increasingly transferred to private actors; the development of "capacities" by private actors that allow them to act at a global level; and a process of "reassembly" whereby these new actors and capabilities become part of global assemblages that are embedded in national settings but operate at a global scale. In this way, the disassembly of the national becomes constitutive of the global, in that "the territorial sovereign state, with its territorial fixity and exclusivity, represents a set of capabilities that eventually enable the formation or evolution of particular global systems" (Sassen 2008: 21).

For the purpose of locating the public in the global era, two important parameters of this process need to be stressed. First, the disassembly is partial – it does not mean the national state is disappearing, or that the state is fading away. Rather, particular components of the state are undergoing a process of "denationalization" and rearticulation, and the processes of disassembly in one part of the state may have implications for others, while revealing shifting power relations between different agencies or organizations within the state.[6] Globalization then is not a process whereby "outside" forces are eroding a territorially distinct "inside"; it is entwined with a restructuring of institutions and power relations inside the state through, for example, the neoliberal practices of privatization and regulation. Importantly, this realignment inside the state has generally redistributed power in favor of those elements of the state that are directly embedded in global structures, such as ministries of trade and finance, elements of the judiciary that deal with international regulation, and the executive branch.

These components of the state are in turn central in instituting the normativity of globalization at the heart of the state, and often operate in complex interaction with private, transnational actors, and institutions. They also facilitate globalization by allowing global actors to link directly to globalized state institutions in support of their projects, and to overcome the opposition of other elements of the state. Thus, for example, the activities of politically independent central banks and their formal and informal links with their international counterparts and with other key players in the international financial system have risen in salience, while those of legislatures have in relative terms declined.

These structural and institutional shifts in power within and outside the state affect the articulation and representation of the public. Most importantly, the relationship between the public good and private goods moves beyond the confines of the national good to which it was arguably restricted until the 1980s, and takes on new and complex forms. The relative decline in power of the legislative branch of government,

---

[6] Sassen 2008: 8, and, from different perspectives, Grande and Pauly 2007 and Gill 2003. We examine this process in more detail in the area of security in Abrahamsen and Williams 2011.

traditionally seen as closest to representing the people, has rendered this practice of the public less viable and capable. Instead, both the burden and the power and opportunity to claim to represent the public has shifted onto the executive on the one hand, and on the other, onto narrower, more technical elements of the state apparatus – from finance ministries and central banks to health or environment agencies – which are frequently "entwined" (as Bernstein shows, Chapter 6) with private and global actors. The challenge, of course, is that while this is certainly a practice of the public, it is at some distance from (and sometimes at the expense of) other representative bodies through which the people have, however problematically, been given voice. Far from anachronistic, the Hobbesian problematic remains highly contemporary.

The Hobbesian problematic also challenges influential accounts of the practice of the public in a global era. For Anne-Marie Slaughter (2004), for example, although new transnational structures of governance represent the extension of power and institutions beyond the borders of the sovereign state, this by no means makes them illegitimate as representatives of the public. Since these networks are composed primarily of state actors (judges or regulators, for instance), she argues that they remain legitimate representatives of the people. At the same time, she regrets that legislative branches of governments are "falling behind" in global governance, and regards this as a result of the lack of institutional initiative on behalf of legislators.

From the perspective sketched above, these conclusions are too simple. The declining power and influence of legislatures cannot be reduced to a question of initiative and voluntarism, but is in large part a consequence of a structural transformation of the state that has entailed the relative disempowerment of a key institution representing the constituent power of the people. Moreover, as the analyses in this volume demonstrate, when the actions and positions of private actors and forms of authority are factored in, transnational structures of governance cannot be assumed to represent the public in any straightforward way. As Eric Heillener (Chapter 4) shows, for example, the role of public agents in global finance may be significant, but the public and public good to which their actions are oriented is by no means one that corresponds comfortably to visions of sovereignty that sought to justify the state as a representative of the people. Put differently, just because we are currently witnessing, or seeing more clearly, an increased role for the public in the form of the state, this does not necessarily entail the reassertion of the public in the wider sense of the constituent power of the people, not to mention an answer to the vexing question of how to determine issues of common concern.

Practicing the public?

As we argued in the introduction to this chapter, the public/private question is inextricably a question of representation; a very old question of who or what is capable of representing the people, and which people, and a very new question arising from the changing nature of the state and its relationship with other institutions and actors, both private and public. In fact, it is the entwinement of these two dimensions that lies beneath some of the most striking and puzzling aspects of contemporary global politics. As this volume demonstrates, the problematic of representation is evident across the environmental, security, and economic spheres. As Helleiner (Chapter 4) and Porter (Chapter 10) both discuss, formally public actors frequently engage in private domains and with private actors to produce (or attempt to produce) outcomes that are both guided and justified by a notion of the public as located within the state and the stability of its international systemic connections. These public (or public–private) actions take place in fora, and through mechanisms and individuals that are often only tenuously connected to politics as representation of the public as a constituent power. The tensions are apparent as governments across the world seek stability and stable transformation within expert networks and increasingly formalized structures whose accountability to a public in the wider sense seems strained or, as Paterson (Chapter 7) suggests, involve new spaces of contestation whose implications are by no means clear. The debt crises in Greece and Spain stand as perhaps the most striking expressions of these tensions, but the wider dynamic can be seen across the landscape of early twenty-first-century politics.

One response to these dilemmas has taken the form of calls for a renewed mobilization of the people as the constituent power in reaction to the policies of its own state. Yet here, too, the trajectories are by no means clear. In some of the most dire readings, the challenges of representing the public and its interests in present-day politics may presage the emergence of reactionary political movements or alternatives, such as a synthesis of plebiscitary, executive-dominated democracy with elite political and economic domination that in its extreme form resembles the kind of authoritarian democracy that Carl Schmitt famously described as the combination of a strong state and free economy.[7] A somewhat similar concern has recently been expressed by Corey Robin (2012). For Robin, we today live in "failed Hobbesian states," not in the

---

[7] For one such reading, see Cristi 1998.

conventional IR sense of collapsed states and an impending return to Hobbesian anarchy, but in the sense that states are increasingly failing to live up to their side of the Hobbesian bargain to represent a public beyond a collection of private interests. In his view, the increased use and salience of the language and politics of fear and security is the result of this incapacity. In the absence of a public that is being adequately represented in other ways, the politics of fear becomes a key technique for the creation of such a public and in maintaining support for the state – a situation that he views as highly dangerous, both domestically and internationally.

From a related but importantly different angle, the dilemmas of the public have led others to calls for the renewal of what Andreas Kalyvas (2008) has called a democratic "politics of the extraordinary." In his evocative formulation, within a democratic vision of extraordinary politics "there is an intensification of popular mobilization, an extensive consensus" which "describes the extraordinary reactivation of the constituent power of the people and the self-assertion of a democratic sovereign" (Kalyvas 2008: 164–65). In this view, acts of founding, such as revolutionary moments, are foundational in the sense of "higher" law-making: they express the "constituent power," the will of the people in the broadest sense. Mobilized in the construction of a new political order, this constituent power becomes latent in "normal" politics: it retreats – and must necessarily do so – in order for stability to be secured, and normality to prevail over the vicissitudes of permanent revolution. Ordinary politics thus becomes dominated by the more narrow and mundane competition of diverse interests and elite political management. As Kalyvas nicely puts it (linking the arguments of Bruce Ackerman[8] with those of Schmitt), ordinary politics is "characterized by widespread pluralism and political fragmentation, devoid of any collective project that could unify the popular sovereign around some concrete fundamental issues. This fragmentation explains and justifies the predominance of relations of bargaining, negotiation, and compromised among organized interests, driven by their narrow, particular interests" (Kalyvas 2008: 164). Yet, in this vision, the constituent power remains capable of mobilization. At such junctures, "the people" – the constituent power of the political order – can emerge from repose. The politics of the extraordinary, and a democratic politics of the extraordinary in particular, are thus marked by times when

---

[8] See Ackerman 1993, 2000.

the formal procedural rules that regulate normal institutionalized politics are supplemented by or subordinated to informal, extraconstitutional forms of participation that strive to narrow the distance between rulers and ruled, active and passive citizens, representatives and represented. Extraordinary politics aims either at core constitutional matters or at central social imaginary significations, cultural meanings, and economic issues, with the goal of transforming the basic structures of society and resignifying social reality. To put it in more general terms, the democratic politics of the extraordinary refers to those infrequent and unusual moments when the citizenry, overflowing the formal borders of institutionalized politics, reflectively aims at the modification of the central political, symbolic, and constitutional principles and at the redefinition of the content and ends of a community. (Kalyvas 2008: 7)[9]

In a very real sense, this casts the struggle as one between the people and the state over the "public." Its contemporary resonances are not hard to find. Many analyses of globalization continue to revolve around the ways that the private interests have either come to trump public interests, or claim that private interests have captured public institutions to such a degree that they no longer represent the people. Similarly, the responses – from the Occupy movement, to the protests in the streets of Athens and elsewhere – frequently (and often self-consciously) invoke and seek to mobilize "the people" – or even the "multitude" (Hardt and Negri 2005) – as the constituent power in contradistinction to a state or international system that has lost its legitimacy. Resistance to the usurpation of a national (and sometimes even global) good by private interests thus also provides the conditions for attempts to call into being a common constituent power within and across national boundaries.

Yet as the fate of the Occupy movement seems to indicate, and as the less savory sides of attempts to mobilize "the people" in Greece (such as the neo-Fascist Golden Dawn) confirm, appealing directly to the people as the constituent power of the public is no simple matter, nor is it one without very significant dangers, as critics of so-called Jacobin politics have long argued.[10] To these critics, the centrality of the state and the doctrine of reason of state, correctly understood and structured, was not a denial of the importance of the people: it was an essential element of there being a viable public at all. These concerns, too, resonate today. As the chapters in this book show, the possibilities for politics are shifting in the face of global transformations, and while the place of the public is perhaps more puzzling than ever, it is by no measure disappearing. To

[9] Kalyvas argues, not uncontroversially, that such an understanding can also be found in Schmitt.
[10] Again, on this, see the superb treatment in Hont 2005.

engage with the public and the private in contemporary global affairs is to open up some of the most vexing and yet urgent questions of modern politics, and yet there is little doubt that they are questions that must be addressed, since they are likely to become ever more crucial in the decades to come.

REFERENCES

Abrahamsen, Rita, and Michael C. Williams. 2011. *Security beyond the State: Private Security in International Politics*. Cambridge: Cambridge University Press.

Ackerman, Bruce. 1993. *We the People*, vol. 1, *Foundations*. Cambridge, MA: Harvard University Press.

2000. *We the People*, vol. 2, *Transformations*. Cambridge, MA: Harvard University Press.

Cristi, Renato. 1998. *Carl Schmitt and Authoritarian Liberalism*. Cardiff: University of Wales Press.

Forsyth, Murray. 1981. "Thomas Hobbes and the constituent power of the people." *Political Studies* **29**(2): 191–203.

Gill, Steven, ed. 2003. *Power and Resistance in the New World Order*. Basingstoke: Macmillan.

Grande, Edgar, and Louis W. Pauly, eds. 2007. *Complex Sovereignty: Reconstituting Political Authority in the Twenty-First Century*. Toronto: University of Toronto Press.

Hardt, Michael, and Antonio Negri. 2005. *Multitude: War and Democracy in the Age of Empire*. London: Penguin.

Hobbes, Thomas. 1991. *Man and Citizen*. Edited by Bernard Gert. Indianapolis, IN: Hackett.

1994. *Leviathan*. Edited by Edwin Curley. Indianapolis, IN: Hackett.

Hont, Istvan. 2005. *The Jealousy of Trade: International Competition and the State in Historical Perspective*. Cambridge, MA: Harvard University Press.

Kalyvas, Andreas. 2008. *Democracy and the Politics of the Extraordinary: Max Weber, Carl Schmitt, and Hannah Arendt*. Cambridge: Cambridge University Press.

Meinecke, Friedrich. 1988. *Machiavellism: The Doctrine of* raison d'état *and its Place in Modern History*. Brunswick, NJ: Transaction Publishers.

Robin, Corey. 2012. "The language of fear: security and modern politics." In *Fear: across the Disciplines*, edited by Jan Pampler and Benjamin Lazier, pp. 118–31. Pittsburgh, PA: University of Pennsylvania Press.

Runciman, David. 2005. *Pluralism and the Personality of the State*. Cambridge: Cambridge University Press.

Sassen, Saskia. 2008. *Territory, Authority, Rights: From Medieval to Global Assemblages*. Princeton, NJ: Princeton University Press.

Sieyès, Emmanuel Joseph. 2003. "What is the Third Estate?" In *Political Writings*, edited and translated by Michael Sonenscher, pp. 92–161. Indianapolis, IN: Hackett.

Skinner, Quentin. 1989. "The state." In *Political Innovation and Conceptual Change*, edited by Terence Ball, James Farr, and Russell L. Hanson, pp. 90–131. Cambridge: Cambridge University Press.

Slaughter, Anne-Marie. 2004. *A New World Order*. Princeton, NJ: Princeton University Press.

Viroli, Maurizo. 2005. *From Politics to Reason of State: The Acquistion and Transformation of the Language of Politics 1250–1600*. Cambridge: Cambridge University Press.

Weiss, Linda, ed. 2003. *States in the Global Economy: Bringing Domestic Institutions Back In*. Cambridge: Cambridge University Press.

Index